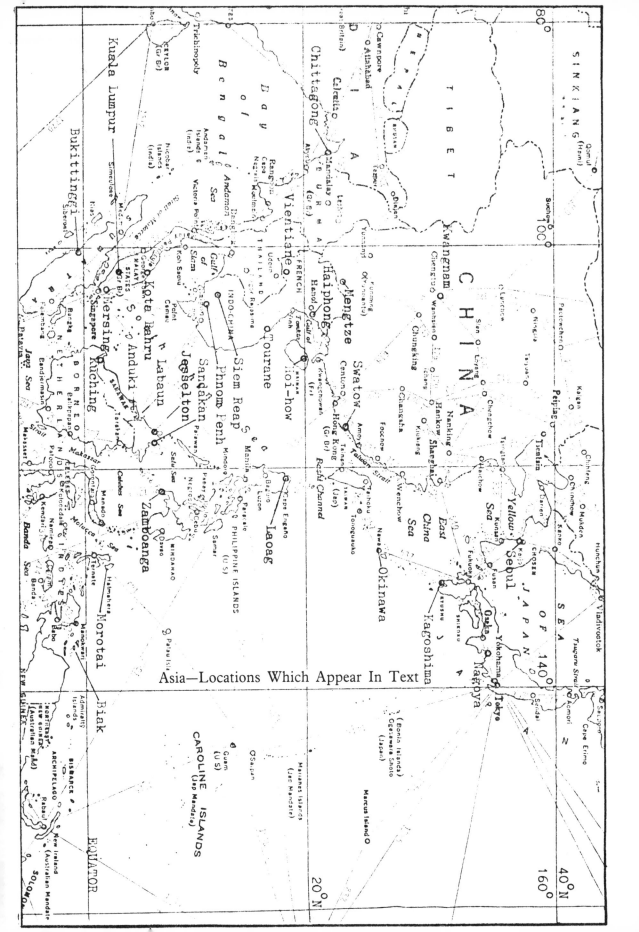

Asia—Locations Which Appear In Text

SYD'S PIRATES

Charles (Chic) Eather

A story of an airline

DURNMOUNT – SYDNEY

DURNMOUNT P/L. SYDNEY

EATHER, CHARLES EDWARD JAMES, 1920—

SYD'S PIRATES

ISBN 0 949756 05 9

1. Eather, Charles Edward James, 1920—
2. Cathay Pacific Airways. 3 Airlines—Asia.
3. Air Pilots—Asia—Biography. 1 Title.

387.7'065'50924

1983

Literary Consultant: Olaf Ruhen

Typeset by: Love Typesetters — Sydney
Printed by: Dai Nippon Hong Kong
Wholly designed and set up in Australia by Durnmount P/L.

To two men – two men of vastly
different life styles – each, however, one of nature's gentlemen.
I dedicate this book. They are
'Mr Cathay Pacific himself, the
late John Kidston Swire, who
looked upon me as 'one of Syd's
pirates' – while the other – the
late George Wilkins Ferguson,
was my companion of the war
years and my very first aeroplane passenger.

Aviation in itself is not inherently dangerous.
But to an even greater degree than the sea,
it is terribly unforgiving of any carelessness, incapacity or neglect.

INM HARDY

Shell Aviation News—Final Edition

"Mr Cathay Pacific"— John Kidston Swire, November, 1974

CONTENTS

FOREWORD

It is customary for the writer of a Foreword to begin by saying how pleased he is to have been asked to do so. This is usually a lie. He may have been honoured to have been asked. He was probably surprised, because, although he knows that he is a man of unsuspected reserves of talent, he did not realise that this closely-guarded secret had leaked to his friends.

He may be suspicious that he will find himself obliged to purchase at least a hundred copies of the book or that he will become responsible for all libel actions launched against the author.

But he is unlikely to be pleased. Anyone whose opinion he seeks will tell him, in the wholly depressing way which is the foundation of true friendship, that his task is a difficult as the author's. The latter, after all, knows the story which he is to tell (or with luck will do by the time he completes the book) whereas the 'foreworder' has to decide what the purpose (if any) is of his contribution.

His dismay is not lessened when he is sharply reminded by the author, that a foreword is not meant to provide its writer with an opportunity to tell an eager public about himself. If, as is probable, this was his main motive for accepting the invitation to write it, he will feel betrayed; in effect, a literary cuckold.

As an unattractive alternative, he feels obliged to say something of the merits of the book (which a cautious foreworder will probably ready for this purpose) and of the less unsavourary characteristics of the author (and of his wife if identifiable and mentionable).

Judge Amsberg has made it clear, in his charitable preface, that he regards the MS as lacking grammarian's polish. If this is true it is, I believe, irrelevant. For this is not the work of a pedant. It is the narrative of a man of action. Here is the boldy coloured view of the actor, not the pale gaze of the critic.

The author tells the story on paper as he would do at home, with nerve, point and humour. It is a story of lasting value, for it tells of an age, and a style of flying, which have gone. Civil aviation is middle aged, with a thickened waistline, and its enterprise dimmed by caution and regulation.

Chic will take you into an earlier world of flying, when being a pilot demanded more than an ability to follow flight control instructions and to read three hundred coloured cockpit dials simultaneously. In those far off times, only a generation ago, the good pilot was a man of courage, tenacity and flair, who controlled the lives of his planes and passengers by his own skill and experience and did not rely on the advice of the faceless monitors who sit in control towers throughout the world.

The book is, however, more than the story of the professional life of a pilot; it is the history of the rise, as seen through his eyes, of a remarkable Asian airline, Cathay Pacific Airways, which has grown from a single Dakota to a fleet of substantial size in thirty-three years.

CPA comes to life through the remarkable gallery of men who have flown for it. The book is scattered with their reminiscences, which show an affection for their colleagues and their airline which is rare and refreshing.

As you may guess from photographs in this book (and that is about all you can do from most photographs) Chic Eather is short, stocky and ruddy faced and looks like a poor man's Bob Hope—with some of the jaunty confidence and irrepressible good humour of his double.

I once sat, at his invitation, in the cockpit of the CPA Convair 880 which he was flying to Bangkok. Before we took off, he asked the flight engineer if anything had been done about the brakes. He was told that there had not. He asked his co-pilot if the latter knew which lever controlled the wing-flaps, as he was not used to Convairs. The co-pilot professed ignorance. He asked me if I had any brandy, as he liked a stiff one before takeoff to steady his nerves.

He knew, of course, for he is a shrewd judge of his mates, that I was the sort of air traveller who will believe anything about the condition of his plane or crew, provided that it is sufficiently macabre. Half-way down the runway, when he asked the second pilot how the hell he was going to get it off the ground, I achieved the difficult feat of getting to my knees while still retaining my safety belt.

When we neared Bangkok, Chic again demonstrated his long experience of his equipment by failing to find the lever which winds down the wheels, accidentally switching off his radio, but inadvertently leaving on the intercom, so that the passengers heard him say what he would have liked to do to the second stewardess, but for the fact that CPA rules forbade it.

As you will have realised, Chic was a pilot with style. Before landing, he donned white cotton gloves, immaculately clean. He wore them as he eased his plane without a bump onto the runway. I am sure that he would have liked to wear a white silk scarf as well, and it would have suited him.

As I believe in maintaining decent standards, even in the trophics, I had taken my rolled umbrella aboard. As the plane came to a halt, Chic asked me why I needed it, I told him that I had heard that CPA planes were prone to leak. 'Not now mate,' he answered, 'but they used to, when I started to fly them.'

This book proves it.

Chic's private life has been as intermingled with CPA as his working life. His wife, Judy, was stewardess with the airline, with an understanding of the stresses and annoyances of a pilot's work which must have been invaluable.

I extend to her my deepest sympathy on her ordeal while the book has been written, a long history of late nights, glum faces and spoiled meals gone cold. She now realises that marriage to a flyer may be trying, but marriage to a writer, is intolerable.

If she had not been nearby, with encouragement, endless patience and jasmine tea, the book would never have been finished.

Perhaps I should have written this foreword for her.

Sir Denys Roberts
Chief Justice
Hong Kong

PREFACE

Just a word.

'Chic' Eather wrote this book—at his request I read the manuscript. Apart from the facts that there were a few spelling mistakes, an adjustment here and there for grammar and syntax, and some additional punctuation, it has been very well done! I endeavoured to correct these errors. Some may have got under my guard; any remaining result from my fault.

This alone has been my function. The text and story are Chic's very own.

The reader may be assured that the work is totally factual. Those events which Chic himself did not see or participate in personally are faithfully described by one or more of the others involved.

The amount of spade work, investigation and research that have gone into the production of this remarkable book has been prodigious.

On this ground alone, apart from its obvious merits, success should follow its publication.

George Amsberg.

Former Judge of the New South Wales District Court and one of its most brilliant legal jurists. (Ed.)

Surfers Paradise 1980.

ACKNOWLEDGEMENTS

There are two people whom I wish to acknowledge before the others who's diverse contributions allowed me to produce a faithful portrait and history of Cathay Pacific Airways.

These two magnificent characters are Mabel Large and George Amsberg.

No words of mine can express the immense debt I owe to Mrs Mabel Large, who unstintingly gave of her time, in typing the manuscript of this 'magnum opus'. Her great effort would be highlighted if one could have seen the extent of the disfigurement of the manuscript from which she worked.

Likewise I am deeply indebted to Judge George Amsberg (ret.), who patiently read my manuscript, and not only kept me free as possible of the more obvious pitfalls of defamatory libel, but also proved a tireless mentor with his constructive criticism and quite unbelievably pedantic correction of my efforts as a teller of tales — I am profoundly grateful for his literary discipline and guidance.

Others to whom I owe immense debts of gratitude, I now list in alphabetical order. If I have omitted the name of anyone who should have been included, I offer my sincere regrets and ask their pardon.

My thanks to Malcolm J Alexander (HK Director of Marine), Andy Anderson (Commercial Artist), Capt. Pat Armstrong, Eric Aylward, F/L Bailey (28 Squadron-RAF Kai Tak), Mrs Jim Barnhart, David Bell, Capt. Phil Blown, Duncan Bluck, The Hon. Sir John Bremridge, Eddie Brown, F/L John Brown (RAF Kai Tak), Ray Bull (OC Engineering Support Flight, Kai Tak).

Ted Campbell, R/O Bill Carew, Capt. Ced Carlton, Margaret Carrick, Mrs Chan (ARB HK), Albert Chan (Radio People, HK), F/P Philip Chen, F/P Johann Chir, Capt. Len Cosgrove.

Don Delaney, Harry de Leuil, Ian Diamond (HK Government Archivist), Bob Dewar, John Dick, Capt. Bob Donovan, F/O Mike Douglas (28 Squadron RAF Kai Tak), Roy Downing.

F/O 'Bo' Egan.

Capt. Roy Farrell, George Ferguson, Michael Fiennes, Capt. John ('Fitz') Fitzgerald, Capt. Bill Forgan-Smith, Dudley Freeman.

Peter Gautschi, Geoff Goodall, Arnold Graham (ex-Shanghai resident), Jenny Grant.

Capt. Alex Hare, Mike Hartley (Air Manager, Jardines), F/L Noel Hitchin (JARIC-RAF Kai Tak), Capt. Peter Hoskins, Guy Howell (HK, DCA), Richard Hughes (Author HK), Mr Hui Lau.

Mrs Ibbotsen (Colonial Sect. Office HK), Frank (Buck) Indge-Buckingham (HK Police).

Mrs Susan Kernis (Hong Kong & Shanghai Bank), Ted Kidner, Capt. Lawrie King, Eric Kirkby, May Kwan (CPA PR HK).

R/O Dick Labrum, Cliff Large, Norm Latham, Mrs Dot Leslie, Capt. Vic Leslie, Fred Lillywhite, Henley Lo, Hon Roger Lobo, Mrs D. Lothian (Chief Sect Office HK), F/O Lyell Louttit, James Laidlaw, Roger Macdonald, Jim Mac-

5

dougall, Willie Main (Harbour Master, Rangoon), Wally Malmborg, Capt. Norm Marsh, Alan Marshall (Author), Angus McDonald, Mrs Janice McIllree, Mrs Robyn McLean, Neil McPherson, F/O Fred Melbye, Michael Miles, Dr. John Morris, Sylvi Morris, Carl Myatt, Capt. Pat Moore, Mike Moran, Dave Nichols (DCA HK), B. Ogden (HK & Shanghai Bank), Peter Onions (HAECO).

Stephen Piercey ('Flight'), Ronnie Poon, Ron Prior (HAECO).

Jack Reid (HAECO), Mrs Pat Richards, Dick Richmond, Sir Denys Roberts, Laurie Roberts, Tim Rossi.

John Saunders, H. Scanlan (Shell), Capt. Roy Sealey, Phil Shakespeare, George Shearer, Keith Sillett, Capt. Bernie Smith, RJ (Bob) Smith, Capt. Dave Smith, Harry Smith, Bill Sowrey, Mrs Lucy Steele, Mrs Clarry Stewart, U Sway Tin, Sir Adrian Swire, John K. Swire.

Reg Thatcher, Jan Theis (Exec Sect China Burma India Hump Pilots Assoc.) Brian Thompson, Trevor Thorpe, Tommy Tomkins.

USA Research Laboratory. John Vader, Alan Van der Sluis. Peter Waitt, Tony Wakeford, Bruce Watson (ESSO), Capt. 'Pinky' Wawn, Tony Weller, Rod West, Ann Whyte (PANAM), Cled Williams, Mrs Wally Williams, Mrs Jack Williams, R/O Ken Wolinski, R/O KK Wong, Cyril Wray, Chris Wren (ESSO), and Capt. Neville Youngs (JARIC Kai Tak). Leon Callaghan (Qantas).

I express my appreciation to the editors of *The South China Morning Post, The China Mail, The Tiger Standard,* (the latter two being now defunct) and several Chinese printed newspapers, whose publications helped me date and in some instances indeed triggered in my mind vivid recollections of long forgotten incidents.

Finally, Daphne Paice must accept responsibility for her part in this manuscript, for she typed the second impression. To this day, how she let herself become involved in such a time consuming task continues to mystify her. Thank you Daphne.

LIST OF MAPS

LIST OF FIGURES

End-Paper Maps:
  Front—Asia—Locations Which Appear In Text
  Back—Australasia—Locations Which Appear In Text

CHAPTER ONE
SALAD DAYS

"My salad days, when I was green in judgment"
Anthony and Cleopatra . . . William Shakespeare.

'Crooked roads . . . are roads of genius,' the poet William Blake asserted in his *Proverbs of Hell*, and the road was far from straight that brought me to the pilot's cockpit, the eminence where I spent most of my executive life. Thirty-five of my years have been centred on flying, a career that has brought me a full share of excitement, adventure and some achievement. Twenty-five of them were spent with Cathay Pacific, a remarkable airline with a significant place in Asia's recent history. Flying found me the wife who complements my more leisured life in retirement and enriches it with her many virtues, of which the long list is headed by beauty and intelligence. It has brought hazards too, and painful losses of friends and associates but in the scenes of action and emergency in which air transport is sovereign this is inevitable. I would not have had my life run in any different milieu.

The winding road that led through my early years revealed no glimpse of this destination. I was born at 3.30 on a Monday afternoon, August 2, 1920, at Balmain North, an inner suburb of Sydney in the sovereign State of New South Wales. My first job was with a local company of gas-stove manufacturers, W.T. Carmichael and Sons, who paid me the princely weekly wage of sixteen shillings and threepence. Later I became a machine process metal-worker with the Glebe concern of G.E. Crane, taking home a splendid 2 pounds 5 shillings each Friday. Then September 3, 1939 and the war with Germany introduced new variables in all our lives.

During May 1940 I enlisted with the 1st Australian Anti-Aircraft Regiment and became Gunner Eather NX 17877. My term was brief; intervention of some sort or other led to my discharge—"not occasioned by his own default". The following January, not at all discouraged, I decided I would still be of combative value to my country and joined the Merchant Navy.

My first trip was on S.S. *Mungana*, a 3315-ton rust-bucket that set out on the seventy-mile trip from Sydney to Newcastle one night in February. She was so unseaworthy that what should have been a routine passage of a few hours developed into a nightmare of forty-eight. Her rudder fell off outside Newcastle and we wallowed round in mountainous seas until a tug came to drag us into port. The tug was delayed because the boom was closed following the bombardment of any enemy ship that had tried to slip out of harbour in a fruitless attempt to break her internment.

I'd had enough of *Mungana*, but the experience had one good result. I had been so seasick that never again was I sick at sea or in the air.

Next month, March 1941, I signed articles on HT *Queen Elizabeth*, then the largest ship in the world, and I recall her with affection. Her turn of speed was absolutely phenomenal, and it earned my heartfelt thanks when we cleared the Suez port of Taufiq (Tewfik) in a hurry because of an impending bombing raid on Alexandria. Returning from Suez, when we crossed the Great Australian Bight the seas were so mountainous that the after gun-deck was untenable. Though it was more than seventy feet above Plimsoll line the seas broke right over it.

I walked from stem to stern under the keel of that massive vessel later, when she was in dry dock at Singapore. Finally on a Sunday morning, January 19, 1972 I saw the beautiful ship, now rechristened *Seawise University* and registered at Panama, racked by explosions and consumed by spreading flames in Hong Kong's western harbour. Her blackened hulk remains there to this day, a mass of useless metal.

I signed off the *QE* on June 25, 1941, and the very next day found me belted into the cockpit of a DH 60 Gipsy Moth (VH-UFV) with craggy-faced Howard K. Morris patiently demonstrating how to fly it straight and level. On a day in August, after I had piled up six hours and ten minutes instruction he climbed out of his seat, removed the forward control stick and, tucking it under his arm, stalked away, saying over his shoulder, "Off you go".

I did, and managed a really good first solo. Immediately anyone set out on his first solo those days, an unwritten rule stopped the operation of the whole airfield until the tyro had concluded this once-in-a-lifetime experience. As I rolled to a stop Howard K was leaning against a Tiger Moth just off to the right, talking to the Air Force instructor who was holding his machine with the prop just ticking over. He bounded across to me with a beaming grin and told me, 'Do another circuit'—something he had never done before, or since, probably. This time I made every mistake in the book, and still wonder that I got through without damaging myself or the Gipsy. The silence from Howard on my return could have been cut with a knife, and we left the scene followed by ungentlemanly guffaws from the RAAF instructor.

As with all private ventures in wartime our fuel supply was limited. This retarded the building up of flying hours in pursuit of the elusive 'B' Commercial licence, the Open Sesame to a job. To get round this we used to introduce new members to the Royal Aero Club of New South Wales. On joining they became entitled to a fuel allowance—so it was important to canvass only those who didn't want to take flying instruction, and our ingenuity knew no bounds in locating candidates for membership who would pass on their share of the priceless gravy. Two of the several new members I brought in were Chinese sisters named Bow, who raised the eyebrows of the selection committee when they listed their occupations as 'champagne bottle turners'.

We tapped another source of fuel supply by flying Army co-operation exercises to give gun-laying and predictor practice to anti-aircraft units at Bantry Bay and Lurline Bay on Sydney Harbour's North Shore. We pilots still had to pay for the hire of the aircraft but the fuel allowance meant we could build up our flying hours towards the coveted licence.

Solo Day – 6th August 1941.
Mascot Airport, Sydney 'Chic' and Howard K Morris
VH-UFV 130 hp Gypsy Major.

My old friend Bob Smith recalls those flights with amusement. We were supposed to fly over the batteries straight and level at about 5000 or 6000 feet but occasionally we would vary this with aerobatics and upset the predictor readings. Then the telephone would run hot with protests of righteous indignation and the dark threat of fuel withdrawal would bring us back to the straight and narrow. When I asked how they would handle the situation if any enemy aircraft did in fact follow an aerobatic course, I met a stony silence.

In this period I had been accepted for the RAAF Reserve, presented with a lapel badge and an instructional booklet and told to report three nights a week to nearby Newington College for technical lectures. I found the evenings very enjoyable and learned a lot from my instructors. The course stood me in good stead when I finally sat the examination for my 'B' licence. But the inactivity of the intervening periods was driving me to distraction and I decided to make another trip on my Merchant Navy papers. My RAAF Reserve status precluded this, but I rationalized that I wouldn't be missed for a few weeks. I was only kicking up my heels waiting for that Air Force call-up, and nothing appeared to be happening even though the Nips had entered the fray.

So in February 1942 I was aboard RMS *Aquitania* when she cleared Sydney Heads, and spent two Fridays the thirteenth dodging enemy subs. One of those thirteenths still haunts me. We ploughed through a vast area of wreckage. There were swollen bodies and, I fear, some which still contained a spark of life. Their weak but joyous calls turned to curses as we made no attempt to slacken speed and pick them up. Stopping to pick up survivors was just what the murderers skulking beneath the placid surface would be hoping for us to do; we would have been sitting ducks. But that knowledge was poor compensation for us, and none for them.

We entered Honolulu's Pearl Harbour, littered with mute evidence of the infamous Japanese attack. After a quick shore leave we found that our task was to transport some 2000 American women and their children to the mainland. The sex which was offered and enthusiastically accepted throughout the run to San Francisco was out of this world. I know of few who missed out, and no difficulty arose until an inexperienced helmsman, whose mind was on far more pleasurable occupations proceeded to turn to starboard instead of to port in response to the blast that signalled the convoy to take a zig-zag sub avoidance. Fortunately no real damage resulted from the near collision. I think we lost a little paint off the starboard bow, but this did lead to a restriction of nocturnal pleasures. Probably just as well, for only the most agile could negotiate the deck and avoid the copulating couples occupying every nook and cranny.

At San Francisco we learned that certain irregularities existed in the articles we had signed, and it became necessary for each crew member to sign off and, if he wished, to sign new articles. I accepted this as an opportunity to leave the ship legally, and put into train a scheme to sneak across the border into Canada and there offer myself to the British Air Transport Command.

The British Consul could offer little advice on joining this command from American soil, but did say many others had followed my proposed route and were now doing sterling service flying replacement aircraft to the British Isles. It was a great pity Bob Buckby, another old mate of mine did not follow this path. He joined a refrigeration ship in Sydney which was ''bumped'' in the Atlantic, with the result that both his legs had to be amputated due to frostbite. I recall going aboard with him while this ship was alongside the Pyrmont wharves in Sydney, and she had death written all over her. When I expressed these fears Bob showed not the slightest interest.

As I sneaked up to the Canadian border a giant American cop grabbed me, gave me a couple of vigorous shakes and marched me off to the local bastille. He mellowed when I explained my reasons for being at the border, but not sufficiently to close his eyes to his duty. Next morning found me standing at attention to the very same Consulate official as had so recently advised me how to join the Air Transport Command.

He was now severely reprimanding me for doing anything so foolish. Didn't I realize I was alienating the great friendship which existed between our now-allied countries? Later, with a mischievous grin, he said I'd blown my opportunity by getting caught. But he became quite earnest when he said I mustn't try it again; this was a condition of the bargain he had struck to get me off the hook of my immigration misdemeanour. I had to phone him each day until he could find me transport back to Australia. This materialized about two weeks later in the form of dear old *Queen Elizabeth* and I became a semi-passenger back to Sydney under a Discharged Seamen's Agreement.

We carried thousands of American servicemen to Australia on what proved to be a pleasant voyage. Of all the remote outposts imaginable we stopped for refuelling at the French Marquesas Islands, northeast of Tahiti in the latitude of Peru. While there, I watched an amphibious aircraft, a U.S. Navy *Kingfisher*, trying to take off with an obvious overload of bombs. Each time the pilot made an abortive run he would drop one more bomb over the side. He finally got airborne but as he left the water his remaining bombload exploded and he disintegrated before my eyes. I guess they didn't even find an ear. But the incident had a surprising and permanent effect on my life. That moment finally clinched my decision to make commercial flying my lifelong profession.

Misfortune awaited my return home. I had missed my RAAF call-up and they had sacked me. When I went to see them they informed me in the most forthright manner that I had committed a crime by leaving the country after my acceptance for the Reserve. After ripping a strip off me for several minutes the officer in charge of the section became interested in my escapades and we spent some time in these reminiscences. Despite his obvious sympathy he could not intervene in my re-appointment. He told me my papers were marked that I was a 'bit of a lone wolf' and not amenable to discipline. He merely asked me to return my lapel badge.

I now devoted myself wholeheartedly to my commercial flying ambition, taking several jobs in protected industries. One was with a minute concern which turned out a range of metal parts for the war effort. Here I became acquainted with Max Grosskrutz, an Australian who had reached the peak of success on the pre-war English motor cycle circuits, the then popular sport known as broadsiding. I spent almost nine months from November 1942 as an air-frame fitter in the repair hangar of Australian National Airways (ANA) at Mascot. My initial assignment was to 'attack corrosion' on Fairey Battle aircraft. This location was ideal, as I could steal away from my post and get to the Royal Aero Club 150 yards away for a quick half-hour in the air, increasing my total flying hours towards that professional licence.

By this time I had spent all my Merchant Navy savings and as the ANA job carried a stipend much less than princely, I was plagued with the necessity of finding the 40 pounds needed to complete my 100 hours flying for the licence. My family was unable to help, and flying was not my mother's favourite subject at that time. My younger brother Richard lost his life in a RAAF Catalina flying-boat on February 28 that year while on patrol duty between Cairns and New

Guinea—it was recorded as overdue. I had never been within coo-ee of any sort of prize in the State Lottery of the time, though naturally I tried. I gave it one more chance and to my surprise won exactly 40 pounds. I deposited it with Miss Joyce Richardson, the Assistant Secretary of the R.A.C.

About this time I had a different sort of surprise which left me shaking for some time to come. As I strutted with windcheater, helmet and goggles in place for another jaunt in VH-UWB (a club-leased Gipsy 2 Moth) a screaming roar dulled my senses as a Vultee Vengeance of the RAAF slammed into the Gipsy I was heading for. Both were destroyed in the fire which followed, but what haunted me for days afterwards was the sight of the head of one of the Vultee crew. Severed on impact it rolled and stopped at my feet.

At ANA I met Dagne Joyce Thorbjornsen, the girl who was to become my first wife. Neither of us was greatly impressed. She thought I looked too self-centred, strutting round in my white overalls with my lathe tools tucked under my arm. I was not at all disturbed—I had many girl-friends who made a mere formality of token resistance, and in the callow bloom of youth I made the mistake of considering myself a lover of heroic proportions.

Also here I met the comedian Joe E. Brown. He was a really funny man, but his humility and understanding most impressed me. He had just lost a son in the U.S. Services.

Finally I entered the magic total of 100 hours solo in my logbook in fiery red. I passed the several technical subjects associated with this standard and qualified for a PMG Morse Code Licence. Then, after DCA examiner John Kerr had shown me how little I really knew my 'B' Licence No. 924 duly arrived. This in turn was followed by a job with Ansett Airways Ltd., where I started as an inexperienced first officer on September 4, 1943. G. Peter Hoskins was chief pilot. The company was flying Lockheed Electra 10B aircraft under charter to the U.S. Service of Supply. This was a beautiful aircraft, but its 3975/E3 engine was the noisiest Wright ever manufactured.

Amelia Earhart, famous for her 1932 solo Atlantic flight and many other feats was flying an Electra, a 10e, on a world circumnavigation attempt when with Lieutenant-Commander Fred Noonan as navigator she disappeared in July 1937 between Lae in New Guinea and Howland Island, a U.S. Trust Territory east of Kiribasi almost on the Equator. Their loss was accounted a mystery which plagues investigators to this day. Charges, never proved, kept surfacing that the pre-war Japanese Government, then in control of the area, instigated their recovery and subsequent murder.

We had many engine failures those days but those skippers were of such expertise that they took each incident in stride, handling it matter-of-factly. One that caused concern began when we lost an engine just south of Beaudesert, across the Queensland border. Since no facility existed for feathering the propellors in-stalled on these 450 h.p. "donks" they posed a major drag/ratio problem when power was not being generated. Our aircraft was losing altitude rapidly and the lights of Brisbane were getting higher and higher above our horizon when Captain Johnnie Presgrave (who figures prominently in Cathay Pacific's initial Skymaster operation later in this record) decided that the situation was serious enough to increase power on the sick engine, and he dragged us to a safe landing at Brisbane's Archerfield airport.

For another encounter of far greater import the blame was later attributed to sabotage, and the story made the newspaper headlines of the day. Fortunately, as it transpired, aircraft maintenance had prevented us from departing at our scheduled time of 2 a.m. and it was not until daybreak that Captain H.F. 'Jimmy' Broadbent gave me the order for 'wheels up' and our Ansett airliner was on the way to our first let-down at Archerfield, en route to Garbutt, Townsville's busy Allied service airport. We had also to make a technical stop at Rockhampton.

VH-UZP was making her climb and the raucous scream of those engines on takeoff power had settled to a sweet hum. The altimeter had ticked off the 5000 foot mark, when suddenly the starboard engine spluttered and immediately lost complete thrust. Our position was approximately over Broken Bay at the mouth of the Hawkesbury River, just north of Sydney. Jim immediately turned back for Mascot and, other than the gradual but inevitable loss of altitude, everything seemed well under control. Naturally the remaining engine was at full power and we closely monitored its operation. Then it too began to lose revs, our altitude decreased at an alarming rate, and the aircraft assumed the glide angle of a rock. We could not remain in the air much longer.

A slamming turn to port lined us up with Narrabeen Beach and with barely a bump Jim put her down on the wet, packed sand; but as she lost way the slope of the beach caused her to slew gently to the left and she stopped with the breaking surf softly caressing her nose.

Jim instructed me to get the passengers out, and in my excitement I nearly cut myself in two, slamming against my seat-belt still firmly locked. I overcame this obstruction and then proceeded to strangle myself with the radio head-set cord. Jim was in hysterics and told me I'd make a good 'straight man' in Vaudeville. I left the flight deck uncertain whether this meant I would be better as a comedian than as a pilot, but he was a true gentleman and never brought up that embarrassing moment again. Naturally I was pleased to put it out of *my* mind as well.

Soon I had opened the rear door and was helping the dazed but buoyant American service personnel to disembark. Then I removed the Royal Mail bags and my duty was at an end. I gave a shriek of 'All Clear!' and the thumbs-up signal. Jim, who had been sitting at his post, came to the cabin door calmly, took in my wet but grinning countenance, and taught me a lesson in forethought which remained with me throughout my flying career. He gave me a smile of sympathy, turned and opened the wing exit window, and left the aircraft by sauntering along the starboard wing and dropping on to dry sand.

With the rising tide VH-UZP became awash. A tractor was brought in and caused the only damage the aircraft suffered. A line had been passed round the lower tail cone and the enthusiastic but bumbling efforts of the driver tore off the tail. We learned later, quite unofficially, that sugar had been found in both engines. Sabotage!

1944
F/O 'Chic' Eather
Ansett Airways,
Mascot Sydney

Narrabeen Beach, Sydney North Shore
21st November 1944

Jimmy Broadbent was an astonishing character, one of the most gentle of gentlemen it was ever my pleasure to meet. He was mild to an embarrassing degree: a man who knew what was required and therefore was in full command of the situation. The first instance I can recall of his prowess dates back to March 1931 when he departed from Hanworth in England in his *City of Sydney*, a Blackburn Bluebird IV registered G-ABJA. His sights were set on Australia but he abandoned his attempt in Turkey following a forced landing which caused structural damage. From May 16 to 19, 1935 he made a record flight round Australia in the actual elapsed time of three days 54 minutes. In that year he continued to keep his name before the avid readers of press despatches that featured the era's 'magnificient men in their flying machines'. In the same Gipsy Major Puss Moth C.J. (Jim) Melrose had made a record solo flight from England the year before, in eight days, nine hours. Jimmy Broadbent set out in it to try for the Australia/England record but the Puss Moth ran out of luck. He crashed it in Basra on October 15, 1935 and finished the trip to London on a regular air-mail service. But next month, flying VH-UVA, a Percival Gull, he set up a solo record, touching down in Darwin after six days, 21 hours and 15 minutes.

In January 1936 Jim and his wife Beryl combined their flying talents and crossed Australia from Sydney to Perth and back. The *Sydney Morning Herald* of March 12 reported that he had been appointed chief pilot of Butler Air Transport (BAT) which then operated the Charleville-Cootamundra link of the Empire Mail Service. At that time BAT was flying DH 84 Dragons, and VH-URV

17

1938
H.F. "Jimmy" Broadbent Vega Gull—Gypsy 6—England
Held 200 gals. 2000 N.M. Range

was the registration of 'Cootamundra'. I have a photo of Jimmy, taken by the famous aviatrix Miss Nancy Bird 'one hot day in Bourke, NSW'. As usual he looks dapper and remarkably cool, in full drab uniform, cap and tie.

In 1937 he flew a DH 85 Leopard (VH-AHB) to England in six days, eight hours, 25 minutes, breaking the record set by H.L. Brook, but, attempting the return flight, he cracked up at Baghdad. In 1940, with RAF Transport Command he ferried various types of aircraft from Canada to the British Isles. Finally, on November 9 1958 he commanded CS-THB, a Martin Mariner flying-boat owned by the Portuguese company Aero-Topografica, on a journey from Lisbon to Madeira. Shortly after midday he dramatically radioed that he was landing in the open sea. Nothing was seen or heard of him subsequently.

March 1944 found me, resplendent in a smart American-cut Ansett uniform, waiting for medical examination at the RAAF recruiting centre in Woolloomooloo where the same NCO paraded me before the same officer as had sacked me from the 'awaiting call-up' list. Much to the disgust of other men waiting to be process-ed, these worthies escorted me to the head of the queue and completed my medical and other examinations with an almost indecent haste. It was something of an embarrassment. But the Commonwealth Gazette of June 1, 1944 showed C.E.J. Eather (267720) commissioned on probation with the rank of Flying Officer in the Citizen's Air Force Reserve, attached to the General Duties Branch, Richmond Squadron.

I remained with Ansett until May 1945. I had had a pleasant and happy association with them and it was a reasonable assumption that my prospects were good, so I was reluctant to leave them. But their headquarters were now in Melbourne, and weatherwise she and I did not click, so I returned to the warmer climes of Sydney town with a glowing reference after an amiable severance. It taught me a lesson. Never since then have I left one job without having another in prospect.

Departure coincided with VE-Day, and although the Japanese would not throw in the towel until September, a great swag of experienced Air Force people were already scratching for the few commercial jobs then offering. I quickly found my first-officer status was not preferred over that of men with time on heavier aircraft, the highly decorated men of Bomber Command. This I understood and accepted without animosity: these blokes had done a magnificent job and were entitled to reap the fruits of their labours. But my spirits were not too buoyant during those lean months.

Though I embarked on several interesting projects at this time, the financial reward barely kept me above the poverty line, and like so many others in similar straits I seemed to go out of my way to increase commitments rather than reduce them. In a more affluent period I had married Joyce and soon I had another mouth to feed: son Wayne was born on July 26, 1946. The marriage was not destined for success; under a lack of compatibility it just drifted into a state of non-being.

Five months earlier I had teamed up with Leo Bennett and Willie Walters to secure a New South Wales certificate of registration for 'The Australian Aeronautical Company' with offices at Ross Smith Avenue, Mascot. My card said

'Flight Superintendent', Leo was Managing Director and Willie was our money man and photographic superintendent. Professor Gerhard R. Felser, the present Consul-General of Austria oversaw the establishment of the company, prepared income-tax returns and became my life-long friend.

Our best asset was a Genairco, a biplane with a roomy front cockpit in which two passengers sat side by side, with the pilot operating from a rear cockpit. All were exposed to the elements. This was a real money-spinner when we made joy-flights from abandoned wartime airstrips, such as Tuggerah Lakes, Ablion Park and Goulburn.

We had also paid the Receiver of Public Monies 250 pounds to become the proud owner of a Wackett Trainer. To take possession we rushed off to the RAAF Care and Maintenance Station at Narrandera, 360 miles from Sydney, on the Murrumbidgee. This was the first time I had ever approached a Wackett but we successfully survived a hairy takeoff which, unassisted by a binding port wheelbrake, gave us a flight path directly above a thoroughly terrified—even grovelling—Station Commander. On our return he appeared to suffer an apoplectic fit and, dancing with rage, banished us from his field. Leo and I quickly set out for Mascot, and in the air I found that our compass had failed. It would have been prudent to return to Narrandera which was still in sight, but the wrath of the Station Commander discouraged us. My log book notes 'Steered by the sun'—whatever that might have meant—and to intensify our grief we ran into a violent electrical storm just north of Nowra. All this went to show how inexperienced I really still was.

Norman Bush, a carcass butcher and meat exporter from Homebush wrote that Wackett off near Bankstown on January 7, 1947 when his engine failed on takeoff, killing himself and his nine-year-old niece and critically injuring his brother. The aircraft, of course, was licensed for only two occupants.

Though Leo and I gave it our best efforts, the air taxi side of the business was a total flop. The only weekday assignments we ever managed to find were occasional air-photography flights. Our choice of unsuitable aircraft had doomed us and we were finally forced into liquidation by April 1946, an event terminating weeks of disillusion for me.

The next two months brought various ferry assignments, the most note-worthy being my part in a mass flight of eleven Tiger Moths from Western Junction, the airport of Launceston, Tasmania, to Mascot, Sydney. Then I teamed up with another Sydney pilot, Frederick Stokes, to fly two Tigers from Mascot to Bundaberg. That flight ended at Palmer's Island in the Clarence River, where we force-landed on the local cricket ground because of a mechanical fault in Stoke's engine.

Fred was an unlucky pilot. Next month he and John Mulholland crash-landed in a field at Ballina despite the efforts of civic-minded local residents who turned on the lights of seventy motor vehicles in a fruitless attempt to draw his attention to the local emergency landing area. Neither was injured and the aircraft suffered only superficial structural damage. But Fred Stokes was killed one month later when his Tiger Moth nose-dived into a farm at French's Forest near Sydney.

1946
Genairco . . . VH-UOD The Australian Aeronautical Company
The front cockpit holds two passengers side by side)

JANUARY 1972—WESTERN HARBOUR, HONG KONG
Seawise University, Panama. Ex-Queen Elizabeth of 83,600 tons and
1031 feet in length. Chapman College of Orange, California. Owner:
Bland Navigation Co. Fire started Sunday 19th January 1972 at 10.30
am. Mr C.Y. Tong purchased for HK$3.2 million in 1970 at a
Florida auction.

I am not happy about recording the next phase of my career because therein I failed to face up to commitments I owed to Mandated Airlines, a company which, in good faith, offered me a hard-to-get position, command of one of their DH 84 Dragons in New Guinea. From the outset the country jolted my confidence with a disturbing conviction that if I hung round there long enough it would claim my life. In June 1946 I had a familiarisation flight on VH-AOS at Lae, and two weeks later it was also the mount for my swansong. The interlude absolutely terrified me, and the most casual observer must have judged me as 'lacking moral fibre'. I attempted to rekindle a career there five years later with my old friend Eric McIllree, but the country still had this ominous effect on me.

Eric McIllree, of McIllree Motors in Sydney was one of those farsighted entrepreneurs with ready cash who reaped riches from war surplus aircraft bought through the Disposals Commission. My first task for him consisted in making the technical preparations for flight and then ferrying to Sydney some twenty-five Avro Ansons from all parts of Australia, a commission carried out without mishap. He also asked me to organise and take charge of a proposed formation flight of Ansons for re-sale in the United Kingdom. He always toyed with the most grandiose plans, some of which must have interfered with his sleep, but this ferrying of Ansons to England could have been a real money-spinner.

The original cost of the Ansons to the Australian public was about 15,000 pounds. Eric bought some of them for less than 500 pounds. After conversion for a Civil Certificate of Airworthiness (then not the formidable hurdle it presents today) and taking into consideration the vast distance to be flown and the concomitant expenses of fuel, insurance, flight personnel etc., his calculated selling price of 30,000 pounds sterling would still have netted him a handsome return.

Though all these preparations were my responsibility I was no longer working for him when the first batch of three Ansons took off from the Camden airstrip on March 19. They switched off in Croydon airport on April 19. But on the Tuesday morning of December 17, 1946, an interview with Harry de Leuil, Sydney manager of the lusty infant Cathay Pacific then was, brought me into that great organisation, and except for a short break when I joined the Union of Burma Airways, the association lasted for the next 29 years.

CHAPTER TWO
WORLD'S FIRST INTERNATIONAL
AIR MERCHANDISERS

With a cargo of ivory,
And apes and peacocks,
Sandalwood, cedarwood and sweet white wine.

Cargoes, John Masefield

When the Second World War ended a group of young flyers who had developed a mutual respect in the air campaigns of the East, pooled their worldly resources to form an air-merchandising company with its eyes primarily on the China/Australia axis. Americans, Roy Clinton Farrell, Millard Kadot Nasholds, Robert S. Russell and William Geddes-Brown and the Australian Sydney de Kantzow had all been involved in the transport flying of the China National Aviation Corporation, an offshoot of Pan-American which had ensured air supply to the Chinese Nationalist forces.

The natural leader of the group was Roy Farrell, who hailed from Vernon, Texas, a city of about 12,000 people, the county seat of Wilbarger County and situated on the Pease River at its junction with the Red, which here forms the northern boundary of Texas. Wilbarger County has many oilfields and Vernon is also a shipping point for the farm produce of a region rich in cotton, wheat, alfalfa and cattle. Here the Farrell family kept a large general store and assumed the role of community leaders, very much at the centre of the wheeling and dealing which typifies the independent Texan.

These pilots met in late 1945 in Miami, Florida. They shared a common problem: how to adapt from the 'all-found' environment of the forces to the dog-eat-dog competitive all-in fighting of Civvy street. They solved it by pooling resources to buy a war-surplus aircraft in New York. It was an oil-stained, unsalubrious, deceivingly-camouflaged scow of a DC3 of questionable antecedents and dubious age, but when they first beheld it their pride of possession far exceeded any doubts. Her registration was NC58093.

With a cargo mainly of clothing they flew it to Shanghai by way of Dakar, Karachi and Calcutta. At Kunming, in Yunnan Province they renewed an acquain-quaintance with CNAC's flight-despatch officer K.K. Wong, who promptly asked them for a job. This bad timing brought a reluctant refusal, but he was to get his wish before the end of the year. They made a landing at the Central Chinese city of Kweilin before rolling on to Lungwha airport at Shanghai. The route had been well thought out and anyway was familiar to them as the one they had used

VR-HDB (DC3)
Certificate of Airworthiness Photo No 22—Hong Kong Department of Civil Aviation—14th
January 1947. (NC 58093— BETSY)   Cathay Pacific's First Aircraft

for replacement aircraft during the war years, so that they had a friendly rapport with flight despatchers and oil company representatives, thus coming in for the little perks of service freely given between airmen of that era.

One thing marred this inaugural flight. When they landed at Shanghai they found that a lot of their immaculately sealed cartons were empty, their contents quietly milked away at each set-down. They should have been aware something was amiss: NC58093 (affectionately now called Betsy) had been showing an astonishing climb rate which improved on each leg of the flight.

In that area, war-starved of commodities of most kinds, these cargo filchers had to be accepted as a fact of life, and, I suspect, their descendants live on. I recall the roar of righteous indignation just a few years ago when Aussie waterside workers threatened industrial action against the introduction of cargo containers which would prevent them pilfering, thus inflicting a massive loss of personal tax-free income.

With throttles set just below the over-boost line the partners set out for Australia, their arrival on February 4, 1946 inaugurating the first direct air-merchandising service between China and Australia. In Sydney they loaded a full cargo of suits and suitings which would more than compensate for their initial loss. They gave the consignment full protection at all stops, determined to give no more chances to free-loaders or pilferers, and rapidly distributed it through their Shanghai head office at 25 Rue du Consulate, where Bill Geddes-Brown took over the management. In his less liverish moments Bill answered to the name of 'Ged'.

By hard work and dedication they moved a mountain of freight. By March 1946 accumulated profits convinced them of the necessity to buy another aircraft to handle their rapidly expanding business. Roy Farrell convinced the others that it was politic to make the purchase in Australia, where practically all their supply originated. A jaundiced eye or two had already been swivelled towards their Betsy, still operating under United States registration. Ownership of an aircraft regularly inspected by the Australian Department of Civil Aviation would tend to keep that august body on side. As an additional link, the now thoroughly tired pilot partners planned to employ Australian-licensed aircrews. In their first move they bought VH-ASJ, a sleek, silvery DC3.

The partners had designed an emblem to stencil on their aircraft. It depicted, within a circle, a kangaroo jumping towards the three flags of Australia, the United States and China, along with a protective dragon. The same motif on their letterhead showed the kangaroo jumping off an upside-down Australia, and the flags foregrounded by a DC3. It was effective symbolism.

In Australia they recruited John Aubrey ('Pinky') Wawn, Neville Hemsworth and Robert Donovan, the first two as 'instant captains', in April 1946. They also hired a stalwart first officer, S.V. ('Vic') Leslie and an excellent radio man, Lyell William ('Mum') Louttit. Of these only one remained with the company more than three years, though Bob Donovan returned in 1949 for another stint. Mum Louttit stayed almost thirty years, becoming a fully qualified pilot. An appreciative company transferred him to pilot duties when radio operators became redundant

THE ROY FARRELL EXPORT-IMPORT CO. LTD.
Roy C. Farrell and Robert S. Russell at Mascot, Sydney, 4th February
4th, 1946, after establishing the first direct air service between China
(Shanghai) and Australia.   The aircraft was C47 NC 58093 (VR-HDB).

August 1946

Captain Roy Farrell, Founder of the Roy Farrell Export-Import Company, the forerunner of Cathay Pacific Airways, waves to Sydney Reporter from the company's first C47 NC 58093 which later became VR-HDB

(Form 5.)   71054

New South Wales.

BUSINESS NAMES ACT, 1934.

(Section 16.)

Certificate of Registration

I hereby certify *that registration pursuant to the Business Names Act, 1934, has been effected in respect of a business carried on at*

Rooms 21-22, Prudential Building, Martin Place, *under*

the Business Name of   Sydney

—— — ROY FARRELL EXPORT-IMPORT CO. ——

Given under my hand, at Sydney, this

eleven   *day of*   March,

one thousand nine hundred and   forty-six.

Registrar-General.

N.B. This certificate is required to be exhibited in a conspicuous position at the principal place of business.

Whenever a change is made or occurs in any of the particulars in respect of which any firm, individual or corporation is registered, a statement in the prescribed form should be sent by post or delivered to the Registrar General within fourteen days after such change. If any firm, individual or corporation ceases to carry on business or abandons the use of its business name, notice thereof in the prescribed form should be given to the Registrar General.

FIGURE 1: ROY FARREL EXPORT-IMPORT CO., BUSINESS CERTIFICATE OF REGISTRATION, SYDNEY

THE FIRST DIRECT AIR SERVICE
between
CHINA AND AUSTRALIA
was established on 4th February, 1946
By Roy C. Farrell and Robert S. Russell Flying
"BETSY" (VR-HDB)

THE FIRST DIRECT AIR SERVICE
between
HONG KONG AND AUSTRALIA
was established on 12th July, 1946
By An Ex-Royal Australian Airforce Crew Flying
"BETSY" (VR-HDB)

THE FIRST AIRMERCHANDISE SERVICE
between
HONG KONG AND THE UNITED KINGDOM
was established on 28th October, 1946
By An Ex-Royal Australian Airforce Crew Flying
"NIKI" (VR-HDA)

The Roy Farrell Export-Import Co. (H.K.) Ltd.

Originated with "Betsy", an Army surplus Dakota Aircraft [illegible] twelve months ago. It now operates several aircraft over self established and pioneered Air-routes. By the experience of very [illegible] flights a reliable **AIRMERCHANDISE**, accident-free record [illegible] successfully maintained, combined with what is the only

TRANS-OCEAN EXPORT-IMPORT BUSINESS BY AIR IN THE WORLD.

The Directive of the company are all "War-Veterans" from [illegible] Air-forces employing almost exclusively ex-Servicemen and [illegible] all assisted by their individual experiences gained during the [illegible] of War-service and now rehabilitated in what we believe to be [illegible] most enterprising and interesting business in the World.

The Roy Farrell Export-Import Co. (H.K.) Ltd.

The First International **AIRMERCHANDISE** Service In [illegible]

402—403 York Building,
Chater Road, Hong Kong.

Telephones 31360
31350

AND AT

SYDNEY (AUSTRALIA), MANILA (PHILIPPINE ISLANDS), SHANGHAI (CHINA) AND LONDON (UNITED KINGDOM).

Fig 2: "First Direct Air Service Between China and Australia" advertisement as appeared *South China Morning Post.*

1947
L to R: Roy Farrell, Neill Buchanan and Millard Nasholds
Kai Tak Airport, Hong Kong

to their operation on August 12, 1959. He and I were to share in countless adventures, including the world's first air-piracy, the shooting down of our Skymaster at Hainan Island (this nearly precipitated a war!) and the hush-hush snatching of Bao Dai, the Emporer of Annam, from Tourane.

Vic Leslie had begun his career in aviation in 1935 by joining the RAAF as an aerial photographer, and later qualified as observer/navigator. In 1939 he gained his coveted pilot's wings, and for the first three and a half years of the war was a flying instructor, conducting 41 courses. He was then assigned to No 46 Squadron, and engaged in supply-dropping missions to Allied troops in New Guinea and the South Pacific area. His qualifications were of the best. He was a quiet type, content to let his reputation and ability speak for themselves. He was a major influence on the less-experienced airmen, always ready to assist.

As business continued to flourish the partners opened branch offices. Captain Nasholds became manager of one in Juan Luna Street in Manila. Captain Bob Russell presided over rooms 921-922 in the Prudential Building in Sydney, where I was soon to join the company. Ex-RAAF Squadron Leader Neil Buchanan directed their fortunes from 311 Prince's Building in Ice House Street, Hong Kong. On August 28, 1946 the partners registered the Roy Farrell Export-Import Company (Hong Kong) Limited, its cable address, 'Broncho, Hong Kong' suggesting the American involvement.

The various premises proclaimed them 'the first air-merchandising service in the world' and their stationery carried the line 'Merchandising Australian products in the Far East—China products in Australia'. They gloried in the reputation that they carried everything from soap to nuts; their Hong Kong newspaper advertisements covered 'Scamp' swimsuits, dual wave radios and Challenge tennis balls.

The mainly ex-RAAF personnel took over the flying reins with enthusiasm and to such good effect that the remaining two active flying partners, Roy Farrell and Syd de Kantzow, devoted more time to locating the more profitable cargoes and the snowballing paperwork.

The element of novelty had undoubtedly aided these early efforts, along with a paucity of competition. They had been able to sell plastic picture frames from Sydney at $HK 30 a time, men's plastic belts at $HK 60, and get rid of the consignment almost before Betsy was inspected, fuelled and taken off again. This occupied little time, for an aircraft resting snugly against wheel-chocks is a liability, with its parking, insurance and other charges. But they were entering a period of diminishing success. August brought the return of an increasing number of ships to ply China's eastern coast and challenge their near monopoly. Cargo consignments were becoming more elusive and when they were obtained they stayed on the Hong Kong and Shanghai outlet shelves for longer and longer periods. Even as they registered their company they were aware that a change of direction would benefit them. Since the end of flying their own merchandise to sell at profit was in sight they would concentrate on charter flying with, they hoped, scheduled airline routes to follow.

In September they met to form a new company. The venue was on the

FIGURE 3: "WING YOUR WAY BY CPA" ADVERTISEMENT
"CHINA MAIL" WEDNESDAY, 1st JANUARY, 1947

tenth floor of the modern Sassoon Building which spreads along the Bund and into the main shopping thoroughfare of Naking Road, in Shanghai. This building housed the Cathay Hotel, now renamed the Peace Hotel, and in 1947 it was accurately described as 'palatial'.

Guided by Roy Farrell and Syd de Kantzow the meeting was soon in agreement on the formation of a legitimate airline, flying private charters as well as charters for other airlines. This was confirmation of a preliminary move by Farrell, de Kantzow and Nasholds to secure office space in the premises of P.J. Lobo and Company in Hong Kong's Chater Road. They had discussed their plans with the eldest son, now the Hon. Rogerio Hyndman Lobo, OBE, JP, concentrating on the prospect of a possible schedule service to Macao, the overseas province of Portugal on the China coast only forty miles away. When they finished talking they had Roger agreeing to act as general agent, beginning an association that would endure and develop in the years ahead.

Farrell especially had his eye on the Macao run. The shorter hauls were the best paying; an aircraft could complete several return trips every day. With the short lines of communication, ever-present engine problems could be rectified quickly.

The meeting in the Cathay Hotel quickly decided that the new company's location would be in the British Colony of Hong Kong, as being more resistant to Communism than mainland China. They took rather longer to decide on a name. The others generally rejected Pinky Wawn's suggestion of 'Air Cathay' as being too limiting a description, though it had merits, and was adopted for a telegraphic code still gracing the letterheads, a fact which Pinky admits gives him a great deal of pride.

The word 'China' in the title would not have been helpful, because Communism was spreading rapidly and would shortly be consolidated under Chairman Mao Tse-tung. 'Cathay' would escape the opprobrium. As defined in the *Encyclopaedia Sinica*, 'Cathay [is] a form of the name by which China is known in Central Asia. It is derived from the race called Khitans who occupied the Sungari Basin and established the Liao Dynasty in China (AD 937-980)'.

The Pacific was where their fortune was to be found. Combining the two names was both rhythmic and romantic and, like the slogan 'Wing your way with CPA' was striking and easily remembered. Setbacks were to occur in the form of accidents, both avoidable and otherwise. Dear Duncan Bluck, currently Cathay Pacific's Chairman, had an aversion to mentioning such things, but they were part of the pattern of growth. The main obstacle to forward progress was to come from Government red tape which, in the flick of an eye, would blot out the Oriental system, centuries old, whereby individuals made their own bilateral agreements without outside considerations.

On September 24, 1946 the new company registered as Cathay Pacific Airways (Hong Kong) Limited. Its nominal capital was $HK5,000,000 in the form of 5,000,000 shares of a dollar each. The directers were Farrell, de Kantzow and Neil Buchanan. The combination of money, faith and effort ensured that the company flourished from that time, so much so that a vigilant Board of Directors

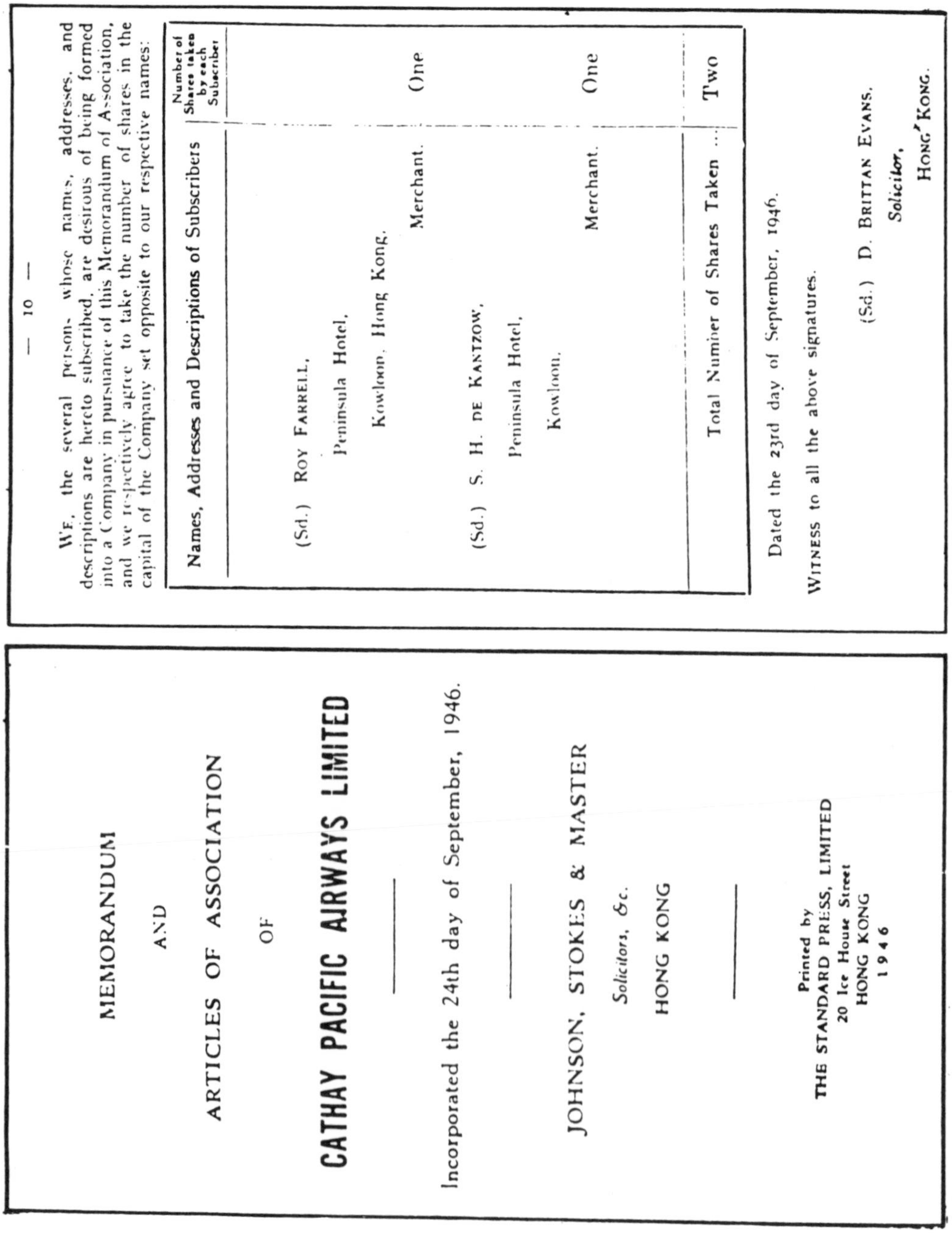

We, the several persons whose names, addresses, and descriptions are hereto subscribed, are desirous of being formed into a Company in pursuance of this Memorandum of Association, and we respectively agree to take the number of shares in the capital of the Company set opposite to our respective names:

Names, Addresses and Descriptions of Subscribers	Number of Shares taken by each Subscriber
(Sd.) ROY FARRELL, Peninsula Hotel, Kowloon, Hong Kong. Merchant.	One
(Sd.) S. H. DE KANTZOW, Peninsula Hotel, Kowloon. Merchant.	One
Total Number of Shares Taken ...	Two

Dated the 23rd day of September, 1946.

WITNESS to all the above signatures.

(Sd.) D. BRITTAN EVANS,
Solicitor,
HONG KONG.

MEMORANDUM

AND

ARTICLES OF ASSOCIATION

OF

CATHAY PACIFIC AIRWAYS LIMITED

Incorporated the 24th day of September, 1946.

JOHNSON, STOKES & MASTER

Solicitors, &c.

HONG KONG

Printed by
THE STANDARD PRESS, LIMITED
20 Ice House Street
HONG KONG
1946

FIGURE 4: *CATHAY PACIFIC AIRWAYS LIMITED INCORPORATED*
24th SEPTEMBER, 1946

of the British Overseas Airways Corporation now decided that their monopoly should include the China coast, an area they had ignored in the past. Now that Cathay Pacific demonstrated the potential BOAC obtained the sympathetic ear of the far-removed British Government which, weary of supporting a sick national carrier, agreed that the East should be BOAC's monopolized preserve. To this time, BOAC's contribution to the welfare of Hong Kong had been a single weekly flight made in five and half days by a lumbering Hythe flying-boat terminating at Hong Kong's Kai Tak Sea-drome. Hong Kong was not a free Dominion, but very much a colony of Britain.

In the beginning the noises of discontent were barely audible, no more than a prelude to the approaching confrontation. But the ready compliance and short-sighted policy of the Home Government would produce a gradual escalation of intrigue at first, and then viscous in-fighting, the Home Government supporting BOAC, the Hong Kong Government manfully standing up for their local Cathay Pacific.

From 1930 to 1939 civil aviation in the Colony had been under the control of the Harbour Department, a reasonable arrangement as the sea-drome was utilis-ed more frequently than the tiny grassed landing area. Civil aviation was suspend-ed when Hong Kong surrendered to the Japanese on Christmas Day, 1941. The subsequent occupation, however, had one beneficial result: the reclamation and extension of Kai Tak aerodrome. Surrounding buildings and private property were resumed by the conquerors' simple annexation ploy—'a quick boot up the arse'.

With peace restored, authorities removed control from the Habour Board on May 1, 1946, and formed the 'Civil Air Services' under A.J.R. Moss, a full-time Director. His title was changed the following year to 'Director of Civil Aviation'. He proved a staunch advocate of Cathay Pacific's aims, and got along famously with the company. Syd de Kantzow asked his intervention for the allotment of a schedule service, using DC3's between Hong Kong and Macao, carrying passengers, mail and cargo and requested interim approval of a non-scheduled service, while awaiting the Government decision. Moss not only approved it, but cleared it with the Macao Colonial Secretary at a time when Cathay Pacific was not yet incorporated.

The Hong Kong community quickly assessed the value of the company's offerings, and several charters came the way of the viable but still shaky organisa-tion. They provided a sufficient income to keep the wolf from the door, and the company directors were vigilant also that the crows did not fly through the window.

Their first venture was to Manila, and then when charters to Siam (now Thailand), Burma and Sydney were satisfactorily completed they knew that their entry into legitimate airline operation had been timely. The charter operations were making a small profit at a time when better-known companies with more modern equipment still recorded alarming losses.

The Manila *Daily Tribune* of October 28, 1946 announced that the local Farrell office, acting as Cathay Pacific's general agents in the Philippines, had opened a non-scheduled air service between Manila and Hong Kong to start about November 9. Cathay Pacific had thus received the first commercial air rights granted to a British-registered company by the Philippine Foreign Affairs department since

CATHAY PACIFIC
AIRWAYS LIMITED

have pleasure in announcing

their initial CHARTER FLIGHT

To The

UNITED-KINGDOM

ON

WEDNESDAY, 23rd OCTOBER, 1946

ASSOCIATED WITH WHICH IS THE

EXPANSION OF THE SERVICE OF ——

The Roy Farrell Export-Import Co. (Hongkong) Ltd.

The First International AIRMERCHANDISE Service in the World

Australia—Manila—Hong Kong—China and now United Kingdom

FIGURE 5: *CPA's FIRST CHARTER FLIGHT TO THE UNITED KINGDOM*
"SOUTH CHINA MORNING POST" ADVERTISEMENT
MONDAY, 21st OCTOBER, 1946

the end of the war. It would give Philippine residents a direct route to England via Cathay Pacific's charter service from Hong Kong to London. The first of these latter flights had left the Colony for the Old Dart in November, with seventeen Chinese students. Captain Neville Hemsworth was in command, with Bob Donovan as first officer and Alex Stewart as radio officer. 'It was one hell of a long trip,' Bob recalls. 'Thirty days from October 23, 1946.'

At this time the Roy Farrell Export-Import Company had chartered a DC3 from Cathay Pacific and in October were able to state that they had established the first air-merchandising service between Hong Kong and the United Kingdom, with an ex-RAAF crew flying 'Niki', officially VR-HDA.

The inauguration flight to Singapore via Bangkok on December 9, 1946 had standing-room only. In fact, Managing Director de Kantzow, arriving in a flurry of dust, found that an enthusiastic ticket-clerk, drunk with power, had sold his seat. But he was aboard when the DC3 left Kai Tak at first light; the airfield being closed to night operation except in emergency. They rolled in Singapore's Changi field right on the dot.

Thereafter, this flight departed Kai Tak each Saturday morning and left Singapore on Sunday at 2 a.m. 'A bloody awful time,' flight crew agreed, but it allowed them a four and a half hour rest period. One got a rest where one could— the aircraft itself being as good a place as any other until the close, humid atmosphere and the inevitable bugs and mosquitoes drove the would-be sleeper out for a walk and some fresh air. The same crew did the entire flight, the round trip demanding a duty period of some thirty hours. Flight-time limits, palatial hotel accommodation and interesting stopovers were still far distant in the future.

On reflection I don't think such rat-race operation could be justified, but the general dedication and willingness to do a little more than one's share must have contributed to the future fortunes of the company. It could be argued that if this attitude had been absent there would have been no Cathay Pacific and none of the comfortable flying jobs of today.

Using Hong Kong as axis and currency comparison base, flights to Manila cost $600, to Bangkok $528, to Singapore $880 and to Sydney a massive $2,200. Freight cost $11 a kilo, and 55 pounds was the general baggage allowance. Cathay Pacific undercut schedule competitors by at least $200 on both the Manila and Shanghai sectors, but this variation came to an end. By March 1947 the regional operators had stabilised fares to around $300 for Manila and $380 for Shanghai.

CHAPTER THREE
CONSTRUCTION ELEMENTS

And far across the hills they went,
In that new world which is the old.

The Day Dream—The Departure
Alfred, Lord Tennyson

The thews and sinews of Cathay Pacific, the factors responsible for its fast-growing strength and efficiency, were rooted in the variant personalities and experience of a remarkable grouping of men. Managing Director Sydney Hugh de Kantzow was born on November 9 in the lazy seaside town of Austinmer, near Wollongong in New South Wales, and in his 43-year span packed several lifetimes of adventure, displaying a rare talent for flying and organisation as well as steadfast courage. The de Kantzows were a family of Polish origin which transferred to Sweden during the Swedish domination of Poland, and thereafter became prominent in many parts of the world, especially as Africa and the East came under European influence.

I found Syd difficult to get to know. He had a moody and retiring disposition and throughout the time he maintained an active association with Cathay Pacific he remained something of an enigma to me. Brought up in the Sydney suburb of Roseville, he learned flying at Mascot in 1934. He is credited with the formation of Canberra's first Aero Club, in partnership with Rod Julius, son of Sir George Julius who was the first chairman of the Council for Scientific and Industrial Research and in 1934 was appointed Chairman of the Australian Council for Aeronautics.

Rod held the agency for Piper aircraft. The two aviators would persuade several enthusiasts to contribute 50 pounds each towards the purchase of a Piper, one of the purchasing commitments being an undertaking to teach each co-owner how to fly. They taught many who were to make their mark in wartime flying. One of their earliest pupils was the future Lady Casey, wife of Lord (R.G.) Casey, the celebrated Member of the War Cabinet and Governor of Bengal. Rod Julius unfortunately met an early death when he flew into a hill during a restricted visibility approach to land.

Syd renewed his acquaintance with Pinky Wawn who, with G.P. Hoskins had learned flying at the same time. With their 'B' certificates licensing them to fly 'for hire or reward' de Kantzow and Wawn now applied for first officer jobs with the New South Wales-based Southern Airlines and Freighters Limited, the former Intercity Airways. The Managing Director was Ian H. Grabowsky.

The two became 'co-jocks' in what in that year were modern giants, the Codock and its derivative the Tugan Gannet, disrespectfully dubbed 'Pregnant

Junior Captains Sydney de Kantzow and John ("Pinky")
Wawn—Great Western and Southern Airlines,
Shoreham, England, March 1939.

Percys'. In my own callow youth I thought them monstrosities dreamed up by designers in their cups, but they were really quite exceptional for the period. The Codock was built, of all unlikely places, at Cockatoo Island Dockyard in Sydney Harbour, a yard better known for its ships. Hence the aircraft name. It was completed at the beginning of March 1934 and its initial test-flight on March 6 was made by my beloved hero Sir Charles Kingsford Smith.

The design evolved into the Tugan Gannet, built at Mascot where Leo Turl and Frank Gannon had taken over the hangar previously occupied by the General Aircraft Company, for whom Gannon had developed the Genairco. Tugan Aircraft Limited lifted its name from those of the partners. Of most interest to me were the two Tugan Gannets VH-UVU and VH-UYE, the former because de Kantzow and Wawn flew her, the latter because of Charles Gatenby. He was a skipper with Ansett Airways while I was with them during the war; but with the late Sid Marshall as engineer and co-pilot he skippered VH-UYE when it became the first Australian-designed and built aircraft to fly across an ocean. In June 1937 their return flight took them from Sydney to Rabaul by way of Brisbane, Rockhampton, Townsville, Port Douglas, Port Moresby and Lae.

This first commercial flying took them, with Sydney as a base to Narromine and Broken Hill, with stops at Bathurst, Mudgee, Orange, Dubbo, Nyngan, Cobar and Wilcannia as inducement offered. As first the DC2, then the DC3 superseded the Gannet and Codock they were phased out, but during the war years Butler Air Transport flew one on the 'Bega or Bust' service down the New South Wales Coast.

The red-dust country landing-fields afforded magnificent though Spartan training, but Syd and Pinky were tiring of the limited round and the prospect of a European war was in the air, so they resigned and sailed together on the P & O liner *Ormonde* for the United Kingdom. On the voyage they struck up an acquaintance with two other young fellows going to take up short service commissions with the RAF—but destined, alas, to early deaths when blasted from an unfriendly sky. The rather rare photograph I have included shows Junior Captains de Kantzow and Wawn at Shoreham, England, proudly but awkwardly wearing the uniform of the Great Western and Southern Airlines, a subsidiary of Imperial Airways, the forerunner of British Overseas Airways (BOAC) and the present British Airways (BA). In this service they skippered DH 89As, Short Scions, Percival Gulls, and those old faithfuls the Dragon DH 84s. Their bread-and-butter route was to the Scilly Isles, off to the west of Lands End. As war drew nearer, Wawn decided his prime allegience was to Australia. He hastened back and was commissioned in the RAAF, in which he served with distinction.

On the outbreak of war de Kantzow joined 24 Communications Squadron in Britain where, after about five months he met C.W.A. Scott who, partnered by Tom Campbell Black won the speed division of the England to Australia MacRobertson Air Race, finishing at Flemington Racecourse in Melbourne on October 23 1934—the year that de Kantzow was learning to fly.

Scott and Black's sleek red aircraft was a de Havilland 88 Comet, christened 'Grosvenor House' and registered G-CSS. They finished the race in the then incredible elapsed time of 70 hours, 38 minutes and 18 seconds. The importance of the aircraft was its design which was later incorporated in the famous World War II Mosquito.

De Kantzow and Scott now began delivering Blenheim bombers to Greece. They were hazardous days with the Middle East ready to explode into intense and vicious fighting. Their delivery duties included training members of the Greek Air Force to operate the Blenheims.

De Kantzow's experience and expertise had built his reputation to such consequence that when he expressed interest in the Atlantic Ferry Service those in control signed him up with almost indecent haste. He served in this hazardous operation for more than twelve months until the RAF had gained the necessary strength to take over this vital phase of aircraft supply and replacement from America.

With the legion of contacts he made during this shuttle he quickly found a niche in the embryo Pan-American South Atlantic ferries, flying supply and replacement aircraft through Dakar to the war zones. From there his employers, Pan-American Airways (PAA) seconded him to a company in which they held 20% of the stock, and he now became a valued acquisition of the famous China National Aviation Corporation (CNAC). En route to this China posting he briefly visited the Crown Colony of Hong Kong. It was then in late 1941, a few weeks before the Japanese attack on Pearl Harbour, and the city so impressed him that he decided he would seek his fortune there when peace came.

At least one reliable account credits him with opening the air route over The Hump, a link between India and China made essential by the Japanese advances; and certainly it was with this link that he was mainly associated until the end of the war. The Sino-Japanese war had been bitterly fought since 1937, and was conducted brutally, with mass killings and refinements of torture, each side attempting to outdo the other in ruthlessness. With the Japanese Navy blockading China Sea ports the Chinese carved out the Burma Road, a ribbon of terrifying hairpin bends transversing the malaria-ridden terrain between Yunnan's capital of Kunming and Lashio in Burma. Only 625 miles (1005 km) in length it took the average truck six days to negotiate because of the gradients, the high operating altitudes and the ever-present humidity. Engines overheated and had to be kept in low gear all the time. Consequently the maximum road speed rarely exceeded eight miles an hour uphill, and to the weary drivers it seemed all uphill. Effective life of the vehicles averaged one and a half round trips. As the cost of a truck was between $US 500 and $US 600, and freight rates were $100 a ton, overloading was the name of the game. The clapped-out vehicles could be sold in China at the end of the second inward trip for around $US 1000, and were therefore pure profit.

After October 1940 this was the only route of supply available to sea-blockaded China. In April 1942 the Japanese overran Burma, sezied Lashio and closed the Burma road. So Generalissimo Chiang Kai-Shek, who had shifted his capital to Chungking in the Far West, turned to CNAC, of which the pilots rose to the challenge, pioneering several routes over the mountain complex they called

The Hump, feeling their way through uncharted mountain passes of the Himalayas. They were soon joined by the U.S. Air Transport Command, and the supplies continued to flow.

The transports also carried equipment, aircraft replacement parts and gasoline for General Claire Chennault's 'Flying Tigers' organised in 1941 as the American Volunteer Group (AVG), deliveries actually increasing in volume. More supplies were flown over The Hump than ever were hauled over the Burma Road. Technically 'The Hump' was the sky route from Dinjan in the Northeast Indian province of Assam, to Chungking. It might have been the meanest air route of World War II with its multitude of hazardous problems. Aircraft operated round the 23,000 foot mark with engines specially supercharged, though the mountains attracted a liberal supply of rain, electrical storms, snow and glazed ice which often forced the unfortunate jockey below the safe altitude line. When these were combined with darkness the pilot was always on tenterhooks; when the weather was clement vigilant enemy warplanes pounced on the unwary, heavily-laden transports.

For de Kantzow each assignment was one of adventure. At an early stage of his CNAC service he followed the example of Captain Royal Leonard, another hero of mine, to become the personal pilot of Generalissimo Chiang. W.G. Burchett, in his book *Wingate's Phantom Army* tells of a flight he made with the Generalissimo, Madame Chiang Kai-Shek and Brigadier Orde Wingate, whose Chindits were harassing the Japanese in the Burmese jungles.

The aircraft had hardly reached cruising level when de Kantzow acknowledged a radio call from one of the many observation posts that CNAC had established throughout the mountains. The message went like this:

'Do you know there are Jap planes on the lookout for you?'

'Where?' asked de Kantzow

'Well, I can see you, and I can see fifteen Nips stalking you from above!'

Sydney's answer was not recorded—a pity, because he was noted for an exceptionally descriptive and lurid turn of phrase. It must have been short; the intelligence galvanised him into action and the subsequent display of cloud and close terrain flying would have gladdened the heart of the most ardent hedge-hopper or given him an inferiority complex. The only casualty was Madame's breakfast, of which she is reported to have said, 'It doesn't taste so good as going down'. Otherwise the episode apparently did little to disturb the equanimity of the VIPs, but the Generalissimo conferred the prized Chinese *Order of the Flying Cloud* on de Kantzow some little time later.

K.K. Wong, the radio officer taken into Cathay Pacific soon after its formation recalls that de Kantzow was not only senior pilot of CNAC's passenger fleet and the Generalissimo's personal pilot but, when these duties did not preclude, flew almost daily on the Chungking-Kunming-Dinjan and Calcutta route. Farrell, Nasholds, Russell and Geddes-Brown were mainly engaged in the freighter operation. Many outstanding pilots were involved, including two Chinese who became almost legendary: General P.T. Mow and Captain Moon Chin.

The secondary sky route between Dinjan and Kunming shared many of

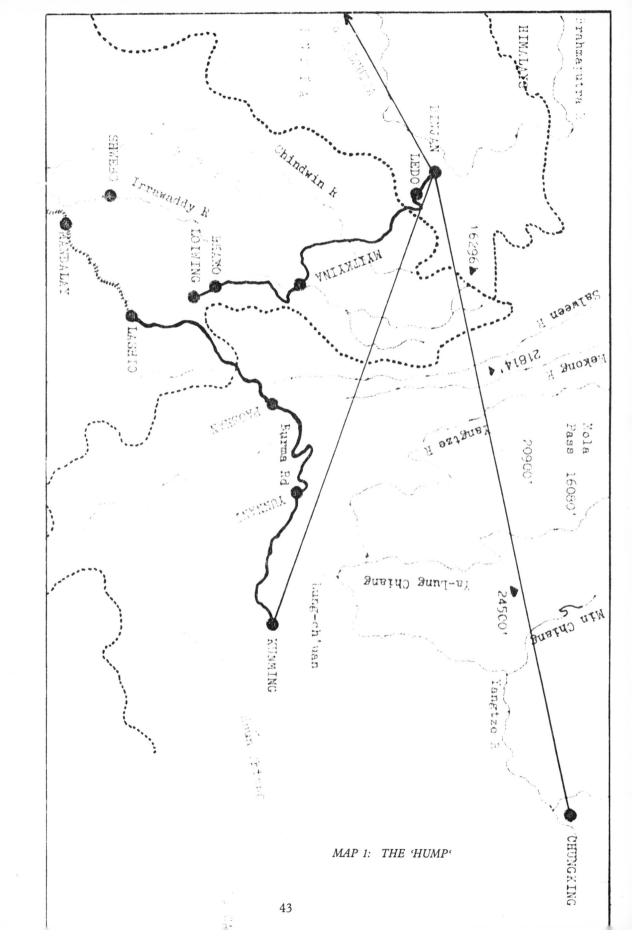

MAP 1: THE 'HUMP'

43

the problems of that between Dinjan and Chungking, but its lower altitudes meant a reduction in engine supercharging. It crossed the foothills of the Himalayas and could be flown at altitudes of from 8000 to 12,000 feet, but Japanese fighters were in great numbers. They operated from the expanded installations of four satellite airfields at Myitkyina, seventy or eighty miles to the south. The Japanese airfields at Lashio at the end of the Burma Road held an even greater force of fighters and were little more than 200 miles from CNAC's assigned track on the Chungking route. The pilots preferred the hazardous direct routing and didn't really think it much safer to operate out of Kunming. Nevertheless, on the rare days that the weather was calm and the hunters resting, this route was spellbinding as it crossed the land's great rivers.

First the Brahmaputra slashed through the gorges of Tibet, next the little Chindwin trickled from the Patkoi Hills, a tributary of Rangoon's Irrawaddy, like the next two rivers, the Mali Kha and Nmai Kha. The Nam Khong or Salween followed, then the great Lan Ts'ang. Saigon's Mekong revealed a section of its 2800 mile length. Within fifty miles of the Kunming strip (6,240 feet above sea-level) the route crossed the great Lung-Ch'uan, a tributary of the 3,500 mile Yangtse which enters the East China Sea just north of Shanghai.

In September 1945 the American involvement in the safer southerly route, which had been made possible by the military victories of General Joseph W. Stilwell ('Vinegar Joe') and Orde Wingate's Chindits, came to an end. RAF Transport Command continued for a few months, flying the last mission on New Year's Eve.

The significant British part in this regular service dated from July 1944, when it had been entrusted to 52 Squadron, a unit with an unusual history. Formed in May 1916 it served from November that year until the Armistice as an Army Co-operation squadron. In the Second World War it began with an instructional role, helping to maintain the Advanced Air Striking Force in the field, one of its duties being the training of pilots in spraying poison gas from Fairey Battle aircraft. After various vicissitudes it reformed with a bomber role without becoming operational, and carried out reconnaissance duties from Iraq, Egypt, Sicily and Gibraltar. Disbanded in 1944, its number was allotted to two DC3 flights of No 353 (a transport squadron) based at Calcutta, and it entered upon these arduous duties of supplying China. After the war it remained in the Far East and, still as a transport unit, played a prominent part in 'Operation Firedog', the campaign against the Communist terrorists in Malaya. Its motto was *Sudore quam sanguine*—'by sweat and blood'. On the Kunming route it operated daily runs for eighteen months and logged some 15,000 hours of flying with the loss of only one aircraft.

The workhorse of those years was the estimable DC3, designed by Donald Wills Douglas, born in Brookland, U.S.A. in 1892. He built DC1 in 1933 and used it as a flying laboratory for his next project, the DC2, of which he constructed 138. He then evolved this type into the unbeatable DC3, commencing its manufacture in 1936. By the time the Douglas Company ceased production in 1945, more than 29,000 had been built, of which many are still flying.

In 1934 Australia had her first glimpse of a Douglas transport when Parmentier and Moll, flying a DC2 for KLM—the Royal Dutch Line—came second in the England-to-Australia MacRoberston Air Race. Two aircraft which would help enormously in winning the war developed from entries in this race, the Mosquito and the DC3.

The latter had a variety of designations. The initials 'DC' stand for 'Douglas Commercial'. The U.S. Army called her the C47; their Navy, with customary contrariness, called her R42. The British and Canadians knew as the Dakota or Dak. But the Russkies took the biscuit. Given 700 of them to help fight the common enemy they obtained tooling rights from Douglas and proceeded to build 2000 more. they gave the type a name of their own, the Lissimov 2, a presumptuous mouthful. The ground troops of the Alliend nations, a discerning body, knew her as the Grand Old Lady, or the Biscuit Bomber, or on the frequent occasions when a landing proved less than a daisy-cutter, the Gooney Bird.

The pilots of the several services had in common a respect and affection for this aircraft. They were linked also by the nature of their work, the airfields and accommodations they used in common and their day-to-day contacts. As with all servicemen in that war (and perhaps in all others) they discussed the future, and a good many of them elected to turn their tested skills to peaceful uses when the time came. Surely it was in such conversations that the idea of Cathay Pacific was born.

After he parted from de Kantzow to return to Australia at the beginning of war, John Wawn's destiny was also to head him into the war in the East, but his experience there was dismally different from that of the run-of-the-mill pilot. Flying Liberators from Corunna Downs, a strip 25 miles south-south-east of Marble Bar, he was assigned to a target in Central Java, a diversionary tactic covering the landings at Balikpapan and Tarakan on the east coast of Borneo. His Liberator was last into the target area which had become so obscured by mist and the heavy smoke of bombardment from the earlier bombers that he diverted to the secondary target, the aerodrome of Den Pasar. As he recalls:

'We made a good navigational landfall and nearing the target descended to make the best use of the bombs. At a low altitude we encountered heavy flak and we think a night fighter or two set one of our engines on fire. We couldn't control this. Other damage caused by the intense defence set up a vibration so severe we could hear the skin rivets popping on the fuselage. We could never get back to Australia in that condition so we made a crash-landing on a beach at Sumba Island. We had all suffered in the action and the crash-landing and we were wandering round in a state of shock. After a few hours of intensive search the Japanese rounded us up, and we spent the remainder of the war in various prison-camps throughout the islands of the Dutch East Indies.'

In an attempt to extract information they believed he might have the Japanese tortured him, pushing sharpened slivers of bamboo under his fingernails. In later years, Alan Marshall, in Hong Kong composing a travel brochure for the company, asked him how he had withstood the excruciating pain. (No stranger to pain himself, Alan was the author of *I Can Jump Puddles*, a novel which explores the subject.)

'It's like everything else,' Pinky replied. 'You make a little pact with yourself just to try to withstand the pain a little longer before you give in, and then you find either that you have resisted long enough to discourage your tormentors, or that nature has intervened and you have passed out.'

The Kempei Tai, the Japanese Gestapo, practiced refinements of torture, sometimes in unspeakable forms, with callous efficiency. The father of two of my friends was another victim. The friends were Leo Landau of 'Jimmy's Kitchen' and his brother, the late Emile, of the 'Parisian Grill', both restauranteurs of Hong Kong. Their father had all the knuckles of his hands broken, and I recall with dismay how he winced when I first shook his hand with a youthful enthusiasm.

Soon after I arrived in Hong Kong I was scuttling down the Nathan Road to the Cathay Pacific office in the Peninsula Hotel when a good-looking Chinese accosted me. Dressed in spotless black he had pads tied to his knees, and two withered legs dragged behind him. At that time I regarded Chinese as inferiors and wasted no time thinking of them. But this man smiled and I found my normally hesitant hand unpeeling a new dollar bill. He stretched it out, rubbed it round his stubble-free face, and then deflated me by exclaiming in precise Oxford English 'Goodness me! Folding money!' We became good friends and, other than telling me that the Japanese had hamstrung him he would never give me details. The last time I saw him was thirty years later and he was a chirpy as ever.

Pinky was discharged from the RAAF in September 1945 and shortly afterwards began with Australian National Airways as a trainee pilot. He left after two weeks. 'The utter ruthlessness of Air Commodore types scrambling roughshod on my shoulders and over each other in attempts to get to the top became too much to stomach,' he said.

His family eventually convinced him that he should learn his father's business in the Sydney suburb of Leichhardt. The older Wawn had developed 'Wawn's Wonder Wool', an excellent pain-reliever which still enjoys the support of a vast following. Though he was brilliant in his own field his lack of business acumen was heading his company towards the rocks, and Pinky embarked on a rescue bid which soon showed results. In March the following year, hurrying along a Sydney street to keep a business appointment, he rounded a corner and ran full-face into Syd de Kantzow on a similar errand. Appointments forgotten, they renewed the friendship the war had interrupted.

He met Roy Farrell, accepted a job, persuaded his brother Bob to run the Wonder Wool business and on April 2 was off on the first leg of the long haul to Shanghai. On the same flight were to other newly-recruited pilots, Bob Donovan, whom he knew by reputation, and Neville Hemsworth, an old friend from his Air Force days.

About this time Farrell signed up Harry de Leuil for the Sydney Office. Though never in the limelight, Harry was one of the true pioneers of Australian aviation, his particular contributions being a fine technical grasp and a dry sense of humour. In January 1930 he began his career as an engineer with ANA, the company Kingsford Smith and Ulm had formed in 1929. After he secured the

A.H. (Harry) de Leuil—Kingsford Smith Air Service
Mascot, Sydney 1936.

four ground engineer licences (A, B, C and D) from the Department of Civil Aviation he was put in charge of engine maintenance, and also did some flying training. But ANA failed in the depression year of 1932 and he joined Guinea Airways, spending four years in Lae. He returned to Australia in late 1935 and joined Kingsford Smith Air Services Ltd at Mascot and the following year took over control, administering a distinguished group of technical experts. Their school covered the full range of aviation subjects: navigation, engines, airframes, radio and meteorology to Commercial Flying Licence standards.

In September 1940 the Air Force impressed their training aircraft and directed instructors to train Air Force cadets. After eighteen months they integrated the instructors into the RAAf and de Leuil was manpowered into the position of Australasian Manager of Paul and Grey's Aircraft Division. He was appointed Sydney manager of Cathay Pacific soon after its inception, and in 1947 given a seat on the Board of Directors. This gave him the authority to negotiate with Air Marshal R. Williams, Director-General of Civil Aviation and Mr. A.S. Drakeford, the Minister. He arranged landing rights into Sydney on a basis of three a month, to be renewable each quarter. He was also empowered to act as Managing Director in Hong Kong when de Kantzow's commitments took him from the Colony for a month or more.

My acquaintance with him did not begin on that December morning when he enlisted me in the Cathay Pacific team. Ten years before, aged 16, I had read a prospectus of Kingsford Smith Air Service, and was especially attracted by the line of Page Six which stated: 'For the best pilots—1000 pounds a year'. Harry de Leuil soon realised I hadn't the wherewithal to take the 325 pound course or even the prospect of finding the terms of 25 pounds deposit and 25 pounds a month. But he was kind enough to have his chief flying instructor, G.S. Coleman give me a quick run around to feel the controls of an aircraft in flight. After the short hop he saved my face by suggesting I was still a little young to take the course.

CHAPTER FOUR
EN ROUTE

Things are always at their best in the beginning.
Pascal

Into the dangerous world I leapt . . .
Infant Sorrow . . . William Blake

From the moment I walked into Harry de Leuil's office at 9.45 on the morning of Tuesday, December 17, 1946 my life changed direction with a confusing velocity. Harry gave me the job on the spot, much to the disappointment of a fellow named Vernon Harold ('Dick') Hunt, who plays a significant part in this story later. He was one of two applicants waiting for a decision. Each had more varied flying experience than me, but my possession of a Second Class Navigator's Licence, then a rarity, gave me the edge.

A talkative office minion then assisted me in filling out countless forms and attending to other formalities like checking the China visa on my passport. I had obtained the visa in anticipation of taking Eric McIllree's flight of Ansons to the U.K. The impressively large entry filled the whole of Page 9. My starting salary was $US400 ($HK1603) made me feel like a prince, but a little of the gratification evaporated when other first officers joined in late 1947, and I found their Sterling salary was equal to $HK1610.

With barely a break in the furious activity of departure I found myself in the co-pilot's seat of VR-HDA, our heavily-laden DC3 under the command of Pinky Wawn, heading for Manila and Hong Kong. Roy Farrell was aboard, and so were Jack Williams, who was to become prominent in the Hong Kong Aircraft Engineering Company (HAECO), and Charlie Rowe, an instrument man of rare ability. We carried a cargo largely of woollen goods in 180-pound bales.

The first part of the journey was without incident until after we arrived at Pitoe strip on Morotai, an island near Halmahera in the Moluccas. Morotai lived up to a well-deserved reputation for bad weather, and our heavily-laden bird staggered off the coral strip in restricted visibility. My reaction to that takeoff, with the coco-palms flashing periously past did little to reassure me that I had made a good choice of employment. Once in the air the continuous turbulence and lightning flashes increased the tension, and about an hour out of Morotai the port engined packed up. It had taken us all this time to reach cruising level at 9000 feet. There was still no real emergency until I heard Pinky's usually calm and lazy voice suddenly pitched an octave or so higher.

"I can't feather this bloody port prop!'

He repeated it twice more in the next fifteen seconds, *con fuoco* and with a rising inflection, and the rate-of-climb indicator, revolving counter-clockwise, underlined the urgency of his warning. The propellor turning the dead engine under the air-stream pressure was increasing our drag savagely.

'Chic, get back and start tossing the cargo off,' Pinky ordered me. We were flying on 'George', the automatic pilot, just monitoring its operation.

'We've lost three thousand feet of altitude and she's going down fast,' he added, rather unnecessarily I thought. My protruding eyeballs had recorded every lost foot.

I jumped out of the right-hand seat, proud of the fact that I had remembered to unclasp my safety belt, but was unceremoniously jerked back. As on the occasion with Jimmy Broadbent in the sabotaged Electra I'd forgotten the stout head-set cable, and my savoir-faire took a bit of a tumble.

As I pushed past Roy Farrell his face was white and strained. With his background of flying The Hump this emergency would not have frightened him, but jettisoning his cargo of woollen merchandise would put a strain on his company. With the assistance of Williams and Rowe we had the door open in a flash, and were soon dumping the expensive bales. As each took the deep six Farrell's face became more grey, as Pinky told me later.

As one bale left my hands the plane took a jolt more severe than the others, and I swayed through the door. To this day I am certain that I saw the fuselage rivets under the belly but as I lurched forwards the strong hands of Williams and Rowe fastened on my belt and hauled me back on top of the bales which were at the door ready for dumping.

At this moment Farrell appeared exclaiming that the prop had feathered and that we were holding altitude. Rowe and Williams closed the door and I scrambled back to my place. I could hardly believe my eyes when I read on the altimeter dial that we had stabilised at 1500 feet. Being a new boy and reluctant to make more of a fool of myself than was absolutely necessary I stared for what seemed a long time before I could trust myself to speak. I was convinced I must have misread it, but there it was: a loss of 7,500 feet, a very sobering thought indeed and one I would recall all through my life.

Reaction to the near miss did not set in until some two days later, but then I was beset with graphic visions of the natives of those beautiful islands beneath being bombarded with woollens, and then, perhaps, getting a portly body come through the thatched roof.

Some 20,000 pesos of cargo had been jettisoned 150 odd miles from Davao (incidentally starting a 'gold-rush' that rivalled Alaska's), but this was not the full extent of the loss. We had also pitched out two life-rafts, two stretchers, sundry aircraft tools, safety belts, lifebelts, control surface chocks and other small but expensive pieces of equipment. Our reprieve had been due to Pinky remembering that the erring prop had been changed in Sydney in something of a rush. He figured it may not have been bled correctly. He thought he might overcome this by rapidly changing the pitch of the blades as the propellor revolved in the

July 1947 view of Statue Square—showing Department of Civil Aviation premises in foreground.

Police Inspector F 'Buck' Indge-Buckingham stands at right. This photograph is very rare as it shows the tents utilised for Port Health, Immigration and Customs before they moved to a more permanent location in 1947. This terminal building was some 300 yards west of the tented area on the sea-wall and adjacent to the flying boat slipway.

JANUARY 1947
F/O 'Chic' Eather at Bangkok Snake Party
(Note american style uniform—CPA's initial uniform)

Japanese War Memorial
Mount Cameron, H.K. January, 1947

airstream, at the same time pressing the feathering button. The experiment worked.

We proceeded to the old Japanese Libby strip of Davao in southern Mindanao. Pinky accomplished this with the ease of a fine experienced pilot, and en route my respect for him rose even higher as he managed to coax his lame aircraft up to 3000 feet, as its load grew lighter with the usage of fuel. We stayed at Guino's Hotel where I was subjected to the attention of the biggest mosquitoes I have ever encountered. Cables flashing back and forth through the night informed Farrell that there was a spare engine in Manila and that one of Cathay's DC3s was overnighting there. At first light this aircraft delivered this spare to Davao and took Pinky and me aboard for its return. Pinky waited in Manila to join as supernumerary crew a seaman charter on its way to New Zealand, while later that same afternoon I arrived in Hong Kong for the very first time. The date was still only December 20.

For the next three decades its Kai Tak airport was to become very familiar to me as I trudged through its sludgy mud or its powdery dust. That afternoon it was mud. Our touchdown had followed the clearance of a heavy rain squall and Runway 13, which a few minutes before had been a lake, had drained quite rapidly to either side. I minced my way along a precarious system of duckboards to the immigration, customs and medical facilities then located in a series of Army tents along the southern seawall. Three hundred yards west and adjacent to the flying-boat slipway the first postwar terminal building under construction was a hive of industry. My spirits lowered with every squelching step.

My impressions are somewhat hazy, but I remember meeting 'Buck', one of the biggest policemen I ever saw. His full name was Superintendent F. Indge-Buckingham, but it was to be thirty years before I learned that, and then only in a chance conversation with his daughter Peta, who married my cricketing pal Buddy Carnell of the Kowloon Cricket Club. At the farther end of the check-in tent a smiling Syd de Kantzow intercepted me. The smile proved later to be quite uncharacteristic, displayed only rarely. He introduced me to Bill Dobson, our Public Relations man, and the three of us walked to the centre of the field where Syd gave me a quick yet concise familiarisation briefing.

He showed me the hills which rise quite alarmingly to embrace the field to east and north. Though the ground to the west was somewhat lower it also presented pilot hazards. Fixing me with a beady eye Syd said I must never be party to a takeoff on Runway 31, which pointed almost directly to Lion rock. To drive home his point he described in gory detail the crash of the RAF's DC3 three months before, on September 25. Nineteen lives were lost when it crashed into the foothills of Kowloon Tong after such a takeoff.

He drew my attention to the Japanese War Memorial which gleamed in the afternoon sun atop Mount Cameron, towards the south. It had been built to dominate the four corners of the Colony and it reflected the sun's rays from about eleven o'clock onwards. It could then be seen from Pratas Reef, ninety-odd miles away in the China Sea. Other than on the cloudiest days it was a good navigational landmark. It was to prove of great value in the weeks ahead.

Press Conference: Kai Tak Airport, Hong Kong, 21st October, 1946.
L. to R: R/O Alex Stewart, Public Relations Officer Bill Dobson, reporters, Captains Neville Hemsworth, Robert (Bob) Donovan, and Roy Farrell. This rare photograph shows the tents used by the Port Health, Immigration and Customs in the background.

Although I was quite weary the excitement of new surroundings buoyed me up as de Kantzow drove the five miles to my new lodgings. He must have covered them in as many minutes over the then unobstructed route. The same trip today takes twenty. The accommodation was a comfortable looking camp bed in the two rooms the company rented for crew accommodation in the imposing Peninsula Hotel—sometimes referred to as 'the upholstered sewer'.

The bunk looked full of sleep, but two nights ended my occupancy of it. Early morning of December 23 found me winging my way back to Sydney, the intervening time a rat-race of filling company forms, obtaining visas and licence conversions and seeing to similar small chores.

That first fortnight, the final two weeks of 1946 saw me completing one and a half return trips to Sydney and logging 94 hours in the air. The longest 'day's work' included flying time of 18 hours and 25 minutes. During the fortnight I had two days off. I wondered how they managed to forget me for this time; perhaps they had no spare aircraft.

The *South China Morning Post* hailed the return trip as a route record, and for a time Captain Hemsworth, radio officer Alex Stewart and I held this somewhat dubious distinction. The newspaper gave the actual flying time as 27 hours and 35 minutes whereas my logbook (which is never wrong) listed it a non-record-breaking flight of 31 hours and 15 minutes. It was obviously a publicity stunt, perhaps one of Bill Dobson's.

Such record-breaking anyway is not worth the trouble; it only arouses suspicion. The *Straits Times* of August 14, 1963 recorded that Captain C.E. Eather, heading a crew of nine which included Flying Officer L.D.C. Cowper and Flight Engineer L.H. Weston, flying Convair 880 VR-HFS had established a record flight of 2 hours 53 minutes from Hong Kong's Kai Tak to Singapore's Paya Lebar. The entire flight took place in the hours of darkness and carried 92 American tourists who broke into wild cheering when our public address system announced the record time.

Flights of those days which excluded intermediate landings might be scheduled as 'direct', but because of internal strife in some countries the routing might provide a track at right angles to the line between terminals, even heading away from it, and the word 'direct' becomes academic. So various Civil Aviation departments vetted every part of the flight log to see if corners had been cut, while the company engineering section ran a similar comprehensive check on all the power-plant flight paperwork, and it was some time before the record was accepted at face value by my colleagues, especially those whose previous records had been slashed. Commercial departments were the only real enthusiasts, possibly recording the sale of a few more tickets. Nevertheless I think that particular record still stands, and Pat Armstrong, a former captain in Cathay Pacific still holds the record of 2 hours 54 minutes set in the opposite direction on May 30, 1963, again with a Convair 880 M.

Bill Dobson, the first public relations man, enjoyed a relatively brief association with Cathay Pacific. I could not have guessed when I met him on that first day in Hong Kong that I was in the presence of an artist, in spite of the debonair bush-jacket he wore and the rakish tilt of his cap. He was certainly able to command the attention of the Press.

On April 13, 1947 he was flying on an exercise in a Stinson Sentinel aircraft belonging to the Far East Flying Training School with FEFTS Chief Instructor Sel Halls at the controls. About 9.40 a.m. twenty minutes after their takeoff from Kai Tak, they were lined up with the grass strip at Macao, and at a low 400 feet they heard what they thought at first was their engine backfiring, but in fact was a Nationalist Chinese machine-gun post firing at them. Down to their right they could see the flicks of light from its muzzle, and these continued till they touched down on Portuguese territory. There they inspected the rows of bullet-holes stitched into the starboard fuselage in an emotional stew of concern, relief and anger.

Both the Hong Kong and Macao Government were advised and threats were made to bring the matter to the attention of the Home Office. But nothing was done. The matter was quietly dropped as a hot potato.

A year later, on Wednesday April 21, Hong Kong's *China Mail* ran a headline RAAF PILOT HELD AFTER MANHUNT. The origin of the story was Shanghai where it was alleged that Bill Dobson had swindled the Wing On department store (then under the management of George Kwok) of 150,000,000 Chinese dollars worth of goods. In the galloping inflation of the time this equated about 100 pounds Australian. He had posed as an official of the American Legion and the commander of its Shanghai branch had besought the entire International Settlement to assist in his apprehension. What is interesting is that in a predominantly yellow-faced metropolis he was able to avoid recognition in an intensive week's search. When he was finally taken the goods were recovered from his room, but Mr Kwok, at the time of the press release, couldn't decide whether to prosecute or not and there were no further reports in the newspapers.

We had more news of him from the headlines in the *South China Morning Post* of November 9, 1949. They read: CRUDE ESCAPADE–FALSE REPORT OF RED ASSAULT–JUDGE'S CRITICISM and emanated from Sydney. Dobson's wet, bedraggled figure had been dragged from the Harbour waters at Nielsen Park, protesting bitterly that he had been assaulted by three Communists, robbed of his briefcase and thrown in the drink. He was then assistant secretary of the Australian Labor Party group of the Federated Clerk's Union, in which position he was perturbed by the influence of elements of the extreme left. He became an outspoken and ardent advocate for their removal, was subjected to what he described as a 'Russian trial', was expelled from the union and abused on the street, and developed a persecution complex. In evidence it was established that he had immersed himself in the water.

In cross-examination it also came out that during 1945 he had obtained a Press pass, altered it to show he was an accredited war correspondent, and on that authority had travelled on several warships as the guest of their captains, visiting England, Japan and Hong Kong at taxpayer's expense. He was fortunate in being defended by the prominent and able barrister Jack Thom, who told Judge Holt in Sydney Quarter Sessions: 'Certain political beliefs held by Dobson caused him to take these rather extreme steps to bring into discredit those politically opposed to him with a view to getting public sympathy against the Communists.' He tabled a report wherein Sydney psychiatrist Dr H.L. Spearman said, 'In my opinion Dobson was obsessed by anxiety, fear and hostility, acted intensely over a long period and temporarily lost his sense of moral and legal responsibility'.

'Hectic' is the best description of the month of January 1947. Lisbon and London were still considering Cathay Pacific's application to start a Hong Kong/Macao service, but in the meantime permitted them non-scheduled carrier status. Some proving flights showed that, due to the short length of the grassed field, a very precise speed-controlled final approach was essential. An official reception was planned for the inaugural flight on January 5 with local dignitaries in attendance, and a red carpet stretched from the welcoming stand to where the aircraft would shut down her engines.

The aircraft was the DC3 VR-HDA, skippered by Pinky Wawn with Syd de Kantzow as co-pilot. One of the partners who was standing between them became agitated at the flatness of the approach. He stood it as long as his nerves would let him and, with an ejaculated comment to suit his feelings scuttled back into the cabin. At this moment the field lay just beyond the retaining wall of the Reservatorio de Aqua, the reservoir of the province.

Whether his action upset the balance of the aircraft at a critical moment is immaterial. The lowered wheels clipped the retaining wall of the reservoir, folding back the undercarriage, and the DC3 skidded along the grass for a considerable distance with its airscrew tearing up great divots of earth and grass. It came to rest appropriately positioned to the red carpet. The door opened and a thoroughly sheepish crew stepped abjectly down, to the accompaniment of the spectators cheering with great gusto, apparently under the impression that it was all part of the show, and the band's jubilant ovation providing an entirely inappropriate flourish of trumpets.

The crew lined up before the welcoming committee and its spokesman went into his congratulatory address as though nothing untoward had happened. A magnificent example of *savoir-faire*, maybe. Naturally the Cathay Pacific personnel were upset by the damage to the aircraft and the possible threat to any scheduled Macao service, but later on they could see the funny side of the affair. Company engineers Neil Norquay and Jack Williams fitted a new centre section to the DC3, an extensive job taking several weeks.

DC3's of Cathay Pacific at Kai Tak Airport, Hong Kong VR-HDG crashed at Braemar Reservoir, near North Point Hong Kong Island during a heavy fog in February 1949.

Chief Engineer Bill ("Hokum") Harris, R/O W.J. (Bill) Carew and Neil Norquay putting finishing touches to VR-HDA at Macao.
This DC3 hit the Macao reservoir wall on 5th January 1947 and was flown back to Kai Tak on 20th April, 1947 by Capt. John ("Pinky") Wawn.

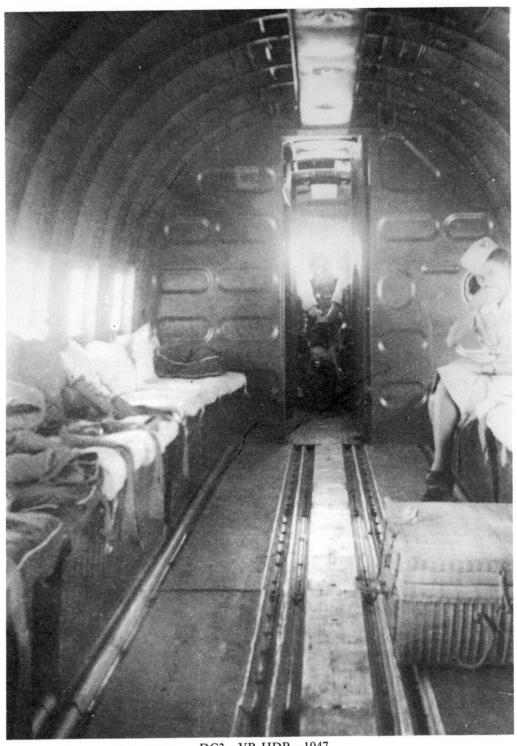

DC3—VR-HDB—1947
Note: Bucket seats, Hostess Uniform and Catering
Basket.

March 7th, 1948
Catalina PBY/5A VR-HDT
Macao Bank Agent, Captain Don Teeters, F/E Larry Cabot and F/O 'Chic' Eather, watch transfer of Gold Shipment to launch. Shipment was from Saigon, and location is the Macao breakwater.

JANUARY 1948 . . . MACAO BREAKWATER
The Gold Run . . . Left to Right: F/O Ced Carlton, Bank officials and Captain Don Teeters with Captain Dale Cramer beaming in the foreground, on the wing of Catalina PBY5A VR-HDT.

61

24th January, 1948
L to R: M. Paul Gurnay's houseboy, Captain Dale Cramer, F/E Larry Cabot and
Captain Don Teeters, Penthouse roof of Banque De L'Indochine, Saigon,
"Our Home from Home"

Catalina PBY5A VR-HDT "Miss Macao" landing on Runway "31" Kai Tak Airport, Hong
Kong 6th February, 1948.

FEBRUARY, 1945
Catalina with damaged port wing trailing edge at Macao, damaged due to striking foreign
object whilst landing.

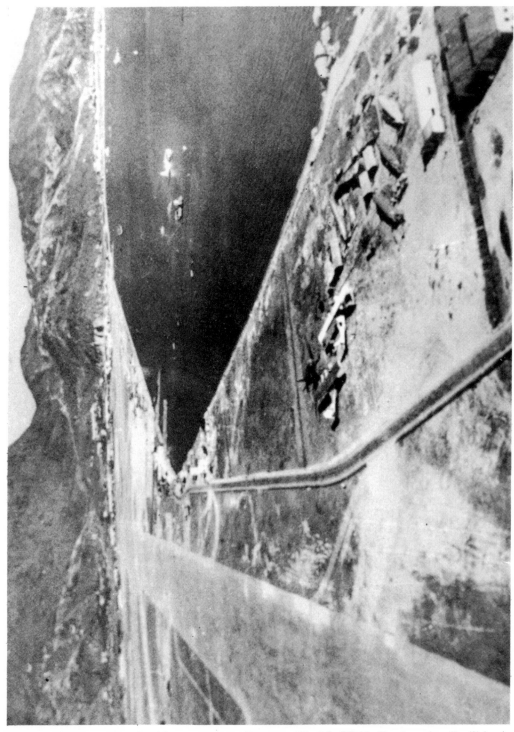

Kai Tak Airport 1947—Looking east along Runway 07 with CPA's Engineering Facilities in right foreground. This is approximately the threshold of the present runway. Photo taken just above the Sacred Hill which was demolished.

The Terminal Building which replaced the tent facilities used by
Port Health, Immigrationn and Customs

Another successful Gold delivery, Macao. Catalina PBY5A VR-HDT—15th March 1948.
Portugese soldiers, Captain Dale Cramer, Macao Bank Agent, F/E Larry Cabot,
R/O Ken Wolinski and F/O "Chic" Eather.

Showing the method of offloading used when the Catalina PBY5A
was brought onto the landing ramp.
Note the wooden box in which the gold was shipped.

The importance of the Macao run had been forecast in discussions the Cathay Pacific partners had had with Roger Lobo, their office landlord. The P.J. Lobo company was the acting agent for the Banco Nacional Ultramarino, and Roger Lobo discussed with de Kantzow and Nasholds what was to prove a real money-spinner, and in fact bring their balance sheet out of the red. At that time an embargo, formulated by the International Monetary Fund and signed at Bretton-Woods, New Hampshire, excluded signatory countries from importing or dealing in gold. Macao was one of several countries that did not sign and in consequence enjoyed a wide-open field to trade in the sought-after metal. Roger Lobo told me of some of the earlier attempts:

'We made the first delivery with a DC3 flying very low over the Macao racecourse, abandoned since the Pacific War as there were no horses. This was quite unsuitable for any but the smallest aircraft, as became apparent when VR-HDA hung up her undercarriage on the reservoir wall. We used a DC3 flying very slow and low along the greatest run of that field, and we selected full flaps and were just "hanging on the props" while all hands pushed and shoved fifty-pound bags of gold on to the muddy field.

'The difficulty afterwards was to dig the metal out of the mud as many of the bags had burst on contact. Fortunately this had been accepted as a "dummy run" and we had to account for only a few bags.

'We now burnt a great deal of midnight oil discussing how to avoid a similar cock-up. On our next delivery we put the load into sealed 44-gallon gasoline drums and it looked as though we had solved our problem until on the second pass we almost squashed three of the bank coolies we had posted at strategic positions round the field. They just could not be convinced that when it struck the ground each drum was capable of erratic behaviour and became a danger to life and limb. So we had to abandon this idea as well. We toyed with the idea of fitting floats to the DC3s. Other operators had accomplished this with success in Alaska and Canada, but when we learned how this would restrict our payload we quickly shied away from it. This was why the Catalina amphibious aircraft came into the picture.

'Like everything else the partners did in those days we purchased only one for a start. This was VR-HDS, followed by a second, VR-HDT—which particular "Cat" was to gain a niche in history as the air-pirated *Miss Macao*. Finally, VF-HDH was to join the amphibious fleet when Chief Ground Engineer Bill "Hokum" Harris signed for its registration in February 1948.

'This final Catalina had become necessary as our gold traffic had increased out of all proprtion to our initial hopes. The gold bars were now stacked in wooden boxes. No doubt you remember they were about fourteen inches long by nine wide and nine deep.'

Indeed I remembered. I was to get so fed up with this operation that I marked several of these boxes and was amazed to discover that on one day I would take a load of these from Saigon to Macao, the next day I would take the same boxes from Macao to Saigon; two days later from Saigon to Batavia and within a week they would be safely back in Macao once again. I knew by my mark that

December 2nd, 1947
F/O 'Chic' Eather, outside CPA's mess
(Note CPA's summer uniform)

they had never been open. They could have been crammed with lead ingots; nobody appeared to know or even care.

The main business was between Macao and Saigon, and in Saigon the crews developed a first-class rapport with M. Paul Gurnay, the manager of the Banque de l'Indo-Chine. Before being posted to Head Office he had been the Hong Kong manager, consequently closely associated with Roger Lobo. In Saigon his bank occupied a full city block and M. Gurnay occupied one of the four large apartments on the top floor. He frequently played host to our crews, and his constant companion in the apartment was a fabulous honey-bear, a monster in size who roamed the whole place.

Over a long period the bear had developed finesse in pilfering any drink not continuously protected. After a time he would get so drunk he would lie in the middle of the lounge scratching his belly and softly crooning. He was a well-behaved drunk, much better than many of our air-crew colleagues. But I heard later that M. Gurnay had to put the bear in the local zoo. One day one of his servants irritated the animal so much it tore his right arm off.

On those gold charters we had to have a midnight takeoff in order to arrive at Macao at dawn. This meant we had to reach Saigon's Tan Son Hut airport by 6 p.m., a necessary arrangement as the insurgents held all of the roads out of the city immediately the light began to fade. They would remain in undisputed control until the morning when the French manned their check-points again.

On one of these runs between Macao and Saigon I joined the Mile High Club in the top bunk of a Catalina flying-boat practically on top of a consignment of gold bullion. This club has no overheads, collects no fees and is, in the main, the exclusive preserve of the early aviator, though it demands agility and on occasion an approach to double-jointedness. The venue of the initiation is an aircraft winging its way above the 5000 foot mark, and in the days before sound-proofing the engine roar successfully masked the squeals of delight.

The lady was the mistress of a prominent Saigon Government official, a petite French girl returning from Macao after a short holiday, and she had all the qualifications of the heroines of my early manhood dreams. I was assigned the duty of seeing her aboard before our skipper saw her, otherwise I might not have been so lucky. I placed her small overnight pack on the top bunk and, having been given the first leg off, curled up on the bunk immediately below. Soon a delicate little hand touched me on the shoulder and the lady's soft voice asked me if I would sit on her bunk with her, as she was a little nervous. Up I went, with the simple-minded intention of calming her fears. But talk was far from her mind, and soon we were threshing round. As I climbed from the bunk later I expressed the inane hope that I had helped her to settle down, and with a demure lowering of her eyelids she assured me that I had.

I hoped it had all gone unnoticed, but the skipper, the other co-pilot and the engineer had traced the unusual vibrations and witnessed the vigorous therapy. Some time later I saw in the skipper's personal (and unofficial) logbook the entry: 'Joined the Mile High Club'. Between 'the' and 'mile' he had inserted the word 'two'. This is highly circumstantial.

OYSTERS!

SYDNEY ROCK OYSTERS

BY AIR

From Australia,
In 32 Hours

AND NOW AT THE HONG KONG HOTEL

These very fine oysters, well known in Hongkong, as a great delicacy, have been brought, alive in the shell, to Hongkong from the Sydney Oyster Beds in the same time as they reach the Sydney Householder.

YET ANOTHER SERVICE FROM

The Roy Farrell Export-Import Co., (H.K.) Ltd.

The First International **AIRMERCHANDISE** Service in the World

402-403 York Building,

Chater Road, Hongkong.

Telephones: 31350
31360

and at

SYDNEY (AUSTRALIA), MANILA (PHILIPPINE ISLANDS),

SHANGHAI (CHINA) and LONDON (UNITED KINGDOM).

FIGURE 6: ROY FARRELL EXPORT—IMPORT COMPANY ADVERTISEMENT
"SOUTH CHINA MORNING POST" WEDNESDAY
JANUARY 22, 1947

About the time of the inauguration of the Macao flights an advertisement of the Roy Farrell Export-Import Company appeared in the *South China Morning Post* testifying to the diversity of Cathay Pacific enterprise. It announced: 'OYSTERS—Sydney Rock Oysters by air from Australia in 32 hours and now at the Hong Kong Hotel. These very fine oysters, well known in Hong Kong as a great delicacy, have been brought alive in the shell from the Sydney oyster beds in the same time as they reach the Sydney householder.'

This was a reasonable statement. But the consignment which followed next took more exertion than the happy gourmets would know. Our DC3 landed on the coral strip at Morotai where tropical moisture affected the ignition harness. The run-up before takeoff showed a massive magneto-drop. We carried a spare harness, but when the Dutch mechanics installed it, it was found to be equally faulty, so we were faced with a wait until our next service charter came through. As luck would have it, this was due in about seven hours, but what was of immediate concern to Roy Farrell was the load of oysters now drying out on board.

With a flash of inspiration he soon had us all struggling with those bags down to the beach which was only a few yards beyond the waving palms. What Roy had forgotten, it was an ebbing tide and we had to carry the bags well out, and when the tide was full they were covered by several feet of water. Apart from his Cunate dance of rage when we tried to retrieve them and an impatient wait for the tide to fall again, all went well, and apart from the loss of a few oysters which had gone off, he once again managed to save his investment.

Dick Hunt joined the company on January 8 and was to remain until February 18, 1952. During his five years of war service with the RAAF he had risen to the rank of Squadron Leader, and had earned the rare distinction of forming, equipping and training the first squadron of Australian Mosquito aircraft. He was one of the few men who really got on well with Syd de Kantzow; they understood each other and Dick's ability to jolly Syd up was an art.

He had been one of the two pilots rejected when I was employed and he didn't readily forget it, though the preference was merely because of my holding a Navigator's Licence. He once told me I was responsible for the delay in his joining the company, and though his face did crack a smile of sorts his eyes held little humour. He needn't have concerned himself; his progress would be meteoric and I happily concede his flying ability to be streets ahead of mine. My progress was akin to that of the slow plodding moon which continues on a well-regulated course and due to familiarity is often overlooked. Dick went to Kenya when he left the company and gained great respect for his flying against the vicious Mau Mau when their outrages began later that same year.

On January 25 an air tragedy shook Hong Kong. The Philippine Airlines DC3 PIC-12 slammed into the side of Devil's Peak on Mount Parker, just a couple of miles from haven at Kai Tak. It carried American-born O.T. Weymouth and three crew. Just across the next hill a Saturday crowd was enjoying the fourth race at Happy Valley. The shock of impact seized the sensitive workings of the skipper's wristwatch at precisely 3.02 a.m., a fact learned when his severed hand was pried loose from a mangled control column.

Fortunately they had carried no passengers, but their cargo was worth more than $US1,000,000 in gold coins weighing 4,565 pounds, something over two tons. The Philippine peso value exceeded 4,000,000. This great treasure was scattered over a large area, and with the impact settled into the disturbed sand and slush. As he surveyed the debris Police Inspector W. Kinlock predicted that much of the consignment would never be recovered, and 'destitute' locals proved him right by filching something like a third of the load. Much more would have been lost had the police not drawn a cordon round the area quickly, and made a body-search of each sight-seer as he left it. To a point this worked well, but shrewder citizens who found a few coins buried them at some suitably marked spot and returned for them days later. It is difficult to out-smart a Chinese who is bent on ill-gotten gains.

The following day, January 26, gave me a first chance to use the magnificent Chinese visa on my passport, after a flight to Shanghai. The Cathay Pacific fleet had been increased to five DC3s: VR-HDA, HBD, HDG, HDI and HDJ. We were flying HDG which was equipped with bucket seats recessed into a metal bench which extended along each side of the cabin, leaving space for cargo in the middle. In those days we flew along the coastline using low-powered radio beacons at Swatow, Amoy, Foochow, Wenchow and Ningpo.

Pre-departure 'met' briefing had promised good weather throughout the route, and we crossed Swatow in beautiful conditions but as we approached Amoy the cloud cover became intense. Soon we were struggling in heavy turbulence and Amoy's beacon began to swing an alarming amount either side of straight ahead. As we approached Amoy on dead-reckoning we made a slight adjustment to port and headed towards our next check-point at Foochow. Suddenly we broke free of all cloud and were amazed to find ourselves trekking up the eastern coastline of Formosa! We had picked up an astonishingly strong westerly jet-stream which in the space of a bare 150 miles had thrust us 200 miles off course! This was disconcerting, but more frightening was the thought that our track had passed through the mountain ranges which stretch the entire length of that rugged island. Some of the peaks exceed 13,000 feet in height, and our altitude was a mere 9000.

We rolled on to the Lung-Hua aerodrome in Shanghai and booked into the impressive Cathay Hotel, with rooms overlooking the frantically busy Bund. But my eyes kept looking back from the windows to my three-day layover allowance stacked in impressive heaps along my dressing-table. This was for meals and personal items; the company met accommodation costs—and I don't remember the actual amount, but I do recall that if you invested in a newspaper (which I did) and made a telephone call (which I didn't) you would have precious little change from half a million Chinese dollars.

The inflation was enormous. The Cathay Hotel, responding to changing conditions of supply and demand, would revise the menu prices while the meal was in progress. On my first evening the prices had already been changed twice when a lovely elderly missionary lady informed me in a conspiratorial stage-whisper that once I ordered my meal I should hang on to the menu as evidence of what I expected to pay; if not, the bill on presentation would be several thousand dollars more by the time I had finished. Some statistics may give the idea:

	Offical rate	Open market rate	Period covered
To $US 1:	$CNC 2,020	$CNC 1,195	3/4/46 to 18/8/46
	3,350	2,710	19/8/46 to 15/2/47
	12,000	13,000	16/2/47 to 16/8/47
rising to	7,800,000	8,500,000	by the end of 1948

The Hong Kong dollar was approximately five to $US 1 during this period.

The newspaper I bought displayed a picture of a well-dressed Chinese gentleman leaving a bank. He walked beside a wheel-barrow piled high with bundles of banknotes, pushed by a husky coolie and flanked by a mean-looking armed guard. The caption stated, a little too jocularly I thought, 'A man bent on buying his weekend groceries'. The text revealed that market shopping now followed a process of first weighing the goods bought, and then the money tendered in payment. Nobody had time to count the odd millions of Chinese dollars needed, and I imagine waiting for change would have been a thing of the past.

Shanghai is unique. It lies about fourteen miles above the mouth of the Whangpoo River, a small tributary of the mighty Yangtse. It was the most important of the five Treaty Ports formed under the Treaty of Nanking in 1842. The American and British sectors were joined in 1863 to form the International Settlement.

The city is built on a mud delta, and the uneven settling of some buildings constructed earlier became so marked that where you originally walked up steps to reach the ground-floor level you now walked down. Later techniques erected twenty-storey buildings on concrete rafts, since the unconsolidated sand and silt was about a thousand feet deep. The International Settlement combined British, American, German and Japanese areas, with the French Concession in a separate area adjacent to the British part.

Each nationality had its own club and we were made welcome in each, so if one's inclination were to bar-hop one could have a delightful time doing just that. A non-drinker, I only accompanied the rest of the crew to one such establishment and that was only to brag that I had breasted the Long Bar at the American Club. It enjoyed the distinction of being the longest in the world at the time. Its size impressed me, but I remember best the plush night-clubs, in particular the Arcadia, a retreat where the red plush carpets and plush-covered handrails were kept in impeccable condition. To a girl, the stunningly beautiful hostesses maintained they were offspring of the displaced Russian nobility. Their beauty was quite unbelievable.

Although the Cathay was in the British sector my feet kept being drawn towards the French Concession. The Avenue Edward VII divided the two sectors; British Police controlled one side, an efficient gendarmerie the other. The Roy Farrell Export-Import Company had its offices in French Town, as the locals called it. Butterfield and Swire had offices and go-down there too. Of more significance to me, though I didn't know it, was a nine-year-old Chinese girl named Yeun-Ching, or Judy, who was attending school there. She was to become my wife.

Her father, Hui Lau, the editor of a prominent Shanghai newspaper, resisted Communism and all it stood for with every fibre of his being. Earlier he had taken up arms against it. He implanted an intriguing picture in my mind when he told me, with a sparkling of humour, of retreating from tombstone to tombstone of a local cemetry, firing his gun with enthusiasm and dedication but little effect towards the advancing Commies. Intriguing, because Father Hui is not quite five feet tall. He certainly took his politics seriously.

Mum Louttit was radio officer on a Cathay Pacific Shanghai flight shortly after ours. He gets the sobriquet as being the senior radio officer, and radio is his overriding interest, discount, perhaps, his thinly-veiled passion for the female of the species.

'That flight is indelibly traced in my memory' he wrote me years later. 'It was bitterly cold. I had made a flight there three months earlier, leaving Hong Kong with only a few RAF frequencies, and as I couldn't raise a soul with them I had a bloody terrible trip. When we landed there I bolted off to the CNAC office. They gave me some frequencies and I was using these this time. Every mile the old DC3 got colder until clear ice was forming inside the fuselage. But on descent we broke through the cloud, and to our astonishment had a visibility of fifty miles with our haven of Lung-Hua aerodrome directly ahead. The ground was a white blanket, like a fairyland, and every building was etched with ice crystals. The only marring detail was the brown ribbon of sludge-covered runway. We landed to a certain amount of rock and roll on that slippery surface but were soon out of that freezing aircraft and hurrying for the warm terminal building.

'We had been marshalled right beside another Cathay Pacific aircraft which had preceded us by only twenty minutes. At the door of the terminal I glanced back to see the sky darkening, and in a matter of seconds saw the fury of Nature at her worst. Had we not landed when we did we would have had to divert to Japan, and I don't think we would have had sufficient gravy to take us there!'

On approaching the customs area Mum saw the skipper take the senior customs official aside and slip him some money. Later he learned that it was $US1,000. For this he placed the large manifest on top of a gigantic pile stacked in his 'in' tray; otherwise that merchandise would not clear for many weeks.

Corruption had always been the name of the game in China, and these kickbacks were an accepted means of countering the officials' wage erosion caused by inflation. Another disgusting aspect, and one which must have contributed to the Communist takeover of China, was the procedure Chiang Kai-Shek's generals followed. They were given the money to pay their troops in U.S. dollars. They would hang on to it for a couple of weeks while the exchange rate sky-rocketed and they got more inflated CNC cash for the hard currency. They would personally pocket a good rake-off, retaining it of course in U.S. dollars.

Louttit was in Shanghai five days and spent each evening in the Arcadia, which he too found 'bewitching'.

'One evening,' he wrote, 'Bill Carew the radio officer on the other DC3, my Captain Vic Leslie, our hostie Linda Ferguson and I went there. Bill won a bet that he could drink more of the local grog than any of us. Although an easy winner he didn't look good as, with an imbecilic grin stamped on his chops, he gently slid off his chair under the table. The competition had taken a long time and Linda rather resented the attention we lavished on those beautiful young blonde Russian hostesses as they flitted between the tables. I often wonder what happened to them when the Commies became masters. What a terrible waste of pulchritude!

'The Arcadia had a small intimate shooting gallery where, if you hit the target, one of these fabulous girls (in a skimpy Scamp swimsuit imported by Roy Farrell) would be ejected into the tepid water of a pool. Bill Carew was a good shot and made some "kills" but as the grip of the grape tightened his direction became so wild that everyone in the vicinity became mindful of their health, and were glad when he passed out. We rounded off the evening at the French Club and forgot him. When we remembered we returned to find him still sleeping under the same table, quite ignored by the new revellers in occupation of it.'

Back in Hong Kong I watched the demolition of the Japanese War Memorial, an event which deprived the aviation fraternity of a wonderful land-mark, but was heartily approved by most others. According to an old cricketing friend Tony Weller, the memorial had been sited where some of the fiercest fighting had wiped out a section of the Second Royal Scots to a man.

Weller had been one of the builders of Kai Tak aerodrome, under the less than sympathetic direction of the conqueror. He and his co-builders had made the concrete so thin in places that some Japanese aircraft bogged through it. On the early morning of December 8 1941 Japanese raided Kai Tak and in five minutes or so gained control of all Hong Kong airspace.

Weller hurried to enlist. The recruiting sergeant asked his age and when he said 'Seventeen' told him to come back when he was eighteen. After lunch Weller told the same sergeant '*Now* I'm eighteen' and was told to sign on the dotted line. In early afternoon Weller and his friends found themselves at Cape d'Aguilar, wondering how they would learn to operate the massive siege guns there. They needn't have worried. The Japs landed elsewhere and they were told to spike the guns and take off. They joined the ineffectual resistance in Hong Kong until the surrender. As prisoners they spent an arduous year enlarging and levelling the Kai Tak field.

Routine flying for Cathay Pacific was never routine for long. Old Faithful VR-HDB was grinding away the miles on the direct route from Bangkok to Hong Kong. Just below us were the beautiful sandy beaches of Vietnam and our naviga-tion landmarks of the tiny Tonkin hamlets of Ron and Ba Don. Just after mid-day on April 24, 1947, and flying conditions were perfect. Alex Stewart, the radio officer pushed a message into the skipper's hands and, smiling, said 'Pick the bones out of that'.

Dick Hunt passed the message to me and with a wry grin disengaged the auto-pilot and smoothly rolled the aircraft to starboard. 'We'll just follow the coast' he said. It was a company directive to proceed to Tourane (now Da Nang) and await further instructions.

Tourane was a port of north-eastern South Vietnam on the South China Sea. In March 1945 the Japanese had interned all Frenchmen and proclaimed Vietnam an independent state under Emperor Bao Dai. In August the Viet Minh overthrew this administration and installed Ho Chi Minh. He, after long negotiation, signed an agreement with the French in September 1946 and the Vietnam War erupted at the end of that year.

I had the impression that the skipper knew what this message was about, and enjoyed his private knowledge. Also, we had off-loaded a full cargo of freight at Bangkok, a most uncharacteristic procedure for Cathay Pacific. After a landing free of the usual hassle usually experienced round French-controlled airfields an officer who was actually smiling passed us through immigration and we were soon screaming along tree-lined boulevardes in an un-Gallically clean car.

All right for Dick Hunt; he spoke French fluently and explanatory conversations seemed to go on continuously, but he didn't impart his information to Alex or me. We screamed to a halt outside a large stone building guarded by policemen who waved us through massive wooden gates. We were conducted to sleeping quarters which, though spartan, were bright and seemed to indicate that at least we were not enemies of the State. But I developed new fears when I was advised not to sleep with the window open: the Viet Minh had developed a talent for lobbing hand-grenades accurately through these particular windows from the foliage of the tall tamarinds and rubber trees. The regular residents of the building had selected accommodation that opened on to the parade ground quadrangle.

Here, at last, the skipper told us what it was all about: We were to fly out the Emperor Bao Dai and his entourage at first light. Until then we were confined to barracks.

In spite of my continued malaise I protested violently at this, but the skipper's grin only broadened. I didn't sleep well that night; I was restless, and as I rolled from side to side I heard regular explosions and small-arms fire creeping even closer. As we had heard, the French held sway during daylight; Ho Chi Minh's Communist Viet Minh ruled the night.

On the way to Hong Kong next morning I kept mainly to the cockpit, but I glimpsed two frothily-dressed French girls in the party; they would have stopped the traffic in the Champs Elysees.

Our rescue remained a hush-hush operation which to my knowledge escaped the ears of the Fourth Estate. Apparently it had been mounted because of French concern for the Emperor's safety. Of two assassination attempts the most recent had come uncomfortably close. Throughout the next year the French continued to hold the towns while the Viet Minh controlled the countryside. Then on June 6 a Cathay Pacific flying-boat took Bao Dai to the signing of an agreement aboard a French cruiser in the Baie d'Along, near the city of Haiphong. This document established the three separate kingdoms of Cambodia, Laos and the central government of Vietnam. It incidentally spurred Ho Chi Minh's Communists to greater efforts since it allowed him no participation in government.

While the Bao Dai rescue was being effected Cathay Pacific was lending aid in another conflict far to the south. It accepted a charter with the Indonesian Republic, of which the administration, set up by the Japanese, had proclaimed independence immediately after the end of the war, but had not yet established a rapport with the Dutch. Some skirmishing was going on and the Dutch were in the process of establishing a blockade of Indo centres of power. The charter envisaged a sale to the Indonesians of the DC3 VR-HDJ, which the Indonesians were already referring to as IR1—for Indonesian Republic Number One. Vic Leslie and Dick Hunt were to rotate as skippers on this dangerous venture, K.K. Wong and Mum Louttit the radio men, and a pilot named Roy Hazelhurst opted to do the entire charter as first officer.

K.K. Wong has vivid memories of the entire operation:

'The charter was to run the air blockade being enforced against Dr Ahmed Sukarno's new Republic of Indonesia by the Dutch masters of the tottering Dutch East Indies. We arrived at Singapore all ready to go as soon as a few minor details were clarified. That same evening we were dining at Raffles Hotel and our skipper was as much in the dark as the rest of us. We didn't really have the slightest clue of what was expected of us. Our company was playing its cards close to the chest.

'The dining-room was a bedlam of suspicion, and we kept intercepting glowering stares which would be quickly averted as we made eye contact. The room held a motley of nationalities. Suddenly two evil-looking Indonesians oiled their way to our table and after a few words, raised our worst fears by croaking that the room was full of spies. They told us where we would be going on the morrow; apparently everyone knew our objective but us. Later that evening we received official instructions and at first light were winging our way towards Java and Sukarno's battle headquarters of Djokjakarta. From there we would fly to the island of Sumatra, to a place called Bukittinghi, a summer hill resort on the western side.

'The three-week tour was quite strenuous as we made the return trip each day. With the oppressive heat and the additional strain of routing fairly close to the Dutch strongholds of Bandung and Batavia (now Djakarta), each trip left us fairly thoroughly wrung out.

'I had responsibility for communciations. I had to maintain a continuous listening watch of all the signals crackling through the air waves, but for obvious reasons my orders were to keep strict radio silence. The atmosphere was filled with static but my main objective was to copy every signal sent by Changi airfield at Singapore, where some arrangement had previously been made. I don't know how the company managed to obtain this co-operation as this was an RAF base and the Dutch were not our enemies.

'Anyway, we had no interceptions and had not a single fright during the

July 1948
Kallang Airport, Singapore
L to R:F/O 'Chic' Eather, F/H Judy Chui and R/O Dick Labrum proudly stand in front
of VR-HDW

CPA's DC3 VR-HDA dumping fuel. Possibly one of the few DC3's
with Dump Chutes fitted.

two tours I did. What did bug me was, for the whole of that period the company had told my family nothing—not a good way to engender espirit de corps.

'Dick Hunt skippered my second such tour and on this occasion the family co-ordination was fine, but when I returned to Kai Tak all dirty and tired I was instructed to proceed straight on to Australia as I was the only key-basher around. They overcame my objections and bought me new laundry and away I went.'

Wong's qualifications were not recognized by the Hong Kong licensing authority and because the company was operating charter flights mainly to Australia it had no alternative but to let him go, a victim of the eternal confusion, existing to this day, regarding the interchange of one country's flight crew licences with another's. Paradoxically, the very authority that had refused to support his qualifications quickly snapped him up. He joined the Department of Civil Aviation in July 1947 as an Air Traffic Controller, retiring in October 1972.

Transfer of the aircraft as forecast by the charter arrangements did not eventuate, the Indonesian Republic having failed to show the colour of its money. The Singapore Government impounded it. On May 3, a thoroughly worried general manager Harry de Leuil convinced Max Oxford of the Hong Kong DCA of company innocence. He in turn advised Singapore authorities, who had impounded the crew with the aircraft, that VR-HDJ was still the property of Cathay Pacific, and was at no time owned by Sukarno's Government. The letter explained that it had indeed been the company's intention to sell it, but owing to 'various technicalities' the deal did not go through.

Behind the scenes at Djokjakarta, Roy Hazelhurst had found favour with the aviation aspirants of Sukarno's regime. When the Singapore authorities seized HDJ these planners released the purse-strings, bought another DC3 from another source, and employed Roy to command it. He was to form their flag-carrying airline when they achieved world recognition. At the same time a pilot named Cunningham was appointed to establish their Air Force later. In the meantime these two would continue to fly the Djokjakarta/Bukittinghi milk-run as co-captains. One morning two Dutch Mustang fighters based at Kemajoran field thundered into the air, intercepted the lumbering cargo plane, and blasted into oblivion the aspirations of all on board.

CHAPTER FIVE
GROWING PAINS

So many hours must I tend my flock;
So many hours must I take my rest.
King Henry VI ... William Shakespeare

The indisposition I had felt on the evacuation flight for the Emperor Bao Dai developed in intensity. On April 28 Dr Tony Dawson-Grove, called to my complete collapse, diagnosed it as typhoid fever and arranged my entry to St Theresa's Hospital. Through my delirium I could hear him advising my wife Joyce against taking me there in the bone-shaking Army ambulance. He recommended a taxi, which would be cheaper and smoother.

Nine weeks of almost complete unconsciousness followed, with almost continuous delirium. I would imagine I was a Knight of the Realm and demand that visitors kneel in my presence. To the relief of my doctor I began to make a slow recovery. As a side-effect, my toes had collapsed and I developed so-called 'electric feet'. The official designation, I understand, is peripheral neuritis. By either name it was absolute agony; I couldn't even bear the gentle pressure of bed-sheets.

At this time I was far from *compos mentis,* but I knew enough to dread the arrival of a particularly vicious amah. She would sidle into my room and tweak those pinkies. I would scream in agony—sometimes before she even got close. That seemed to please her more than the final tweak. The commotion would bring the Nursing Director, Sister Patrick on the run, but the amah, a cunning mover, would be well away, and Sister Patrick would never be convinced that 'one of her girls' could be capable of the dastardly deed. One day I made my preparations, bending my knees and getting my toes to the right-hand edge of the bed, a move that took time and caused considerable pain. My tormentor came round the bed for a better go at them and as she slowly reached out I swung and made contact with her chin. I can still see her disappearing through those swing doors, black skirt up and bloomers displayed. I convinced Sister Patrick I was far too ill to have played the part of which I was accused. She took my word and the discredited nurse never came near me again.

Those electric feet stayed with me for several years and I had to treat them with great care. A major hazard was showering in a bathtub at outports. I had to take my shower sitting on the edge of the bath. This used to amuse Dick Hunt, and I just had to bear with his childish mirth. He had made his meteoric rise in the company and I couldn't give him the slightest inkling that my health was in doubt. Only the understanding attitudes of Roy Farrell and Syd de Kantzow had retained me in my job during the days of illness and recovery and, the company being new and forced to watch every penny, I shall be forever grateful for the way they stood by me.

For a period I became something of a thinker—perhaps 'brooder' would be a better word. Convalescence guided my thoughts into channels deeper than usual. I'm not deeply religious but, convinced that I, perhaps more than most need an Interceder from on high, I have accepted God quite unquestioningly. I feel no embarrassment when I record that at times I have been absolutely terrified, mainly by the contrary whims of the weather, and regard prayer as having been my salvation on numerous occasions. My thoughts were morbid to a degree when I considered the many situations that even the most accomplished aviators could not handle, though he be trained to a stage where his knowledge of technical matters and emergency procedures were at a maximum.

For example, an uncontrolled engine fire breaks out while you are at 30,000 feet on a dark stormy night over the sea at least twenty minutes flying time from the nearest land. Where do you go? Emergency descents from these altitudes are a recurrent requirement of training and you can get down to sea-level fairly quickly, but by this time the fire may have spread to the wing spar, and all that fuel is stored behind it. In the given weather conditions the sea will be rough, so it seems a safe bet that whatever the pilot does achieve in this ditching most, if not all the souls aboard, will have their lives snuffed out.

With such thoughts I developed an interest in the arcane. I spent vast amounts trying to explore it. I became a Rosicrucian. I contributed to a magazine called *Prediction* and acquired some beautiful books. One was J.C. Street's *The Hidden Way Across the Threshold*. I still enjoy reading it: his name and the title seem such a providential mating. I read with avid interest books on palmistry, analysed my dreams, followed the prediction of the great Cheiro, sent prints of my palms and even my feet for analysis. Most bizarre of all I sent for summaries of my past and future lives on this earth.

This was to Abdurahman, an Indian gentleman who operated from 41 Pembridge Road, London, a most unlikely address from which to contact the occult. He proclaimed himself a specialist in Oriental psycho-astrology, and although he dealt with matters not of this world, he was very earthy with his fees. My previous incarnations took place in Italy, England, Greece, India, Egypt, Tibet and Peru, but the one I like best inhabited the ancient Babylonian city of Ur during the 12th century B.C. I was then tall and slender, with high cheekbones, large beautiful black eyes, long thin neck, long arms and fingers, dark suntanned shining complexion, aristocratic and beautiful facial features and physical excellence. All these things are of course missing from my present incarnation and—oh yes!—best of all I was female! I have been a little derisive of our sage, but anyone able to extract payment for a such a nebulous service needs no protection. His clients need it more—and I had become one of the most gullible of men.

Another disturbing development dated from my recovery. Where I had been a contented and happily married man, rarely looking at another woman, I now found myself eager to make another conquest at every opportunity. Joyce and I began the slow drift towards the eventual dissolution of our marriage, a dissolution not legalised for many years, and mainly my own fault.

After a brief convalescence in Australia I managed to convince Dr. Hood-Stobo, one of DCA's medical examiners, that there was nothing wrong with me, even though my weight had dropped from 180 to 128 pounds. October 13 found my old pal Keith Robey of the Royal Aero Club of New South Wales giving me a few circuits and bumps on a Tiger Moth. After about thirty minutes of rounding out too high for the landing he decided I wouldn't get any better and turned me loose to accumulate the five hours required for Licence renewal. The same month found me operating as co-pilot on a Cathay Pacific DC3 en route to Cloncurry. From there our track took us to Keopang on Dutch Timor, Surabaya in Java, Kallang at Singapore, and then our tyres rolled along Runway 31 at Kai Tak. I had returned.

I was to find some changes. Pinky Wawn had retired in May. His marriage to the lovely Kay the previous December had sown the seeds of a slight discontent. The month had started with the company accepting more charters than their fleet or personnel could handle and tempers became a little frayed. Then a now-pregnant Kay decided she needed a husband in more than name and it was inevitable that her quite reasonable arguments would prevail. But to the company this loss of a friendly, humorous and efficient pilot was untimely. The story of his final flight from Hong Kong illustrates some of the difficulties of those free and easy days.

All went well until they landed at Morotai, where they learnt that they would have to over-run Darwin because the fuel loaders there were on strike. They decided they would shorten the next sector by landing at Ambon, on the northern boundary of the Banda Sea, a few miles south of Ceram. The Dutch Air Force controlled two Japanese-constructed air strips on this tiny island, and they told Pinky to use Liang, about seven miles northwest of the town of Ambon. Pressed for more details the Dutch controllers at Morotai airily told him it was the strip with the low-powered radio beacon on it. When they got over Ambon they found that the intertropic conversion front was, in Pinky's words, 'stirring up the weather a bit' but the radio beacon was giving a steady reading so down they went. The rain was heavy but the windscreen wipers were handling it pretty well and soon the strip came into view. Just before the wheels made contact the co-pilot yelled that dozens of palm trees were obstructing it. Pinky poured on the power and, after stooging round, located the other strip and landed on it. There he found that the Dutch had removed the beacon from Liang to Pattimura in expectation of occupying Pattimura as it promised to be the better of the two, but the radio beacon had moved in ahead of the bulldozers. The 'strip' was still obstructed and no one had thought to inform headquarters at Morotai of the progress of the changes.

Refuelling didn't take long; they bypassed Darwin and overnighted at Daly Waters. The next leg should have taken them to Charleville but suddenly the fuel gauge dropped at an alarming rate and they made an emergency stop at Blackall, on the Barcoo River, only to find that one fuel tank had collapsed. When they attempted to get fuel they found they had to wait for a tanker from Longreach.

KAI TAK 1950
F/O Ced Carlton, F/H Vera Rozario (later Mrs Jack Williams),
Jack Williams, Captain Frank Smith.

After half a day's wait they took off and completed their flight.

'But the memory of the two following takeoffs with unbalanced fuel will always haunt me,' Pinky told me recently.

With his departure his brother Bob entered the Cathay Pacific organisation. He too had served with the Air Force in Europe, but was shot down by the Germans in 1940 and remained a prisoner until VE-Day in 1945.

Francis Paul Smith brought his intransigent individualism to the Cathay Pacific service on July 1, 1947. He also brought an admirable war record. He had been a pilot of the Lancaster 'G for George' which has been a major exhibit in the Australian War Museum since it was flown there from the European theatre by another of its operational pilots Flight Lieutenant Peter Isaacson DFC, AFC, DFM. Smith also earned a DFC for his thirty bombing raids over Germany. His flying ability was above the average; by the time he left Cathay Pacific on October 23, 1952 he was its chief pilot.

Like many other Australians he rebelled against authority as a matter of course, also against most of society's conventions. He believed that every Australian had the inalienable right to a good punch-up. Unfortunately he could not hold his liquor; he was a mean drunk and in this state couldn't fight his way out of a paper bag. Probably the rest of us should have avoided his company. Nobody likes a loser, but his likeable nature when sober won him a legion of friends and we grieved when he was killed in a crash. The aeroplane, owned by Lebanese Trans-Mediterranean Airways, had to make a refuelling stop at Brindisi when returning from Frankfurt to Beirut. An eyewitness saw flames belching from one engine, two terrifying explosions, and the craft plunging into the water just half a mile from the runway.

Cathay Pacific spent the rest of the year wheeling and dealing, focussing attention on their activities. Roy Farrell arranged a series of charters flying freshly-caught fish to Singapore from Kuantan on the Malay Peninsula's east coast, near where the Japanese had sunk the *Prince of Wales* and the *Repulse* at the beginning of the Pacific War. He had a contract for two months beginning in September, and the crews were very glad when it was completed. Surely never again, they thought, would they be rid of the smell of fish. Of more concern was the condition of the control cables which ran the length of the fuselage floor and were continuously splashed by the salt water in which the fish were carried. In periods of turbulence the tubs would overflow, and salt water and control cables are bad friends.

Then in November Eric McIllree entered the scene again. He brought two more of his Ansons, VH-BFL and VH-BFK to Hong Kong by short stages, and demonstrated them as de luxe ten-place feeder-liners to an interested Cathay Pacific, driving home their short-field operating characteristics with demonstration flights to and from Macao, where our DC3 had lost her landing gear earlier that year.

Syd de Kantzow and Roy Farrell immediately projected their vision to the pocket-handkerchief strips abounding in Burma. They clinched the deal, subject to Eric's flying the Ansons to Rangoon after the serviceability checks which would permit Hong Kong registration. On Boxing Day Cathay Pacific became owner of the Ansons, now VR-HDX and VR-HDU.

Perhaps Eric McIllree put in a good word on my behalf, for during the first week of December I found myself summoned to de Kantzow's office. Roy Farrell and Nash Nasholds were also there, lounging in comfortable chairs. Immediately I was seated Roy enquired about my health, whether I had fully recovered from my bout with typhoid. I replied I felt first class, and then was somewhat staggered when, with a broad grin, Syd said he hoped my knowledge of the Brumese language was progressing and that I possessed a good wardrobe of longyis (the gaudy Burmese sarongs). They were appointing me to take charge of the Anson fleet they were buying from McIllree. I told them how grateful I was for the opportunity, and that I would give the job my very best, and was assured that not only did they know this, they expected it. I left the office accompanied by their congratulations, hand-shakes and slaps on the back. I felt on top of the world.

Then as I walked towards the stairs which led from P.J. Lobo's office to Chater Road I saw Morrie Lothian, another first officer who had joined the company whilst I was out of action. I hailed him to tell him my good news, the words tumbling from my mouth in almost incoherent confusion.

His reaction was not quite what I had anticipated but I didn't give it much thought at the time. In a voice which I could only describe as menacing he growled,
'Oh, they did, did they?'

He swung around and bounded back through the door leading to Sydney's sanctum. Morrie went to Burma in charge of that Anson fleet and I remained a first officer!

During my convalescence Cathay Pacific became involved in a lucrative carriage of the migrants who flocked from several European countries to Australia, carrying its first load in October 1947. Some of the plentiful difficulties of the trade sprang from the thwarted ambitions of the Australian Labor Party under Prime Minister Ben Chifley, who had assumed leadership on the death of John Curtin a month before the Japanese surrender. Chifley's vision saw the people, under Government, the rightful owners of all air transport in Australia. He told Parliament that the only proper monopoly was a Government one and he hoped that the whole of air transport would come under this control. His initial measures, which passed both Houses of Parliament in 1945 included setting up a company called Trans-Australia Airlines (TAA) which would monopolise interstate air transport. This measure barely concealed his hatred for Ivan Holyman's Australian National Airlines Pty Ltd., which he meant to force completely out of business. This was the second company to carry this name, and was registered in Melbourne in 1936.

The verdict of a test case in the High Court ruled that while the Commonwealth of Australia could operate its own interstate airline, it could not prohibit private enterprise from competing. Mr Chifley learnt nothing from this first attempt at nationalisation. A similar failure to nationalise the banks a little later saw the beginning of his decline.

TAA, which he fathered, remains a successful enterprise and shares Australian airspace with Ansett, which embodies ANA. But not so fortunate was his creation BCPA, irreverently translated 'Ben Chifley's Private Airline', or sometimes 'Belt Christ out of Pan-Am'. More accurately the initials stood for British Commonwealth Pacific Airlines, and the company was owned 50% by Australia, 30% by New Zealand and 20% by the United Kingdom. BCPA had been created to drive ANA from Pacific skies. ANA had made 255 trans-Pacific crossings on an interim licence between September 1946 and April 1948 when BCPA took over. Qantas absorbed BCPA in 1954, when the UK dropped out of the agreement.

Charterers in plenty jumped in to meet the demand from southern Europe to Australia. Trans-Oceanic Airways was charging approximately $300 a head for both adults and children from Greece, and other carriers were in line. Qantas carried only a trickle of these passengers, surely an indication that seating capacity was filled and the Australian protection of air nationalisation misguided.

On behalf of the Government-owned airline the Australian Department of Civil Aviation was making things difficult for all these charter lines and, in consequence, for the migrants. When they reached Darwin, for example, the charterers would be told to off-load their passengers and advise them that TAA would take them onward next day. When the limited hotel accommodation was filled they would have to sleep on the beach or in the waiting-rooms. At times like these Cathay Pacific would be directed to proceed to Sydney whether it suited the company plans or not. The Cathay Pacific management could not formulate its aircraft employment plans without being sure how long an aircraft would be engaged on any particular flight.

The Babbitts of DCA were not in any way influenced by reports of hardship, and their attitude induced some charter operators to dump their human loads in Asian cities, leaving someone else with more moral fibre to tackle the Australian Civil Service bureaucracy. Such operators had put every plane available on the line whether or not it was serviceable, and would rush back to Europe to load yet another consignment of the hopefuls. Singapore, Rangoon and Calcutta at different times became their main dumping grounds and were cleared only when the local government, worried by the plight of the pitiful and abandoned people, would close its airspace to the offenders until the backlog was cleared.

Radio officer Ken Wolenski told me of one of these migrant trips in Cathay Pacific's first DC3, VR-HDB, skippered by John Furley. Their route lay between Rangoon and Darwin, with technical stops at Bangkok, Singapore, Soerabaya and Keopang. At Singapore the ground engineer found a broken rudder-hinge, and naturally, no spares were available. It seemed that Cathay Pacific would lose heavily on its charter as some twenty-eight migrants would soon be eating their heads off at Raffles Hotel at company expense.

Then Furley remembered that some of his old RAF chums would be at Changi airfield, so the crew hailed a taxi and were soon breasting the bar at the RAF Officer's Mess, surrounded by Furley's old friends, each insisting he would buy the next drink. The total mess bill amounted to about twelve to fifteen Straits dollars, but since it was Air Force duty-free grog that is no indication of the amount consumed.

'We were soon making a somewhat unsteady way to the RAF stores,' Ken Wolenski said, 'and were there presented with a handful of the elusive rudder hinges. Someone insisted I should have my very own hinge as a memento of the event. I still have it somewhere. With the repair made we were soon on our way, a little hung-over. When Furley later submitted the small grog account to the company for payment it was refused: "Really, old boy, you can't call that a legitimate expense!"'

'What magnitude expenses might have reached had he not kept the show on the road by his own intervention was not taken into account. Furley footed the bill himself.'

Other forms of bureaucratic interference harassed the migrant runs. In March 1948 a Lockheed Hudson owned by Mr Warren Penny, of Intercontinental Air Tours, a Sydney firm, was delayed in Rangoon for nearly a fortnight pending payment for fuel and hotel accommodation. He needed an export permit for his Australian funds to reach him and it wasn't forthcoming. When it was finally authorized it was forwarded to a bank not nominated in Penny's application, a considered ploy, without doubt. Meanwhile fourteen Greek migrants were delayed with the aircraft.

Cathay Pacific used one of their 'no frills' DC3s at Calcutta to transfer seventeen seamen to Sydney with other passengers. It was one of the war transport types with bucket seats and minimum facilities, and one agitator among the seamen induced the others to leave the plane at Singapore. Captain Furley, persuasive and charming as always when it suited his purpose, explained that these conditions were quite usual on the aircraft then being used to shift a vast backlog of people from Eastern ports. He seemed to satisfy the malcontents. They trooped aboard and the flight continued without further incident. Then the Sydney *Daily Telegraph* of April 24 published a story headlined: PASSENGERS BAN PLANE.

For the next couple of years frequent news reports presented the plight of migrants suffering under government protectionist policy. The *Daily Telegraph* in June ran a story on forty-odd people who arrived in Darwin at 6 p.m., and did not get through Customs and Immigration procedures until 2 a.m., and still were not allowed to leave the airport until 5 a.m.—eleven hours to process these few people.

Ivan Holyman for ANA negotiated an agreewith with the Ceylon Government by which ANA, with a 49% shareholding was to operate in parallel with Air Ceylon, which retained 51%, to offer a London-Sydney service by way of Colombo, using four (DC4) Skymasters. Within three months the Australian DCA refused onward clearance from Darwin to an Air Ceylon Skymaster en route to Sydney. The Department accused Air Ceylon of operating charter flights in Australia without authority, but the following day admitted the government protectionist policy. The fact that the national carrier Qantas was still operating with 'standing room only' made no difference whatever to these uncivil servants.

The childish war of attrition continued until August 14, 1949 Captain Ken

Lockyer did a moonlight flit from Darwin in a Guinea Air Traders DC3. He took off without an approved flight plan, he ignored a red light which meant 'Stop. Clear strip immediately', and he negotiated a series of red flares which came dangerously close.

Ken was quite in the wrong, as he admitted to me off the record some time later, but in the interests of Andreas Sehx, Stylianos Kleanvoos, John Goerchios, Andrew Spanos and his wife and five more migrant passengers who were practically destitute, decided to make the effort to end their inhuman situation.

The newspapers mixed in, perhaps giving more coverage than usual because uniformed watchmen had struggled with investigating journalists at the airport, and the fact that the whole matter had thus been brought before the public did seem to quieten the over-zealous officials. Migrants seemed to get a more humane and less obstructive reception after that, so Ken's courageous but foolhardy action had a worthwhile effect. The usually unbending DCA did not suspend Ken's licence, a punishment they had inflicted a few days earlier on Lionel van Praag for a similar transgression.

CHAPTER SIX
ENTER THE HONG

Hong: A commercial establishment
or house of foreign trade in China

Webster's Dictionary

About the time I was so briefly appointed to take charge of the Ansons in Burma, Cathay Pacific was facing a constitutional crisis. In January 1948 the Hong Kong Government informed de Kantzow and Farrell that the time for allotting official franchises was at hand, and that if they wanted to be considered they must reduce their American holdings to ten per cent. The obvious solution lay with the Hongs, the great houses of foreign trade of which one of the largest was Butterfield and Swire, a subsidiary of the London house of John Swire and Sons Limited. The Chinese called it 'Taikoo', translated as 'Great and Ancient', and its management was anxious to spread its activities into the aviation field. The nearest competitor, Jardine Matheson and Company had earlier floated Hong Kong Airways, which in the spring of 1947 had been taken over by the British Overseas Airways Corporation.

By then de Kantzow and Farrell, faced with the weakness American ownership imposed, were looking for some British partner to buy the bulk of the American interest. Brigadier-General Critchley, Chairman of Skyways Limited, flew to Hong Kong to negotiate the purchase of Cathay Pacific. Skyways represented in Hong Kong, under Jardine's agency, by M.H. Curtis. No doubt Critchley expected to find a thoroughly disheartened de Kantzow prepared to sell the company for next to nothing. But the confident de Kantzow, well aware of the value of his company, was not prepared to be bluffed or bullied into a sale. Though they came close to the point of sale, the negotiations were hampered by an incompatibility of temperament between Critchley and de Kantzow.

In the autumn of 1947 Skyways transferred their agency from Jardine's to Butterfield and Swire, where Curtis was given a seat in the office. Curtis brought full particulars of the Skyways/Cathay Pacific negotiations, to which Far Eastern Aviation Company had also been a party. Soon afterwards John Swire and Sons Limited, the parent company of Butterfield and Swire, began discussions in London with Skyways as to the possibility of starting an Air Repairs Company and the chances of still coming to terms with de Kantzow.

In February 1948 a period of intense negotiation began with the arrival of Mr J.K. Swire in Hong Kong. On May 5 this resulted in the initialling of a 'basis of agreement' by China Navigation Company, Butterfield and Swire, Australian Nationay Airways, Cathay Pacific, Skyways and Far Eastern Navigation Company for the formation of a new Hong Kong company to be called Cathay Pacific Airways (1948) Limited.

Under this, Cathay Pacific should be taken over for the value of its assets with no consideration for goodwill, de Kantzow agreeing to accept the valuation of I.H. Grabowksy of ANA. He would retain a ten per cent holding and management of the company with a seat on the Board. Ten per cent was divided among his American partners. Butterfield and Swire would hold the booking agency, and John Swire and Sons and China Navigation Company would have the right to appoint Chairman and Managing Director.

Presented with these terms in London, Skyways and Far Eastern refused to ratify and dropped out. After more discussion in Melbourne the agreement was ratified on June 1 and operations began a month later. CNCo and ANA each held 35% of shares, John Swire and Sons 10%, de Kantzow 10% and Cathay Holdings Limited 10%. The last-named was a new Hong Kong company owned by de Kantzow's American and other original associates. The company was registered on October 18 with a nominal capital of $HK10,000,000 ($HK3,000,000 issued), C. C. Roberts Chairman, M.S. Cumming Managing Director. The other directors were J.K. Swire, Captain Holyman, I.H. Grabowsky and S.H. de Kantzow. The allocation of the franchises remained to be settled, and an agreement between BOAC representing Hong Kong Airways and J.K. Swire for Cathay Pacific was signed on May 11 1949 and blessed by the Colonial Office and Ministry of Civil Aviation two days later. It read:

> 'The broad basis and spirit of this agreement is that Cathay Pacific shall exploit the area south of Hong Kong and Hong Kong Airways shall exploit the area north of Hong Kong. Any intrusion by one company into the area of the other, except in the case of Macao, for which Hong Kong Airways already holds the franchise, and Manila, where both companies hold equal rights, shall be by agreement on a reciprocal or other agreed basis.'

In November BOAC sold Hong Kong Airways completely to Jardines. The franchised routes were licenced officially on March 22, 1950. The following month de Kantzow sold (at 107.5) 656 shares to ANA, 656 to CNCo and 188 to J.S.& S., making the shareholding ANA 37.19%, CNCo 37.19%, de Kantzow 5% and Cathay Holdings Ltd. 10%. Then at the end of the year the latter company offered the whole of their holdings to the parent companies. John Swire and Sons took up the offer and the transfer (with valuation by the auditors) was registered on June 2, 1951 at a price of $HK 50 a share. De Kantzow severed his connection with the company on April 30, 1951, selling his shares to ANA and J.S.& S. Ltd. Thereafter the shareholdings of the company were ANA 39.69%, CNCo 37.19% and J.S. & S 23.12%.

The aircraft that the company took over were six DC3s and one Catalina flying-boat. De Kantzow and Farrell had bought a second Catalina in September 1947 from the USAAF Federal Liquidation Commission in the Philippines. It cost them 6000 pesos, approximately $HK12,000. The most remarkable feature of the type was its ability to stay in the air for a phenomenal time, as attested by the Qantas Catalina air-link between Koggala, Ceylon and Perth, Western Australia. On 271 crossings between July 1943 and July 1945 the Catalina logged an average time in the air of 27 hours, the longest time being 31 hours 51 minutes. Each passenger was presented with a strikingly printed certificate called 'The Order of the Double Sunrise', having been airborne in excess of 24 hours.

It was designed as a pure flying-boat for the US Navy in the early 'thirties, but with the advent of World War II the Candian Government, aware of its advantages in its vast Northwest, built an amphibious version under licence and named it Canso. This name is remembered in Canada and in dusty archives, but the pilots who wrestled with this hybrid, who cursed it, blessed it, died in it (as did my younger brother) knew it only as the PBY or the pig-boat.

Safely negotiating the 600 miles of restless sea that separates the Philippine Island of Luzon from mainland China, the second Catalina put down at Kai Tak during the late morning of October 2, 1947. Almost before the aircrews stopped rotating an army of engineering minions descended on her. With indecent haste they commenced to strip her, and with the remarkable engineering efficiency Cathay Pacific commanded in those days, the passenger conversion was completed by late November. On December 5 she entered service with the registration VR-HDT. She was then a sleek, silvery lady with the 23 passenger seats which, in those early post-war years, could only be described as 'regal'. As a concession to her new civilian role the airline added an ice-box filled with cold drinks, no other catering being considered necessary. So the airline, for something like $HK50,000 had a first-class asset that was, six months later, handed over to the new interests for $HK173,400.

Some aircrew colleagues spoke of her as a venerable pig-boat. Since on purchase she had logged only 993 hours she was to me a lovely lady in the full bloom of youth. She was dubbed *Miss Macao* when she commenced service there in April, under charter to the Macao Air Transport Company (MATCO). She had logged a total of only 1,596 hours when, three months later, she became a muddied, twisted heap of corroding metal and the tomb of innocent people.

With this metamorphisis she entered history. She had become the victim in the world's first air-piracy, an attempted hi-jack that went miserably wrong.

The China coast shelters perhaps the last strongholds of pirate communities, with the possible exception of the Sea-Dyak lairs in Malayan waters. In their twentieth century routine, according to a 1961 Encyclopaedia Britannica reference, 'the Chinese pirates ship themselves as ordinary coolie passengers on a coastal steamer and at a given signal produce revolvers and hold up the passengers and crew and compel them to navigate the ship to their headquarters at Bias Bay, where the ship is plundered and officers and passengers held to ransom.' Bias Bay is the modern Daya Wan, a bay just northeast of Kowloon; and indeed on April 7, 1891 the mass execution of a band of pirates who had sacked the *Namoa*, one of the worst of Hong Kong's piracies, had taken place approximately on the site of Kai Tak airfield.

A plan for pirating the *Miss Macao* developed in the minds of Chio Tok, Chio Kei Mun and Chio Cheong, three villagers of Nam Mun, which is in the

SEE THE BEAUTY OF
HONGKONG FROM THE AIR

FLY TO

MACAO

NEXT WEEK-END

YOU WILL SEE SO MUCH IN 20 MINUTES

MACAO AIR TRANSPORT CO., LTD.

in conjunction with

CATHAY PACIFIC AIRWAYS LTD.

are maintaining regular services
between Macao and Hong Kong

FLIGHT SCHEDULE

	DEPARTS HONGKONG	DEPARTS MACAO
FRIDAY	4.00 p.m.	[illegible] p.m.
SATURDAY	[illegible] a.m. 1.00 p.m. 4.00 p.m.	[illegible] a.m. 2.00 p.m. 5.00 p.m.
SUNDAY	9.00 a.m. 1.00 p.m. 4.00 p.m.	10.00 a.m. 2.00 p.m. 5.00 p.m.
MONDAY	[illegible] a.m.	8.30 a.m.

SINGLE FARE H.K.$40.00
RETURN .. H.K.$75.00

Passenger Bookings

Peninsula Hotel
Kowloon
Tel. 56260

4 Chater Road
Hongkong
Tel. 31162

FIGURE 7: MACAO AIR TRANSPORT COMPANY LIMITED TIMETABLE
HONG KONG-MACAO "SOUTH CHINA MORNING POST" ADVERTISEMENT
SATURDAY, APRIL 20, 1948

Seong Chao region adjacent to Macao. Tok, the leader, had learned to fly amphibians while he had been living in Manila, and would take over the controls after the pilots had been subdued, the gang having taken passage in the normal way. They had a bank of $HK3000 from the sale of rice-fields.

Tok was aware of two weaknesses in the straight-forward plan. Kei Mun was an opium smoker with a habit costing three dollars a day and therefore probably unreliable under pressure, and none of the three had good local knowledge of the coasts and islands, including a haven to take the captured Catalina. To offset this latter defect he had approached Wong Yu, a 24-year-old rice farmer living on the island of Tao Mun, since Wong had an excellent knowledge of the Seong Chao region, within which, at Peng T'ong, Tok proposed to land the captured aircraft.

Wong Yu agreed with reservations, stipulating that he would take no part in the actual hold-up, reasoning perhaps that if the attack failed he would continue to Hong Kong as an ordinary passenger. His sole contribution would be to direct Tok to the most suitable landing site. He made other stipulations, for example he would not mount guard over the captured passengers after landing; the inhabitants of Peng T'ong being certain to demand large bribes to keep silent.

Both disturbed and influenced by Wong Yu's many conditions Tok redrafted his plans and dismissed Kei Mun. He kept Wong Yu in the scheme, perhaps as a precaution against betrayal, and entlisted another clansman from Sio Chek Kam, another village on Tao Mun. He altered the projected destination of the captured Catalina to his own village of Nam Mun, where the locals, being family, would likely keep their mouths shut. Several village conferences settled the matter; after looting the Catalina the pirates would take the passengers and crew to the mountain of Seong Chao and there abandon them.

They had a Macao base in the home of 29-year-old Chio Iek Chan, a pretty deserted wife who lived at 39 Estrada Coelho do Amaral. She had no connection with crime and was completely honest, unlike an elder sister Chio Min Vo, a tall, thin, ugly and dark 37-year-old. Min Vo was staying there while she awaited a visa that would allow her to join her husband in New York. The next precaution of the pirates was to make a dummy run to check on the procedures of MATCO, the charterers of *Miss Macao*.

A little after 9.30 on the morning of July 16, Wong, Tok, Cheong and Choi met and went to the house of Iek Chan. They had a meal there, and left a small black bag for safekeeping, warning the sisters not to investigate it or indeed touch it. Tok came back and deposited the bag in the middle drawer of a chest of drawers, repeating the warning, and perhaps this over-emphasis was a challenge to the ugly sister, Min Vo. When they had gone she unzipped the bag and, with a rasp of indrawn breath, found herself staring at three hand-guns. She trembled in the grip of an agitation so intense she had trouble zipping the bag up again. Meanwhile the conspirators bought some light-weight European clothing in a shop on the Almedia Ribeiro at a cost of twenty patacas, Tok acting as treasurer. They had coffee at a small restaurant.

The walk and the coffee settled the men down, and when it was time to

Alan Marshall and F/O Bob Wawn (extreme right) at Haiphong, Indo-China—June 1948

1948
The Cathay Pacific single officers mess at 48 Grampian Road, Kowloon, Hong Kong. We would airily direct our taxi driver to 'say sup bart Galimpinto' which seemed to impress the driver but in reality that was the full extent of our Cantonese.

June 1948
Alan Marshall at CPA's mess
48 Grampian Road Kowloown, Hong Kong

return to Iek Chan's house to change their clothing their spirits were buoyant. When it was time to leave for the seadrome Min Vo called from the window to a neighbour who was the proud owner of a telephone, and ordered a taxi for their short trip to the airline's embarkation pier where the company launch was moored.

Just before 5.30 that afternoon Captain Dale Cramer was cleared for takeoff from the Kai Tak tower, and rolled the *Miss Macao* away from the tarmac area. A U.S. Navy pilot, he had soloed in February 17, 1943 and been posted that April to the naval station at Corpus Christi, in Texas. After logging 1000 hours he was posted to Patrol Squadron 45. He finished the war and his Naval career with 1789 hours logged, leaving the service early in 1947. His record and ability earned him a captaincy with INACO, a Philippine company which operated Catalina amphibians. In June he was hired by Trans-Asiatic Air Service operating from Bangkok and checked out on DC3s, and in August Cathay Pacific snapped him up when he applied for a job with them.

On this afternoon he had expected to take as passenger Alan Marshall, freelance journalist and author. Since contracting polio at the age of six, Alan has walked on crutches. (In July 1977 Soviet Russia presented him with the Order of the Friendship of Peoples, one of the highest a non-Russian can receive.) Earlier this day he had left his room in the Cathay Pacific crew mess at Kowloon where he had spent much time learning about air-crew, listening to their thoughts and anecdotes, and their lies about sexual conquests.

He accompanied the *Miss Macao* crew on the hair-raising car ride to Kai Tak. He was enjoying a beer at the airport when the soft sweet voice of 21-year-old hostess Delca da Costa broke through his reverie.

'Captain Cramer has asked me to tell you it is now 5 p.m., and we expect to be leaving for Macao in a few minutes. Perhaps you would like me to help you out to the aircraft?'

Alan lined up his frosty beer-glass with the passenger steps located at the cat-boat's port blister, regarding with dismay the intervening hundred yards of glaring concrete and made a quick decision, one which without doubt would be the most important of his life.

'Delca, dear, please tell Captain Dale that my legs are giving me more pain than usual, and ask if he would mind my taking a rain-check?'

Before she could answer one of Alan's companions, Cathay's sales and traffic officer Rober Lowich Frost, interjected:

'Never mind, Delca. I'll walk out with you and explain to the skipper.'

He confided to Alan that he didn't feel in the mood to kick his heels around the airport and would use the vacant seat himself. His wife was having her hair done and would not be home for several hours. He was at a loose end, and a quick trip to Macao would help him while away the time. Bob Frost, born in Australia in 1921, had joined Cathay Pacific after a successful Qantas association which had brought him to their Singapore Office. For the purpose of insurance he was listed as a supernumerary crew member.

Cleared for line-up, Cramer opened the throttles fully, his feet firm on the brake pedals. As the sound above his head reached a comfortable roar he released

Roy Downing, May 1948. Air Traffic Control Officer Kai Tak Airport, Kowloon.

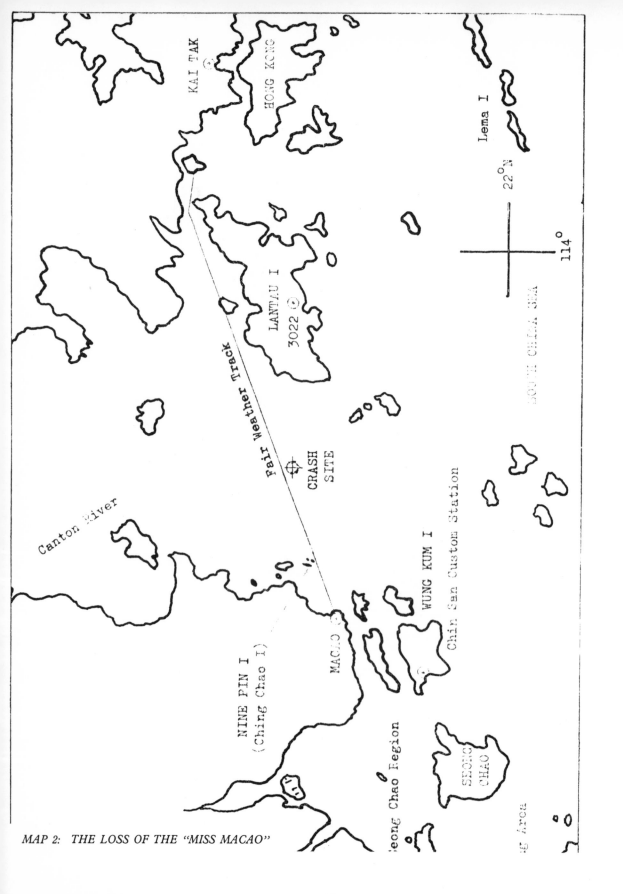

MAP 2: THE LOSS OF THE "MISS MACAO"

Len Cosgrove makes a splendid mooring pick-up which is no mean
task in a flat calm—bad language seems to make the task easier in
such conditions. Macao Breakwater, 1958

1947
Bill ''Hokum'' Harris
CPA's first engineer Kai Tak
(Note: Engineer Store and Flag thereon).

the brakes and Macao Flight Two was rolling on schedule. At 60 knots he lifted the nose-wheel off the concrete and at 75 a solid back-pressure on the control yoke brought the Catalina into the air. On the call of 'Wheels Up' his young first officer, Sydney-born 23-year-old Ken McDuff selected the landing gear to 'up'. The ponderous system took nearly two minutes to tuck the wheels into the hull in a semblence of streamlining. Most pilots believed that undercarriage systems had been designed by Emmet of *Punch*, but surprisingly it seldom failed. Only the nose wheel had a tendency to lag and the watertight doors under it had to be checked fully closed before landing at Macao.

Duty controller Roy Downing recorded takeoff at 5.30 p.m., and watched *Miss Macao* flying out at approximately 1000 feet on a track of about 275 true; then gently turning to port round the northern tip of Lantau Island on the normal good-weather route. Levelled out, the Catalina quickly achieved its flight-planned airspeed of 130 knots, and with power reduced the passengers could maintain a shouted conversation, for sound-proofing was a non-existent luxury.

Lantau Island, eight miles from Hong Kong and flaunting a craggy peak of 3000 feet or more, contributes to the limitation of radio contact between Hong Kong and Macao, a matter of great concern when any aircraft became overdue. After the routine message that they had Macao in sight McDuff, on Cramer's instructions, closed down the radio, not getting an answer, or expecting one. Macao did not maintain a radio station for aircraft, having no space for a landing field. Only the amphibians could operate there. The Government did not supply a launch to keep the landing ways clear of small craft and debris.

Cramer therefore placed his reliance on one low-powered run over the breakwater-enclosed harbour to scatter the sampans. Normally a second such nudge was unnecessary. The more knowledgeable women worked frantically at their sculls when they heard the sound of the engine. Over the breakwater McDuff climbed into the engineer's 'tower' and selected the switch which lowered the floats from the wingtips, completing the transition to flying-boat. Cramer gently closed the throttles and for the very last time settled *Miss Macao* sweetly in Portuguese waters. At the forward hatch McDuff completed the mooring procedure with a glow of pride. This was the first time he had done so without getting a drop of spray on his freshly-cleaned uniform. The reason he was on this flight was that the morning flight's first officer had fallen into the muddy, stinking water when he had misjudged the pick-up. Chief pilot Dick Hunt had been on that early flight too, but had developed a severe earache.

With the passengers transferred to the launch, Delca da Costa settled herself on the lip of the blister, her ankles comfortably crossed. This was the coolest place during the turnaround, which was effected in the least time possible because of the mounting heat within the metal aircraft. She was industriously writing of her life with Cathay Pacific for the benefit of Alan Marshall. He had sold a successful article to *Woman* magazine and planned this as a follow-up.

McDuff closed the mooring hatch, took in the pole on which the moored Catalina displayed her courtesy flag and strapped himself in his seat, ready when Dale commenced his pre-takeoff check to hold the necessary full aileron input

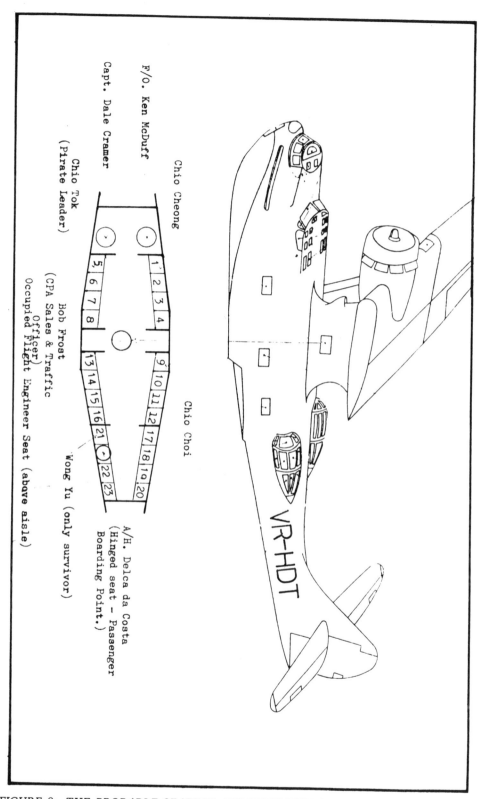

FIGURE 8: THE PROBABLE SEATING ARRANGEMENT ON THE "MISS MACAO"

according to skipper's instructions. On land an aircraft's engines can be run up against wheelbrakes. Operating on water, as each engine is run up individually the aircraft turns in circles, to port when the starboard engine is advanced and vice versa. The test setting for this particular engine is measured as thirty inches of mercury, and each dual magneto is tested in turn. The aileron input is opposite to the turn and the control column is held right back, so that if the aircraft is turning to port the starboard aileron is wound right in. These two actions keep the wingtip floats from digging into any swell and help to tighten the turn, which in the confined area is very desirable.

With an hour to go before low tide Cramer had an ample depth of water, but the wind was slight, so he could not afford to waste time. With a firm continuous movement his right hand opened the two overhead throttle levers and he felt McDuff's left hand following up, holding the throttles in place against the wave-induced jar. At the precisely right time he rocked the wings, helping the Catalina hull on to her planing step. The solid bow-wave gave way to a beautiful feathered wake.

For the passengers, the heavy spray which had blocked visibility was superseded by well-spaced bubbles, and they were able to see through the perspex blister. Once airborne Cramer put *Miss Macao* into a wide, shallow turn, rolling her on to he heading for Hong Kong. When the ramshackle buildings of the Chung-San area of old Macao gave place to the muddy waters of the Pearl River estuary, McDuff unfastened his seat-belt. As he swung round to leave his seat Tok and Cheong sprang to their feet. Tok demanded that Cramer surrender the controls and Cheong's gun backed up his words.

Cramer refused. For a few seconds suspense froze the dumbfounded passengers in their places, while Choi, gun drawn, moved up from the centre compartment to the front area by the flight engineer's companionway. He ordered the passengers to the starboard side. One of them tried intervention. In this confusion mcDuff thought he saw an opportunity. Stooping, he grabbed the flagpole and struck Cheong with it, mounting a vigorous attack from which the pirate retreated smartly. In doing so Cheong cannoned into his leader, who pressed the trigger, and the bullet took Cramer in the base of the skull.

The roar of the gun was the panic signal. Immediately, all three pirates began firing indiscriminately until all eighteen bullets had been used, and even then terrified fingers still clicked the hammers on empty magazines.

More bullets thudded into the lifeless body of Captain Cramer as it slumped over the controls. Under his dead weight the Catalina nosed over in a stomach-turning dive, and in the time it takes for a few heartbeats, broke into fragments on the sea below.

The tail, emblazoned with the Union Jack protruded for a second or two before the muddy maw of the Pearl River estuary swallowed it. As it sank, bits of flotsam began surfacing. Those moments encompassed the deaths of 26 of the 27 people aboard. The time was 1808 Macao standard time, the possition 22 degrees 14' 28"N, 113 degrees 44' 43"E, approximately ten miles northeast of Macao.

THIS IS TO CERTIFY THAT

R.G. Labrum

IS A MEMBER OF THE STAFF OF

CATHAY PACIFIC AIRWAYS, LTD.,

AND IS AUTHORISED TO TRAVEL

ON THAT COMPANY'S AIRCRAFT

IN THE CAPACITY OF CREW

MEMBER.

TRAFFIC MANAGER

14th May, 1948
R/O R.G. (Dick) Labrum—CPA staff pass issued to all flight crew
(signed by Bob Frost)

The amiable John Riorden

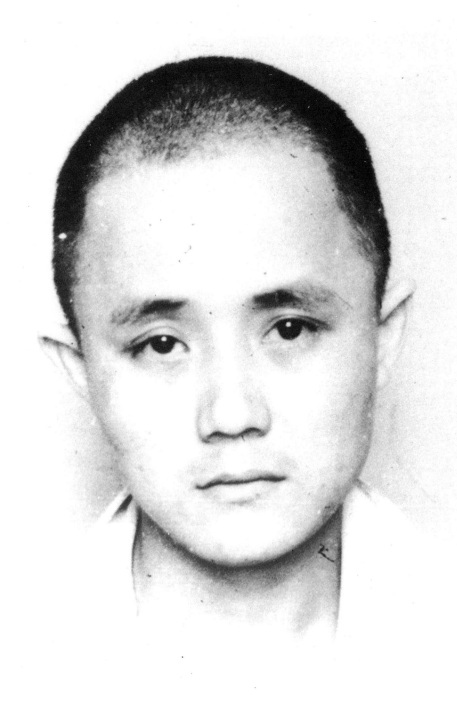

Wong Yu, sole survivor of the pirated Catalina flying boat
"Miss Macao"—16th July 1948.

The lone survivor was Wong Yu. He found himself floating free of the aircraft and instinctively reached for a seat cushion which floated past him. Some time later a Macao motorized fishing junk, captained by Fung Man Yau, picked him up and carried him to Macao, where he was admitted to the general hospital of St Januario and treated for severe shock and a fractured leg.

Not surprisingly, Hong Kong had received neither landing nor departure signals while the Catalina was in the Macao area. However, some 45 minutes after she was scheduled to leave Macao, a now-tiring Roy Downing directed that repeated calls be made on the international distress frequency 116.1 mcs via the forward relay services, with no result. On the stroke of 7 p.m., he reported the situation to his senior air-traffic officer Ben Hewson, who raced to the air traffic centre and repeated the procedures, without success. Alerted by Air Control, both the Hong Kong Water Police and the Chinese Maritime Customs contacted their cruising patrol vessels, but as night closed in they reluctantly abandoned efforts until the morning.

In Macao, Sydney Chan had observed the aircraft line up on her course for Hong Kong. He was spending the evening in his favourite airmchair when, at 9.30, the telephone rang. A police representative advised him that a few minutes earlier a fishing vessel had brought in an inujred male, thought to have been aboard an aircraft that had been seen to crash, shortly after 6 p.m. near the Ninepins Islands, off the coast of Macao. This was Chan's first indication that the *Miss Macao* might not have completed her normal run. The police were experiencing radio trouble and had not even been able to monitor messages from the patrol boats of the British Police or Chinese Customs in the area. Chan's hope was that the aircraft belonged to another company—aircraft on the Bangkok/Hong Kong run passed very close to the port of Macao. He was unable to contact Hong Kong.

But soon, police advised that the fisherman who had brought in the survivor had actually seen the crash. Shortly after 6 p.m. a flying-boat proceeding towards Hong Kong had passed over his vessel, made a sharp turn to the left followed immediately by a sharp turn to the right, then dived into the sea a short distance away. An explosion followed the great splash of contact. He had picked up one survivor, returned with him to Macao and advised the authorities.

Back in Hong Kong Syd de Kantzow about this time was telephoning the flight crew of VR-HDS (the other Catalina) which was scheduled for a Saigon flight the next morning. He advised that the *Miss Macao* had failed to return from her Macao flight, and that their takeoff had been advanced to first light to find out what had happened to her. Dick Hunt, the Chief Pilot was in command, Dick Labrun the radio officer, and Neil Norquay was sent because of his engineering skills.

They flew to Macao, and as their Catalina waddled up the ramp Sydney Chan met them to relay the news from Fung Man Yau, the fisherman who had picked up the survivor. Fearing the worst, Dick Hunt took off again without delay, and carried out a low-level 'recce' round the area looking for wreckage, or indeed the *Miss Macao* herself, in the optimistic hope that she might have merely force-landed. After cruising about for some time they saw a couple of sampans at anchor in the estuary. The crews were waving frantically, trying to attract attention, so they flew even lower. They could see a number of bodies tied behind the sampans and assuming—incorrectly as it happened—that the sampans had pin-pointed the wreckage, Hunt returned to Macao and reported.

Not until 9 a.m. was Sydney Chan able to get through to Cathay Pacific in Hong Kong and report that the *Miss Macao* had indeed departed on schedule the previous day, and give the more distressing news of the sighting and the survivor.

The return of the Catalina galvanized Macao authorities to greater efforts. They called Fung in for closer questioning but he, considering that he had done his duty, was away again in pursuit of his livelihood and did not reappear until late afternoon. Then it was arranged for him to guide police and an official of MATCO to locate and mark the position of the crash. This had to wait until the next morning, which was Sunday.

A great deal of co-ordination had involved other authorities throughout Saturday. During the late morning a RAF Short Sunderland flying-boat joined the search. (Her captain, Leonard Francis Cosgrove was to enlarge this association with MATCO and Cathay Pacific in later months.) The Catalina VR-HDS returned to Hong Kong to pick up Syd de Kantzow, A.J.R. Moss and Ben Hewson. Of these, only de Kantzow returned to Hong Kong that night. In a Press interview he reported:

> 'No accurate picture can be gained of what has happened. Stories told by so-called observers are conflicting.' He added, 'I have been informed that the location of the submerged plane has been found by search launches. I hope the area will be dragged tomorrow morning.'

From a different part of Macao the S.S. *Merry Moller* eased away from the wharves at 2.15 p.m., on what her Captain Blown was anticipating would be a normal cruise to Hong Kong. At 3.20 p.m., just off Ching Chao, one of the Ninepins, his lookout sighted a floating object two hundred yards to port. Blown decided it should be recovered. Swung aboard it was found to be a float, probably from the missing plane. When originally sighted it had been floating in an upright position and on examination was seen to be stoved in on the forward section. The damage was consistent with a crash. What disturbed Captain Blown were several yellow marks on the float and a neat round hole through the fairing. Surely this could only be a bullet-hole! Blown did not convey his thoughts to any member of his crew, but when he docked in Hong Kong early that evening he forwarded the float to the Police for examination.

One more macabre discovery was to be made that day. One of the search craft recovered the battered body of H.G. Stewart from near the breakwater. He had been a passenger in the missing plane.

The police launch cast off its lines in Sunday's pre-dawn light and, guided by fisherman Fung, carried its complement of high-ranking police officials and company representatives to the crash spot. Like most Chinese boat-people Fung had an unerring sense of location in the unmarked waters, but the marker flag

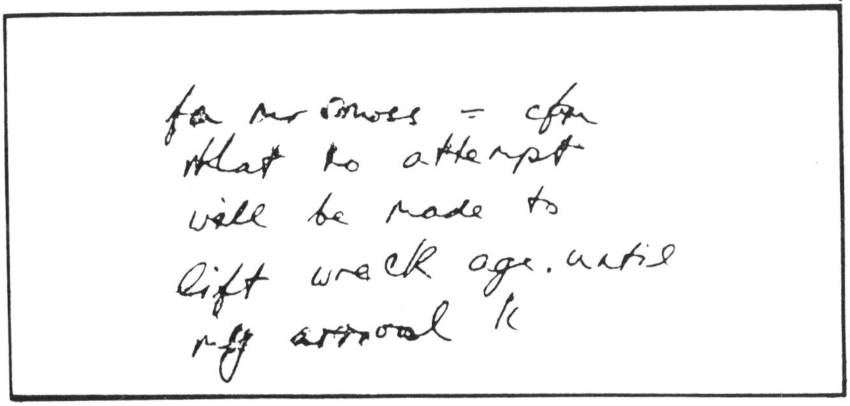

FROM MR A.J.R. MOSS, DCA, HONG KONG
"CONFIRM THAT NO ATTEMPT WILL BE MADE
TO LIFT WRECKAGE UNTIL MY ARRIVAL."

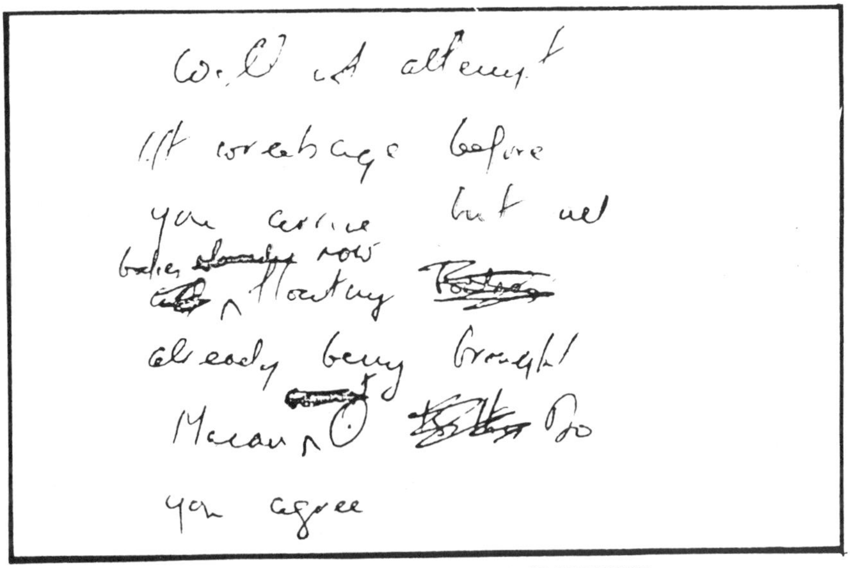

FROM CAPTAIN S.H. de KANTZOW
"WILL NOT ATTEMPT LIFT WRECKAGE BEFORE
YOU ARRIVE, BUT ALL BODIES NOW FLOATING
ALREADY BEING BROUGHT MACAO. DO YOU AGREE."

FIGURE 9 : ORIGINAL SIGNALS RECEIVED & TRANSMITTED BY RADIO OFFICER
R.D. (DICK) LABRUM—CATALINA CRASH SITE JULY 18, 1948

they slipped over the side had to be regarded as the centre only of a wide field to search. The launch returned hastily to Macao to arrange for search equipment and by late morning an armada of fishing junks with dragging-gear had begun operations. By early evening an efficient and methodical quartering had pinpointed a section of the *Miss Macao* lying in four fathoms. The other Catalina had come from Hong Kong to give support, its crew of Dick Hunt, Larry Cabot (a close friend of Cramer's) and Dick Labrum now augmented with de Kantzow acting as co-pilot, Roger Lobo and Roy Farrell. A crane-barge towed to the site formed a natural command-post, and for several days the Catalina shuttled between the barge and Hong Kong, or the barge and Macao. At other times it remained anchored alonside the barge, and even from here Labrum's expertise enabled the Catalina to function as a radio command-post, maintaining communication between the three points.

As time passed more bodies, disturbed perhaps by the operations, came to the surface. A stream of information ran between the Catalina and the shore, sent and received with great difficulty. At one stage a cruiser of the Chinese Maritime Customs came along and they hailed it, because they felt it would make a better radio platform than the bobbing Catalina. The officer agreed and brought the cruiser alongside the barge but he was unable to maintain a radio link with Hong Kong and after a time departed. In doing so he ran right across several markers dotting the area, and this was, naturally a setback to the operations.

Labrum kept samples of the messages in the back of his log-book. An incoming one from A.J.R. Moss, DCA head and accidents inspector at Hong Kong, read: 'Confirm that no attempt will be made to lift wreckage until my arrival.' In reply de Kantzow dictated, 'Will not attempt to lift wreckage before you arrive, but all bodies now floating being sent Macao. Do you agree?'

So far the sole survivor, Wong Yu had contributed little to an explanation of the tragedy. For a time his speech was incoherent. All that investigators understood was that he had jumped from the plane as it struck the water. There had been an explosion.

In the early part of the search the junks dragging nets had located some large portions of the wrecked aircraft. With the passing days bodies continued to be recovered and identified. The meagre news reports explored some of the rumours which came thick, fast and fanciful. One of the passengers, a man associated with a gold bullion firm in Macao, was reputed to have been carrying 3000 tæls of gold—244 pounds, or nearly 99 kilos—he must have been a strong man! Statements were made that looters had dived ahead of the investigation party and had stripped bodies of their valuables. Still another rumour, fortunately unfounded, reported the death of Wong Yu. The *China Mail* on July 22 ran a banner headline which queries: ABORTIVE PIRACY CAUSED CPA PLANE WRECK? It was the first allegation that criminals might have been involved. Three of the bodies recovered continued to elude identification.

The *New Life Evening News* carried an interview with Macao Police Commissioner Captain Luis Augusto de Matos Paletti, who admitted that his department was bending its investigation towards the theory that an attempt to force the plane down to be looted had caused its destruction. But this must be regarded as speculation until the wreckage had been recovered and carefully examined for clues. Two men suspected of being involved had been detained and this brought to seven the unconfirmed total of those 'helping the Police with their enquiries'.

Summer scourge of the China Sea, the typhoon lent a hand. Its effects deferred operations until Sunday July 25. On that day a full team of searchers and a range of heavy lifting equipment were readied for a start at first light next morning.

But, as Roger Lobo recalls:

'We continued to experience great difficulty in lifting the broken aircraft and indeed to find all the pieces which had scattered over a large area. Exceptionally strong currents were doing nothing to help, so we were drifting on barges and launches for several days somewhat aimlessly until Roy Farrell, who was a great thinker, said we had better do some sounding. Everyone should go out with a length of string (piano-wire, said Roy Downing) with a metal weight on the end. We would drop this lead until we hit something hard, and if we thought if felt like a metallic object we would have everyone congregate at that particular spot doing the same. If we were satisfied we would then send down our divers.

'These poor fellows had a terrible time, for the estuary bottom was so soft they found themselves half-buried in the evil, sucking mud before they found a firm foothold; but Roy's system did produce good results. By this method we brought many wayward pieces to the surface, and some of them held entombed victims.'

Having lain in tropical salt water for this considerable period the bodies deteriorated rapidly, and the smell was overpowering. Roy Farrell fished out sanitary towels, and they sprinkled them with Dettol and strapped them round their noses. Dick Labrum recalls that it helped them put up with the smell more easily than before.

The typhoon had not shifted the markers as Monday's resumption proved and the main portion of the fuselage had been raised and swung aboard the barge before the day ended. Under close security it was then taken to the Macao Naval Yard. There the atmosphere became electric when a .38 calibre shell-case clattered to the concrete as the broken, twisted hull was lifted from the barge. Another violent spell of weather hit Macao and prevented the authorities dismantling the recovered wreckage until Thursday.

The *China Mail* published the Police Commissioner's report which provided the first real indication that pirates had been involved, and that one of them had been a trained pilot capable of taking control. Police put a concealed recording machine near Wong's bed in the hospital, and *agents provocateurs* in nearby beds were visited from time to time by elderly 'relatives'. The *China Mail's* further report stated that four Chinese millionaires were on the casualty list and that the wife of one of them had been carrying $US500,000. Four men and one woman had been detained for questioning, but two of the men had been released after intense interrogation.

The body of Wong Chung-Ping, whose personal fortune was estimated at

$US3,000,000 had not been recovered. The recovered body of McDuff had a bullet wound across the back of the neck. Another recovered body was identified as that of Chio Tok, a Manila-trained pilot. Wong Yu was definitely identified with the crime, and of four other suspects held, two were arrested when they visited the mortuary to identify the bodies of Wong's three accomplices. Police Captain Paletti went on record as saying there was no law covering piracy in the air, therefore he was not sure what charges could be brought against Wong Yu.

The *Post* carried a letter from a Mr. C.W.L. Way who anticipated procedures adopted years later by suggesting that a low-priced and extremely efficient army mine detector which one person could easily operate could be the answer to the prevention of such a loss: 'There must be thousands of these war-surplus mine-detectors in the United Kingdom today . . . sensitive enough to reveal even metallic collar-studs and cufflinks, they should put an end to weapons being carried aboard planes, ships or railways carriages.'

Sydney de Kantzow's official statement covered some lesser points:
'On the afternoon of the day following the disaster we at CPA became suspicious of the circumstances surrounding the plane's disappearance. We appointed private investigators in Macao to enquire into the bona fides of all the passengers. By the Sunday morning these investigators had obtained sufficient evidence to justify the company requesting the assistance of the Macao police, which was freely given.

'The pirate pilot carried, concealed in his shoes, bullets for use in the hold-up. When the actual hold-up occurred, a European passenger offered resistance and in the struggle that followed shots were fired at the pilots. Frost must have become involved in the struggle: as a member of the crew he would be seated in the forward compartment.

'So far ten bodies have been picked up including all three dead pirates. The body of the pirate pilot was one of the first to be recovered. One of the millionaire passengers was a retired successful gangster and a bit of a fighter; his body was found with a bullet-hole clean through from chest to back. The plane must have turned right round and dived into the sea at a very steep angle, the impact tearing off the nose. The force of the water as it rushed through the fuselage under extreme pressure tore away the tail and probably flushed out the sole survivor Wong Yu who was at the back of the plane.

'Only the middle part, the nose and section of the wing have been recovered. Still missing are the tail, the engines, most of the wings and the portion where the fight was supposed to have taken place.'

Captain de Kantzow concluded his statement with: 'A gang tried to take Wong Yu away by suggesting he would be better in a private hospital. Wong himself twice attempted suicide in hospital.'

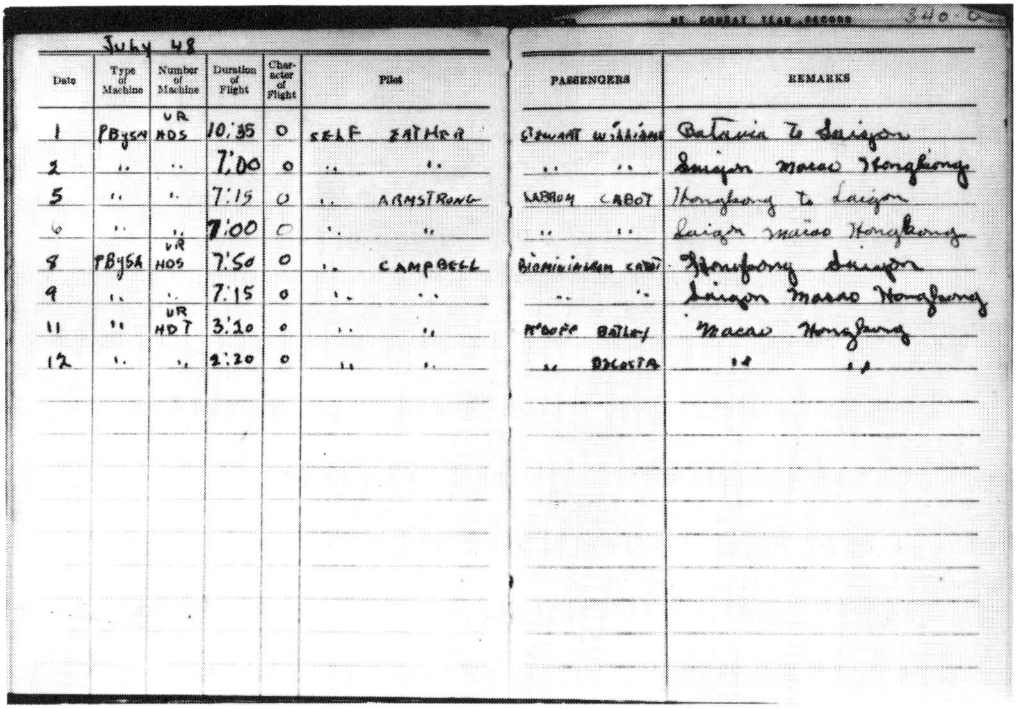

Date	Type of Machine	Number of Machine	Duration of Flight	Character of Flight	Pilot		Passengers	Remarks
								July 48
1	PBy5A	VR HOS	10.35	O	SELF	ZATHER	Stewart Williams	Batavia to Saigon
2	"	"	7.00	O	"	"	" "	Saigon Macao Hongkong
5	"	"	7.15	O	"	ARMSTRONG	LABROY CABOT	Hongkong to Saigon
6	"	"	7.00	O	"	"	" "	Saigon Macao Hongkong
8	PBy5A	VR HOS	7.50	O	"	CAMPBELL	Biamininsam crew	Hongkong Saigon
9	"	"	7.15	O	"	"	" "	Saigon Macao Hongkong
11	"	VR HDT	3.10	O	"	"	M'Boff Batley	Macao Hongkong
12	"	"	2.20	O	"	"	" Bicosta	" "

FIGURE 10: CAPTAIN DALE CRAMER'S FLYING BOOK-FINAL PAGE

In the investigation the sisters Chio Iek Chan and Chio Min Vo proved co-operative; their evidence and that recovered from the clothing of the pirate corpses proved conclusive and clinched the guilt of Min Vo as an accomplice. The engineers' reports showed the aircraft controls, instruments, mixture controls and switches had been in normal cruise position. No fire had occurred.

Wong Yu maintained an obstinate silence but finally, on July 28, having been continually confronted with the mounting evidence, he broke down and spontaneously admitted his part in the crime. In his statement he claimed to have been 'an insignificant element', but I have wondered how 'insignificant' his contribution really was. No one was in a position to contradict him. He had been seated near the rear of the port blister, not merely remote from the action, but in a position where his forward vision would be blocked by several protruding bulkheads that divided the different seating areas. He probably stood up and moved into the aisle, but his vision would have been restricted there too.

A talking point canvassed the question of whether passengers offered resistance, and who might have made it. Europeans gave the distinction to H.M.R. Hodgman, a former Major of the Royal Corps of Signals and a noted Hong Kong jockey. Chinese were adamant that it was the millionaire ex-gangster, a fighter who would resent being the victim of these amateur hatchet-men. The loss of face! Airmen credited Cramer himself.

As late as September 1948 Wong Yu was expected to face a Macao Tribunal at the Loyal Senate. In October Captain Paletti, who doubled as the Chief of the Colonial Governor's Cabinet, informed the Hong Kong Police Commissioner they were ready to hand over for trial the self-confessed air pirate Wong. He told the media he thought the charge might be one of murder. The Macao Court had found itself incompetent to try the matter, presumably deciding it had no jurisdiction over a crime on a British plane in international waters. But in Hong Kong the Attorney General expressed the opinion that there was no admissible evidence on which a prosecution could be brought in a British Colony. He asked that the Portuguese authorities reconsider.

On June 11, 1951 it was reported that Wong Yu had been released from the prison where he had been held nearly three years without trial and had left for China. Though nothing official came to light, it was rumoured that there his life had been snuffed out in a suitably-contrived accident. Chinese authorities had no time for pirates. Min Vo, however, served several years in a Macao jail.

In place of Robert Frost, Tom Bax was appointed Sales and Traffic Manager. He was a friend of Bob Wawn. They had met as fellow-prisoners in the notoriously brutal Sagen prisoner-of-war camp, where the Germans murdered fifty British officers in 1944.

Ken McDuff's remains had been interred in Hong Kong's cemetery, Happy Valley. After a decent suspension out of respect for the dead, Cathay Pacific reopened the Macao route using the Catalina VR-HDS. The proving flight dropped wreaths on the wreck site.

De Kantzow believed that the only solution to the new hazard of possible piracies was the installation of metal-detectors at the departure points. He dismissed as 'impractical' the suggestion of locking the crew door. Frankly I believe it impractical even today. The flight deck is connected by interphone with the several cabin attendants' points and I do not think as pilot I could place myself above the welfare of a hostess or passenger threatened with summary slaughter if I refused a hi-jacker's instructions to open the crew door. I could see a situation where every passenger could be executed while I, with grim determination, held on to the flight deck. This is not the action of a commander: his main duty is to protect each and every life placed in his care.

This was the first of air piracies. For many years I included all hi-jackings in this category. But on March 25, 1972 I received a request from David Phillips, a producer with *Independent News* in London. He had already written a book on the subject, *Leila's Hi-Jack War*, and sought details of the *Miss Macao* affair for a history of air-piracy he was writing. His letter stated: 'The Miss Macao affair was the first sky-jack carried out by a gang for criminal gain. The **seven** that preceded it were all politically activated.'

CHAPTER SEVEN
BURMA SOJOURN

'An' I was the Junior Deacon in my Mother-Lodge out there!'
The Mother-Lodge . . . Rudyard Kipling

Next to the lucrative gold charters and the Butterfield and Swire takeover, the Burma sojourn probably contributed mostly to the early success of Cathay Pacific. This began in November 1947 when Captain A.R. Lewis landed his DC3 on the perforated steel plates of Mingaladon airfield at Rangoon. These interlocking plates, widely used in the East and the Pacific constituted one of the more successful inventions in the war. Each interlocking strip was about eight foot in length and eighteen inches wide, and they could transform a muddy paddy-field into a usable runway in a matter of minutes. They are still to be seen in the form of fencing and rough construction throughout these parts of the world today. November 29 found the company's other DC3 making that distinctive whining sound as the wheels skimmed along that metal. The captain was Neville Hemsworth.

These initial flights were of short duration, with a brief overnight at Rangoon. But the insurgency of brutal proportions about to explode on this rather backward country took a stranglehold on the roads, the railways and the Irrawaddy River's large fleet of barges. Cathay Pacific was prominent in supplying the only means of transport left to the beleaguered government of Thakin Nu. These insurgents were the Karens of the hill country to the east and north, traditional enemies of the Burmans who constituted the other large element of the country's population. Both Karens and Burmans are Burmese people.

During World War II the Japanese on the tropical Chinese island of Hainan in the Gulf of Tonkin had trained a Burman group, the 'thirty comrades' who formed the nucleus of Japan's 'Defence Army' in Burma. The future General Ne Win, currently President of the Union of Burma, had been a clerk at the Rangoon Post Office, and was one of these 'thirty comrades'. Another, U Bo Setka was the founder/owner of Air Burma, the company which rose and fell during the Karen rebellion.

I assume that these thirty Burman comrades accompanied the Japanese invasion which rolled up the Tenasserim coastline, assisted in the capture of Tavoy on January 20, 1942, occupied Moulmein soon afterwards and conquered Pegu and then Rangoon on March 3.

In marked contrast to the assistance such Burmans were giving the invader, the Karens, with a steadfast loyalty to the British, had scourged the Japanese, hunting them with the few arms they possessed—mainly bows and arrows. The British resumed their civil administration in October 1945, reaching an agreement with the Burma Executive Council. In September 1946 Aung San was given the

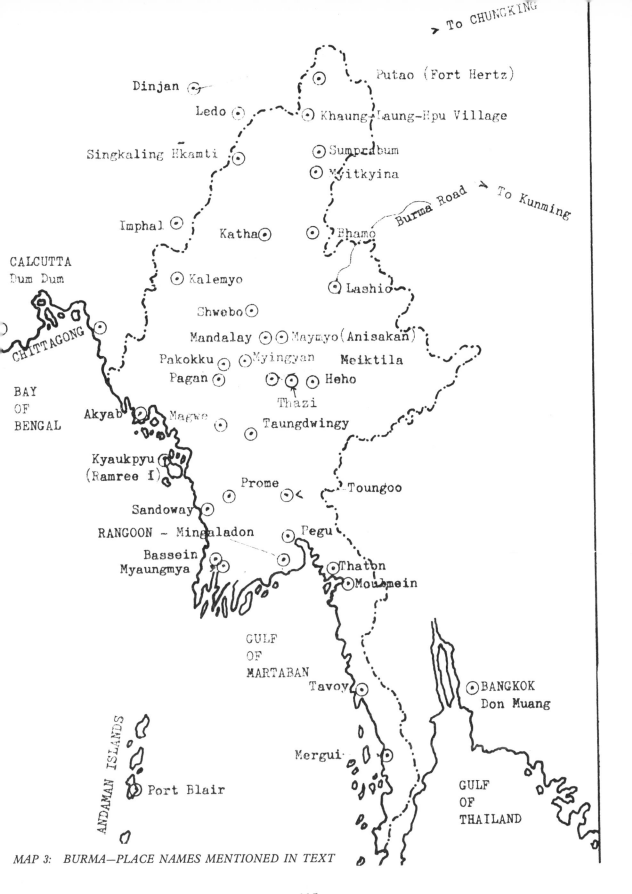

To CHUNGKING

Dinjan

Putao (Fort Hertz)

Ledo

Khaung-Laung-Hpu Village

Singkaling Hkamti

Sumprabum

Myitkyina

Burma Road → To Kunming

Imphal

Katha

Bhamo

CALCUTTA
Dum Dum

Kalemyo

Lashio

CHITTAGONG

Shwebo

Mandalay Maymyo (Anisakan)

BAY
OF
BENGAL

Pakokku Myingyan

Meiktila

Pagan

Heho

Thazi

Akyab Magwe

Taungdwingy

Kyaukpyu
(Ramree I)

Prome

Toungoo

Sandoway

RANGOON – Mingaladon

Pegu

Bassein
Myaungmya

Thaton

Moulmein

GULF
OF
MARTABAN

Tavoy

BANGKOK
Don Muang

ANDAMAN ISLANDS

Mergui

Port Blair

GULF
OF
THAILAND

MAP 3: BURMA—PLACE NAMES MENTIONED IN TEXT

115

disposition of most of the seats on the Governor's Executive Council as leader of a nominally all-party front, the Anti Fascist People's Freedom League. In January this organisation reached agreement with the Attlee Government in London, and in April scored a resounding victory in general elections. The resulting Constituent Assembly met on June 10, and six days later proclaimed Burma an independent sovereign republic.

On July 19 Aung San and six of his Cabinet Ministers were assassinated while holding a Cabinet meeting, but the expected disorder and chaos did not ensue because that same night Thakin Nu, the then Speaker of the Constituent Assembly accepted the mantle of Prime Minister. In September all parties approved the draft Constitution, and next month in London Thakin Nu and Attlee signed a treaty covering future financial, defence and commercial relations. Transfer of power from the British Raj took place on January 4, 1948 and the diverse peoples of Burma were expected to join in allegiance to the new national flag of red, with a canton of dark blue containing a large five-pointed star with five smaller stars nestling between its points.

But The Karens were moving towards the point at which they would be no longer prepared to take Burman dominance. They considered the Burmans to be a race of lazy dreamers, ever ready to let others pull their chestnuts from the fire. The Burmans were growers of wet rice, traders in pottery, lacquer ware and metal products. They had lived in the lowlands of central and southern Burma for at least a thousand years. They had adopted Buddhism at an early stage. A succession of powerful dynasties had displayed sophisticated statecraft and fostered artistic traditions.

Until the British came the Karens had remained isolated within their own mountainous country on Thailand's western border, adjoining the Salween River which enters the Gulf of Martaban near the city of Moulmein. They were mercilessly harried by the Burmans who called them 'Hill cattle' and regarded them as inferior. The coming of the British revitalised the Karens, and in each of the three British wars in Burma they fought the Burmans and gave sterling service to the British invader. They became greatly attracted to the teachings of the Christian missionaries, particularly the American Baptists and the Roman Catholics, and many became devout Christians.

Under the secure conditions of British rule the Karens came down from the hills and establishing thriving communities round Toungoo, Thaton, Moulmein and Pyapon. They became recognised as one of the martial races of Burma and when open rebellion flared against the new sovereign State the Karen contingent was the strongest in the Army. The commander-in-chief Lieutenant-General Smith Dun and the Commander of the Air Force were both Karens. Their adoption of the Roman script introduced by the Christian missionaries had greatly facilitated Karen dominance of the learned professions and the field of commerce.

Until about Christmas 1948 the Communist elements were the chief fomenters of dissatisfaction in the new Burma, these hooligan bands of several persuasions were well armed with the discarded weapons of several armies. Their unco-ordinated efforts were more annoying than dangerous, until a masked gang

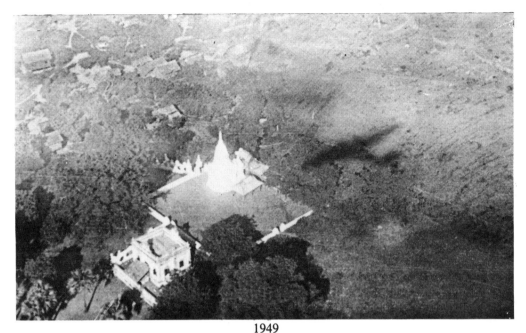

1949
Pagan, On The Road to Mandalay
Site of the first Burmese Empire once held 5000 Pagodas..A CPA Catalina PBY/5A Flying
Boat casts a shadow and contrasts the ancient and modern as it crosses one of the 2,000 pagods
which survive.

25th August, 1948
Douglas DC3 . . . VR-HDB . . . Anisakan Airfield, Burma.
Note: The spartan passenger accommodation.

rolled several hand-grenades into a Roman Catholic church at Moulmein, killing dozens of innocent worshippers and horribly mutilating many more. At that time Moulmein was playing host to a full battalion of Karen infantry with a Karen transport section in support. They took arms against their traditional enemies the Burmans, whom they blamed for this atrocity. They had reached the end of their tether and the war of attrition began. Their rebellion came within an ace of succeeding.

Cathay Pacific's entry on the Burma scene had predated by about a year this organised Karen rebellion, but the Communists were causing sporadic trouble and the company found plenty of work to do. With the despatch of McIllree's Ansons Morrie Lothian began a progress within the company as spectacular as Dick Hunt's. Indeed it seemed sometimes that he could do no wrong. He had been there little more than a month when, on February 9, 1948, while landing on the small field of Sandoway on the coast of the Bay of Bengal he undershot the airstrip and damaged Anson VR-HDX beyond repair. The report which Syd de Kantzow submitted to the Hong Kong DCA referred in the first paragraph to the 'minor accident' during the landing at Sandoway, and in the last admitted: 'It is understood that due to damage of the front spar and undercarriage the aircraft is likely to be a total loss.' 'Minor' in one breath and 'a total loss' in the next! Eyebrows lifted when the word went about.

The Ansons proved unsuitable for the Burma operation; military stores and equipment frequently could not fit in the restricted fuselage, so the company introduced DC3s.

My first tour began on May 3, 1948, when I was detailed as first officer to Captain John Furley. It terminated after the expected three weeks or so. Tour followed tour, and each deepened my affection for that country. At one time I seriously contemplated becoming a citizen of Burma, as did a dear friend, Lance Rutherford. For a while citizenship seemed a wonderful idea, but time has shown it would have been a grave error.

My duties were pleasant and I enjoyed every facet of life. Romantic-sounding names like Tavoy, Akyab, Kyaukpyu, Bassein, Heho, Moulmein, Mandalay rolled off my tongue with an ease which the casual observer might judge to have been gained in years of familiarity, and not merely hours. Most of the sectors we flew were short, and although at times we got an early start, it was rare to finish later than four o'clock in any afternoon. The length of the sector has little bearing on what may happen, and many interesting incidents coloured even brief trips into the Irrawaddy Delta, but the truly rewarding aspect of my time in Burma is still the realisation that those were my hands that safely shepherded hundreds of people taking their very first flight. Naturally other pilots can make this same statement, but it gives me a glow of achievement.

Rangoon, the city, takes its name from the word 'Yangon' meaning 'End of strife', a name bestowed by the founder King Alaungpaya in 1755 to mark a decisive victory. It gladdens the heart of a Burmese if you pronounce the name 'Yangoon', a worthwhile experiment. Two gilded pagodas, Sule and Shwe Dagon, dominate the capital's skyline, and giant figures of mythical lion-like animals called

Chinthes guard the latter's approaches.

During tours of approximately three weeks we were billeted in a large rambling Colonial-style house a couple of miles from the city. It stood in fairly spacious grounds off University Road. A somewhat unkempt lawn sloped gently down to the lapping water of Inya Lake. A punt on the lake from which I would fish gave me many hours of pleasure, and there were times I liked the solitude for I did not drink. But I often think with affection of the 'orrible things that happened in that den of iniquity.

Most of the rooms were fitted up with folding camp stretchers, usually at least four and sometimes six to a room. We had a spartan common lounge fitted with, of all things, a piano, and a separate dining-room centred by a massive oak table. Later on I found that table a Godsend. One break of dawn I sought its protection as a battery of 24-pounders opened up a bombardment of the railway terminal township of Insein. This artillery battery was dug in on University grounds and the chosen line of trajectory barely cleared our Mess. One moment I was dreaming of harems and houris, the next I had thrown off my mosquito net and rushed through several doors—but my colleagues had all beaten me and the normally slow-moving Nash was on the bottom of the panicky pile.

Millard Kadot Nasholds can be looked on as Cathay Pacific's father figure in the Burma involvement. He was one of the original friends who had dreamed of the post-war world while flying The Hump. His approach to life was so casual he could fall asleep anywhere anytime. He could sleep on a barbed-wire fence in a typhoon. He had earned the sobriquet of 'Wheels up, eyes shut', and the failing was famous.

Pat Armstrong told me that once his DC3 was halfway between Darwin and Morotai, he being first officer with Nash in command. Suddenly Syd de Kantzow poked his head in and asked how they were doing. Pat pointed out the islands which showed they were on course for Morotai.

Syd looked at Nash and scowled, 'The bugger's asleep again!' He then gently and slowly wound the auto pilot knob about ninety degrees off course and whispered to Pat to fake sleep as well. He then gave Nash a violent thump on the shoulder and yelled:

'Well, Captain! Where the hell are we?'

Pat told me he had never seen a more startled commander trying to work out his position.

When Nash married Hazel Merritt Royal, Bill Geddes-Brown (another of the founding partners) gave the bride away and Syd de Kantzow was best man. I don't remember how she earned the nickname 'Boots', but I do remember her part in a charity show for the Children's Home and Rangoon Vigilance Society. She recited a monologue on men and concluded with an Indian dance that really brought the house down.

After the American share was bought out by the Butterfield and Swire influence, Pat told me, Nash decided to spend a weekend in Taipei, wallowing in the salt springs.

'I don't know if he was involved in smuggling,' Pat said, 'but I think not.

1948
CPA's 'Infamous' University Road Mess, Rangoon Burma.
Top: Front Precinct   Bottom: Rear Verandah

November 1948
Catalina PBY/5A amphibious flying-boat anchored in the Irrawaddy River off the town of
Magwe, Burma

Magwe, Burma—22nd November 1948
F/O Pat Armstrong takes it easy on a Cat-boat fuslage—VR-HDS

Magwe, Burma—22nd November 1948
Capt Syd de Kantzow is rowed to VR-HDS anchored in the Irrawaddy River (Syd in centre
of group)

Anisakan Airfield, Mandalay, Burma—1948
VR-HDB parked at the spartan terminal facilities

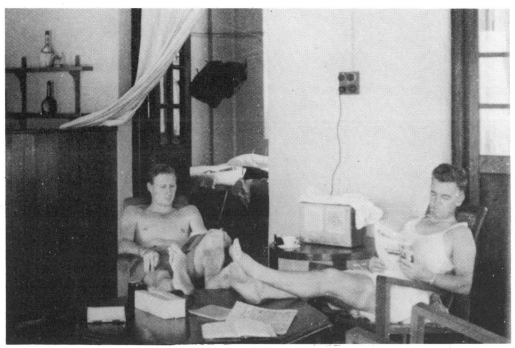

1948
CPA's University Road Mess, Rangoon Burma
Ken Begg (left) and Vic Leslie catching up on the news of the day.

1948
Alan Marshall shares the 'royal' seating facilities on a Cathay Pacific Dakota during an up-country flight in Burma.

That was not his character at all. But the authorities claimed to have found some contraband on him and jailed him for a considerable time. After his release he returned to the States and I've heard nothing of him since.'

Captain John G. Moxham figures in a lot of stories of that mess. Lack of exercise and a gluttonous approach to the larder had rounded his once athletic frame to the point where he was usually called Mox the Ox. The Burmese DCA had authorised two doctors, Dr Lal and Dr Sekaran, to handle medical inspections for licence renewals. Both were first class, but for licence renewals most of us preferred Dr Lal, since Dr Sekaran's approach was somewhat cavalier and his joyous nature sometimes rankled when one sought the solace of an understanding ear. But he was the accepted authority on what polite society knows as social disease, and so got his share of our business.

John returned from Dr Lal with a tale of woe. Lal, taking note of his alarming increase in poundage had passed him as fit, but said he would not do so again unless he lost a stone in weight. He had to exercise.

'I'll play the piano. That's exercise, isn't it?' Mox snarled, and for fifteen minutes, with more enthusiasm than finesse, he belted into it. Suddenly he collapsed over the keyboard and had to be assisted to his bunk.

Bob Smith recalls that Mox used to sleep out on the verandah with a mosquito net covering his canvas stretcher. His night attire was a Burmese longyi knotted round his stomach.

'Each morning,' Bob told me, 'he would follow the same ritual: roll out of bed, walk to the verandah's edge and gaze at the lake. Then he would scratch his great hairy chest, deliberately pick his nose with the little finger of his right hand, and then spoil it all by indelicately wiping the proceeds on the verandah post. Then a look of concern would spread over his face. He would look at the dial on his watch, spread his fingers in calculation, and then gingerly lift his longyi and do a DI (daily inspection) on his pride and joy.

'One morning another Smith named Pete, a movie-camera buff as well as a radio officer, had his camera trained through one of the broken panes of the lounge windows and recorded the ritual. Pete composed the action with quite brilliant expertise, but there was mayhem when Mox wandered in one evening during a private showing. I understand Pete still has that film.'

Ken Wolinski, radio officer, gives the explanation of the broken pane—one of many:

'One of our favourite sports, and a test of dexterity was to throw beer cans into the ceiling fan, with the ultimate target the entrance door. We would anticipate the entrance of an unwary new arrival and clobber him as he stepped through, the prize being another can of beer. I remember you were not a drinking man and spent all your spare time fishing from the punt in the lake. Liquor was quite hard to come by but every now and then Dan Peccorini would arrive with the odd case of beer. Of course it had to be paid for; neither the company nor Mud-guts Peccorini had the slightest intention of spoiling us with such expensive gifts.

'One evening we managed to get an early start. Most of us were running hot and making regular kills. It was Ken Begg's turn. We heard clumping footsteps approaching the danger point and immediately realised there must be a foreigner about to enter. The butler and the bearers had developed a dexterity of avoidance by this time and were increasingly difficult to trap.

'At the right second Ken hurled his not-quite-empty can—for which we disqualified him. It struck the fan blade at just the right angle and arrived at the intruder's shin just as he stepped through the door. Imagine our consternation when the leg left the body! What had we done? Most of us sobered up immediately.

'Ian Grabowsky casually re-strapped his wooden leg and with arms akimbo gave each of us a piercing glare. Ken Begg, first to recover, hailed him:

' "Well, you hoppy-legged old bastard, are you OK?" '

'Ian was quick to forgive the transgression and in nothing flat was glugging the grog with the best of us. He also insisted on his turn at target practice, but he was a pretty rotten shot, a danger to us all. He might have improved with time. We had practiced for weeks.'

For a while John Watson Maurice Furley was Mess President. A real wing-commander type he tried to run the mess on strict Air Force lines and sat at the head of the table. Arriving for a meal he found Mike Russell occupying that exalted position.

'Michael,' he said, 'I believe you have my chair.'

Mike completely at ease, replied,

'Oh, I'm sorry, old chap.' He rose, handed John the chair, took another and sat down in the same place. John was so upset he retired to his camp bed.

Another day we took the mickey out of First Officer Geoff Leslie, a trencherman of heroic accomplishment. Realising that the butler invariably started serving the head of the table first and then moved anti-clockwise he arrived bright an early and plonked himself to the right of the Mess President's chair. As the rest of us answered the dinner gong we realised what was in Geoff's mind, and quietly instructed the butler to reverse the serving procedure. Then we took greater portions than usual, so that by the time the dishes reached him even the gravy had disappeared. He never forgave us for that little joke.

That butler had his standards. One morning with dismay colouring the identifying Indian accent which British comedians love to imitate, he declared to the Mess President that if ever there should be a repetition of the previous night's happening he would have to resign. It seemed that one of the more virile pilots had brought back two women for his evening's entertainment.

'I'm very good Christian gentleman,' said the butler. 'I am not standing for captain coming back with two women! One woman quite all right. Two women not good!'

The romance between Captain Morrie Lothian and our senior hostess developed into marriage. Ann was a very nice young Anglo-Burmese, a bit on the tall side and rather loose-limbed. Some might better described her as gawky. My main remembrance of her comes from a trip we did together from Sydney. I had gone off to sleep along some unoccupied bucket seats on the port side. Ann had done the same on the starboard. Suddenly I awakened with the feeling that someone was staring at me, and sure enough, there was Ann, sound asleep and gently snoring in a ladylike way, with both her eyes wide open! This was pretty disconcerting and I moved away to another part of the fuselage—Ann obviously trusted no male!

Her romance with Morrie was a thing of beauty, but soon our reactions became a bit fragile when she used to arrive early for a flight, and at breakfast take a chair beside her love and proceed to cut up his bacon and eggs and feed him with a spoon. Morrie, not unreasonably, loved every second of this treatment, but it disturbed us so much we got into the habit of eating our breakfasts in the bedrooms. She was too publicly amatory for our peace of mind.

'The Three Wise Virgins'—Olive, Kim and Gracie—normally plied their calling from established premises at 12 Ady Road, but were known to visit the mess at the call of a special client. Olive was the most beautiful, but unlike the others she was so dusky she was not only elusive but downright difficult to find in other than a bright illumination. In the romantic glow of the love bower the brilliantly white knickers she consistently wore proved of assistance to impatient clients. One evening, passing the room occupied by a close pal, I heard the testy remark, 'For goodness sake, Olive, smile so I can find you!'

Bob Smith came back to the mess one afternoon and caught the cook picking his nose—unlike John Moxham, probably with the wrong finger. Smithy kicked the cook up the backside from one end of the room to the other until the offender escaped, screaming that he would have his two sons take care of Smithy. When Eric Aylward returned from the airfield he found all the Indian servants in a group discussing the incident. Eric was one of the butler's favourites, and the butler warned him that the cook had gone off to get his two sons who were two of the toughest gangsters in Rangoon, and would soon return and shoot all the sahibs in the mess, so he had better go elsewhere. When Eric told him he had nowhere else to go he shrugged in a resigned way. Night fell and everyone went off to the sack.

About midnight a flashlight flickering through the windows awoke Eric and Smithy. Neither bothered with night attire, and as the beam settled on their bunks both bounded up, looking for cover, the light following them. Eric wrapped a mattress round himself hoping it would slow down a bullet. Whatever he did Smithy kept pace and right behind him, a difficult accomplishment as he was about six inches taller. As they waltzed round the room in their surrogate armour the light kept right on them, and Smithy was screaming 'They'll shoot us! They'll kill us!'

'Don't tell *me*!' Eric yelled. 'It was you who kicked the cook! You're the one entitled to die!'

Then a voice from the window asked, 'What the hell's going on in there? You look like a couple of poofs pouncing round with a mattress tied round you. Open the bloody door! I've been working half the night and I can't get in—everything is locked and barred.'

It was one of Smithy's ground engineers who had been delayed at

AVRO-ANSON . . . VY-AYE . . . 1946
Eric McIllree's "flagship". Used to co-ordinate the various
ferry-flights of the Ansons he purchased from the Australian
Disposals Commission, from the many locations throughout the
country.
I first flew her on 1st October, 1946.

Meiktila, Burma—1948
F/H Jean Cannon CPA's first Hostess in Burma.

Mingaladon, putting the finishing touches to an engine change.

Jean Cannon was the first air hostess Cathay Pacific employed on its Burma operation. She had no uniform, and a predilection for light printed frocks. We all liked her a lot and soon looked upon her as one of the boys. Along came a handsome first officer, Mike Russell, and it was love at first sight. The airline practically closed down for the day while we attended their wedding.

John Moxham and Mike Russell invariably found themselves rostered together. Neither could stand the sight of the other and here they would be jammed into a small flight deck and expected to think as a single unit. Mox was as rough as a bull, but Mike was in complete contrast, having hailed from the baronial halls of Merrie England. On days when they were completely out of agreement all instructions would be conveyed in a series of notes, even such elementary orders as 'gear up' or 'gear down' would be the subject of hastily scribbled correspondence.

'When they were prepared to accept one another on sufferance was the period that brought most alarm and hours of unnecessary work,' Bob Smith told me with a touch of jaundice. 'When those two stupid bastards were showing vague signs of friendship was the time for an engineer to be concerned. Their favourite little ploy concerned the cylinder-head temperature readings, and it would start with Mox leaning across to Mike and remarking in a confidential whisper:

' "Michael, don't you think the cylinder-head temperature on the port side is a little high?"

'Mike would reply, "Yes John, old boy, I do believe you are right. What would you like it to read?"

'Mox would think for a moment and, being a tidy character in mind if not in appearance, would reply, "Michael, the starboard engine is reading 190 degrees. What about making them even?"

'Mike Russell would now place his finger-nail into the set screw and carefully reduce the output reading to the desired figure. Then he would turn a beaming countenance to his commander and ask if that were satisfactory, to which Mox, in a tone of relief would reply, "Ah, thank you Michael; that's much better. I feel happier now."

'Of course the next fellow who flew that aircraft would immediately notice the difference in reading of those two cylinder-head temperature gauges under static inoperative conditions, and I was forever in and out of the flight deck adjusting the needles. A high cylinder-head temperature was a reportable snag— and an early warning that all was not right with the engine.'

Jean Cannon's father, Major Arthur (John) Sinclair Cannon developed a yen to own an aircraft about this time and it coloured some years of his life. When Cathay Pacific decided to suspend its Anson operation it just left VR-HDU on the end of the taxi-way. The Anson received no attention and soon the terrible heat and monsoonal rain just about rotted it away. Still, Cannon felt he just had to own it.

His troubles began the day Wing Commander Bunce, commanding officer of a small RAF mission at Mingaladon, agreed to have some of his fitters look

VARIOUS PHOTOGRAPHS OF THE WING REPAIRS ON THE BOB SMITH AVRO ANSON VR-HDU *WING WHEN   OWNED BY MAJOR JOHN CANNON.*

Mingaladon, Rangoon—1949
Bob Smith proudly stands in front of the replacement
wing slung under VR-HEN just prior to take-off to
Bhamo.

it over. Their report indicated they could handle the job, making it serviceable with the spares they had in their stores. Bob Smith, when told of this, advised Cannon that if he could get the Anson cheap enough it would probably turn out to be a good deal, with the mission doing the work. Cathay Pacific was pleased to get whatever Cannon offered, but when the RAF fitters found that the entire wing and spars were rotted, they backed off.

Then Bob Smith good-naturedly let Cannon talk him into handling the wing repairs, a job that took nine months, for they had to import the spruce, the birch and the glue from England. The RAF fitters hung and tested the engines, but by that time Cannon was really in a mess, owing a fortune in hangar fees. Some of his political manoeuvres too had come home to roost. Apparently he had been attached to MI5 during the war. A crony in the Burmese War Office advised him that a warrant out for his arrest was to be executed the next day, so he and his wife and his dog Lothie all sneaked out to Mingaladon in the dark and fueled their Anson from dozens of five-gallon cans they had acquired. After stowing extra cans in the rear of the fuselage he completed a successful takeoff at night without either aircraft or runway lights.

'That was quite an achievement,' Bob told me. 'I'd seen his logbook and his total flight experience amounted to sixty hours, and all of that was on a Mark One Moth! He headed off in the general direction of Singapore, and when the light of day arrived he decided he had thumbed his nose at fate enough, and landed at Butterworth. The landing was OK, but he ended up off the strip. Butterworth is an Air Force establishment and when his unheralded, unauthorised flight landed without permission he was placed under immediate detention. I was in Singapore at that time, and later that morning I got a telephone summons from Johnnie Johnson, the Singapore Director of Civil Aviation. When I got to his office he glared at me and asked if I knew anything about Anson VR-HDU, and when I finished telling my story he said, "Well, the bloody thing is sitting at Butterworth".

'He managed to talk Gibby and me into flying the Anson back to Kallang Airport at Singapore. At Butterworth I checked the rocker-boxes and the grease which surrounds those rapidly-moving parts and found it congealed into a substance resembling silver paint. We made a very careful check before flying, and a day or two later I asked Cannon how he had operated those engines.

' "I didn't follow any particular procedure," he told me. "There was a gauge there and I seemed to recall the needle hovered round the '2' or slightly further to the right." I asked him how long the gauges had registered that and he blithely answered, perhaps an hour or two. He had held takeoff power all that time and was lucky not to have blown up both engines, for the manufacturers had put a maximum of five minutes at takeoff power. A subsequent inspection found all bearings worn out.'

Cannon continued to bring grief on himself. In Singapore he got a job managing a garage, and on the strength of owning an aeroplane built up some tremendous bills with big department stores. He ignored payment and several stores took out court orders to confiscate his Anson. It sold at auction for the paltry sum of 400 Straits dollars.

Various Civil Aviation departments may have shared my feeling of sympathy for Cannon and a little spark of admiration of his courage in tackling that moonlight flit, for no action was taken against him. The Anson, centre of the whole episode was transferred to the Malay Register in July 1953 as VR-RCE, and I wonder whether the final owner was ever made aware of its off-beat history.

Cathay Pacific continued to expand the scope of its activities. During October 1948 a Burmese newspaper recorded the completion of its hundredth air-drop of bags of rice, salt and flour. This was to minute Khaung-Laung-Hpu village, some 200 miles north of Myitkyina and nestling against Tibet. This load alone was a money-spinner and at six U.S. cents a pound an airmile must have given the company the impression that it had discovered the legendary gold of Ophir.

We approached most charters now in a mood of almost casual expectancy, but were sometimes surprised. Bob Smith told me of a charter to Toungoo on the Sittang River. Johnnie Paish was skipper, Smith was engineer, and Eric Aylward had gone along for a morning jaunt. When this crew went out to their aircraft, VR-HDA they found the cargo tied down, covered with an old tarpaulin and crowned with an escort of three lounging soldiers. Paish waved the troops off the load—and froze as he heard the unmistakeable sound of an automatic weapon being cocked. In a stage whisper he told the crew to get off, then returned to the despatch office and told the co-ordinating Burmese officer that the cargo could sit and rot unless he withdrew his men until a check could be made.

The officer began screaming, vilifying them, and seeking instructions by telephone. Paish was unmoved, and when he got to do his check found, not the manifested foodstuffs, but gelignite of pre-war vintage, as shown by the stamp on the boxes. The load was sweating profusely, and when aged gelignite sweats it becomes unstable so that even a gentle bump can set it off. The loaders had illustrated their tidy thinking by placing a large box of detonators on top. The three Sten guns lay carelessly round the detonator box, each with a bullet 'in the spout'. Even a gentle sneeze could have set one of those beep-guns off.

They separated the detonators but were unable to disarm the escort. Smith told Paish he would not fly unless the guns were unloaded. Paish agreed, but the guards didn't. Smithy suddenly raced over to 'Moultrie's Palace of Germs', the airport canteen, coming back with half a dozen large bottles of beer. While the guards were glugging away he removed the live clips and replaced them with empty ones. The gelignite was intended to blow the Sittang bridges in the face of a rebel advance, but it would have been as much danger to friend as to foe.

Coming home Paish flew most of the way under a hundred feet, out of respect to the magnificent Swiss Oerlikons below, and enjoyed the sight of the rebels flinging themselves into the paddyfield mud as they passed over. Fifty miles from Mingaladon he climbed to a comfortable 8000 feet, and out of nowhere, without preamble, Smith declared, 'Rudyard Kipling is wrong'. The others didn't know what he was on about. Then he recited: 'By the old Moulmein pagoda, looking eastward to the sea.' He said that if the pagoda faced eastward it would face right into the middle of China. It couldn't possibly face the sea. He raised such an argument that Paish got fed-up, and said they would go across and see. He landed at Moulmein on the other side of the Gulf of Martaban and proved Smithy right and Kipling wrong. Smithy was so pleased he bought them a curry lunch at a little native eatery just below the Pagoda. The meal was first-class. When they went to re-start they could not get a peep out of the starboard engine, and found that a bullet had sheared the connecting drive of the starter. A replacement starter had to be flown over next morning.

Some weeks later Syd de Kantzow tackled Eric Aylward:

'You were on that flight. Tell me, how did you get so far off course? Surely you could see the Rangoon Shwe Dagon Shrine glittering in the sun?'

Aylward told him the whole story, and de Kantzow said,

'Do you mean to tell me you would ground one of my aeroplanes for 24 hours and use hundreds of gallons of fuel just to prove Kipling right or wrong! I know who started that argument—it was Smithy, wasn't it?'

I shared several memorable experiences with John Paish. The morning of January 26, 1949 dawned with a blood-red skyline as we were boarding the crew transport, and ex-army Dodge battle-wagon. The weather was still fine, though a furious storm was to lash Mingaladon Airfield, an explosion of nature at its worst. By that time we would be well out of it en route to Hong Kong, to return VR-HDI for her periodic maintenance check. She had been heavily engaged in flying round Burma; many of her serviceable parts had been cannibalised and we were left with a lot of unserviceable components.

Our radio officer was Dick Labrum, and Eric Aylward, the ground-cum-flight engineer filled out what I thought was a very efficient crew. The Karen rebellion was gaining momentum and it had been found prudent that each trip to Mingaladon should have a military escort of three men in a jeep.

These jeeps were nice and clean, but all needed a thorough tune-up. Not wanting to tempt Providence by merely ambling along, the Indian driver of our station wagon would keep the pressure on and usually outstrip the escort. So it happened this morning, and our transport, with a large Union Jack strapped to its rear, was alone on the deserted Prome Road.

At one of the several well-graded bends our driver lost control, the wagon slammed to the left and in a split second we were in a plantation of trees. In his terror the driver had disappeared under the dashboard but his foot was still jammed down on the accelerator. I had been the last to arrive that morning and my cunning companions had annexed the back seat, which left me riding shotgun. As the trees loomed around me, being thoroughly terrified and having nothing better to do, I grabbed the bucking steering wheel and, more by good luck than ability I not only succeeded in keeping us upright but also avoided head-on collisions with the trees. Naturally, both sides of the wagon came in for hefty damage as we sideswiped trees during our passage.

With a sigh of relief I got the wagon back on Prome Road and as the driver sheepishly took over there was a blinding explosion fifty yards or so along the road from where we had, out of control, left its surface. Our escort had disintegrated in a mass of blood and tangled limbs. They had hit a landmine planted by the Karens just previously.

I never did direct a word of criticism at our driver, but I noticed he was no longer at the wheel of our crew transport on my subsequent tours of Burma.

Although the day had barely begun I felt wrung out, but more misfortune was in store. VR-HDI took off without a hitch but as we passed through 5000 feet we got a terrific backfire. The engine immediately began rough-running and threatened to pull itself out of its mountings. John Paish feathered it and we returned to Mingaladon. Bob Smith soon had us on our way again, but the day was beginning to stretch out and it became obvious we would be a bit tight to make Hong Kong before the airport closed at dusk. However, if we made a quick turn-around at Haiphong, our refuelling technical stop, we would just about manage to make it. John had now gone back into the cabin for a kip, and I was in control.

The clouds thickened up as the miles ticked off. The cloud tops were gradually rising and were soon caressing our fuselage with misty fingers, so after getting authorisation I eased up to 12,000 feet. Soon we were again enveloped and glaze ice began to form on windscreen and wings. It looked unlikely that we could outclimb the thickening cumulus layer, so I sought permission to revert to 10,000 feet, and although we were still in thick cloud there was no turbulence and the ice disappeared.

At this moment our radio communication equipment packed up. This was followed by our directional gyro (which indicates flight direction) and then, as though it did not wish to remain the only instrument in working condition, our magnetic compass settled to the bottom of its bowl and ignored any change of aircraft direction. We were now left with a single artifical horizon; all other aids to finding and checking direction had become unserviceable.

I felt that this was the sort of situation for which a captain was paid his princely salary so I called Eric Aylward, who was trying to help Dick Labrum sort out his radio problems, and after a few minutes discussion asked him to call Paishy. John arrived at the flight deck, smoothing this thinning blond hair and knuckling sleep from his eyes. He told Eric to do something about the compass.

'What do you suggest?' Eric asked, and John answered testily: 'Any bloody thing. It's no good as it is.'

'What if I fill the compass bowl with water? That might give it some buoyance.'

'Try anything,' John snarled.

The water didn't help; the card remained stuck to the bottom of the bowl. The red hydraulic fluid Eric then tried proved no better. Paishy irritably told him to take it back to the 'head' and piss in it.

'There's so much grog in you it will probably float it,' he added unfairly.

Down Eric went and followed his advice. He realised that the cure was working, and in triumph re-positioned the bowl in its mountings. It worked beautifully and I don't think that Charlie Rowe of the Pacific Air Maintenance and Supply Company (Cathay Pacific's engineers) ever changed it.

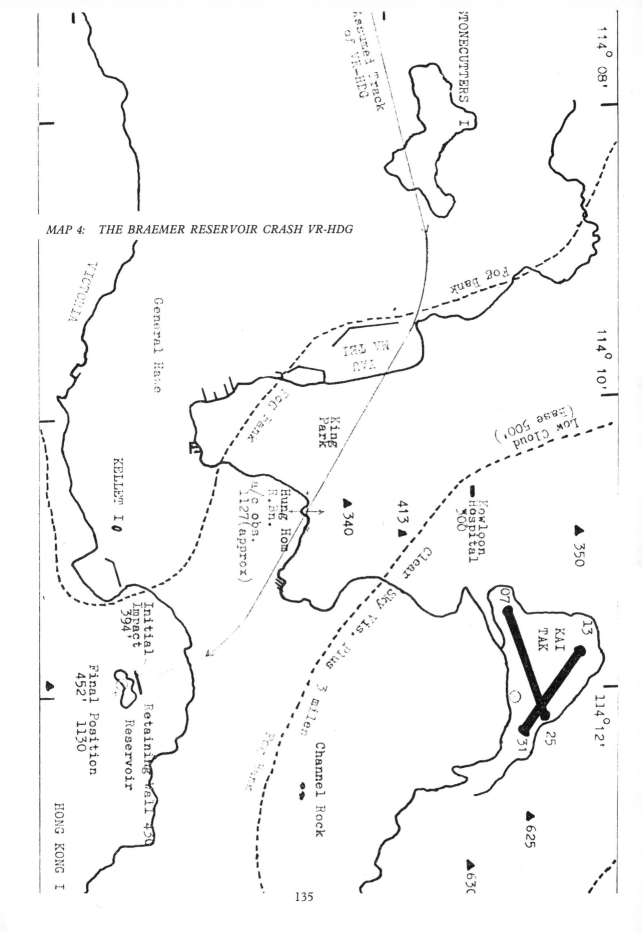

MAP 4: THE BRAEMER RESERVOIR CRASH VR-HDG

That solved only part of our troubles, as we had little idea where we were. After some hasty calculations we concluded we must be somewhere over the Gulf of Tonkin, and our only chance would be to descend through the cloud cover, hoping to make contact with the sea. Eric found no joy in this suggestion and retired to the back of the aircraft. Luck slowly turned our way. At 8000 feet we found a small hole in the murk, and at its foot a glimpse of the sea, gale-whipped.

John had no intention of losing that hole. He kept tightening the turn until the artificial horizon exceeded its limits and finally tumbled. We had been doing a turn rate exceeding 90 degrees, but he kept visually clear in that tight funnel of sky and we were able to descend right down to 900 feet. Visibility here was fairly good, with an occasional heavy rain squall, so turning towards the west we finally made contact with the Vietnamese coastline slightly north of Haiphong. That was just where we wanted to go but unfortunately an extensive line of rain-bearing clouds stretched right across the city. By that time our fuel reserves were getting low, so John elected to fly inland a few miles to clearer weather, and without further trouble we landed at Hanoi.

One final surprise awaited us there. Our fuel carnet, only valid for Haiphong, was not honoured at Hanoi though only fifty miles separated the two places. We couldn't get any gravy without paying cash. Eric was the only man aboard with any Indo-Chinese money and came to the rescue. This didn't give him great cause for mirth; he had had visions of spending that dough on perfume and—you guessed it—grog.

No fortune favoured John on February 29, 1949, when he was involved in the second fatal loss of an aircraft owned by Cathay Pacific since the Butterfield and Swire entry in the previous July. That morning had brought me to the Flying School in Hong Kong where I had an honorary instructorship, and at the precise moment of the accident my Chinese pupil K.C. Lam was strapped into one of the Ryan trainers and I was explaining the operation of the blind flying instruments, for that day the fog was intense.

The Air Registration Board released a bare two-line explanation of the accident: 'The aircraft was attempting an overshoot after an approach during poor visibility and struck the hillside by Braemar Reservoir.'

Practically all observers reported the happening in the same way, while the official findings wasted no time at all: Pilot error. I have all the news reports and some eye-witness translations of the unhappy affair, but the report that covers it in the best taste is in a letter written by Edward Guard Price to John Swire, his London-based co-director:

'I am writing today as little more is likely to be known than we have been told already (by DCA, albeit unofficially) about the disaster. The aircraft was on her way back from Manila with a quite unusually large complement of passengers, the weather was brilliant to within the outskirts of the Colony, but on and within the circle of the hills there was heavy but patchy cloud and mist.

'The pilot, who was one of the soundest and most experienced of our men, after a long wait, asked for permission to come in.

This was granted by the Kai Tak control on condition that visibility was not less than three miles. The aircraft came in safely, seeing Stonecutters from near Lantao, and when approaching Stonecutters reported to Air Control that he was able to see the airfield and asked for permission to land on a certain runway. Immediately this was granted he corrected this request and obtained permission to land on another runway. To do this involved circling, in the course of which he ran into heavy cloud which covered all the hills between Causeway Bay and Lei Yue Mun Point, and the next news was of an aircraft at low altitude being heard to crash in the neighbourhood of the main Taikoo Reservoir. The aircraft is a burnt-out wreck and all the occupants must have been killed instantly.

From all the facts we have it is a case of human error of judgment and I do not see how there can be any reflection on the company's operation. Hong Kong Airways aircraft had landed not very long before, and but for the tragic afterthought about the best runway on which to land, all would have been well.'

This Price Report, honest in intent, was somewhat deficient in analysis.

The downward visibility that day was really first class, but there was little forward visibility. Roy Downing, on duty in the control tower, could see every aircraft as it circled overhead but almost nothing beyond the horizontal panes of his glass house. As an aircraft dropped lower on approach the forward visibility reduced even more. Even when John Paish elected to do an overshoot he could still see every movement of the busy shipping in the harbour as he looked straight down. Unfortunately he had erred in direction. As he crossed the coast near the Ritz Nightclub the ground was rising faster than his labouring aircraft could climb. For many seconds the crew on that flight deck must have known that they were about to be dashed to pieces.

The aircraft of Hong Kong Airways came in from Canton perhaps a dozen times a day and knew every landmark like the backs of their hands. The pilots would time each leg of a particular approach with a stop-watch, starting it at a carefully identified position, say, for instance, Green Island in the western harbour. They would then fly so many seconds on a pre-determined heading towards the southwestern tip of Stonecutters Island, and if this point did not come up precisely on the second, they would get the hell out of there and make another attempt. If however it did come up as expected they would carry on to the next point of, say, Yau Ma Tei typhoon shelter, and so on.

The method required only downward visibility. The more important forward visibility required by the less experienced users of Kai Tak made little difference to their brilliant record of arrivals in even the most adverse weather conditions. The pilot of the aircraft that landed before Paish had reported ample visibility, but that was for the method the pilots of his airline had perfected, albeit without official sanction. Probably the knowledge that another aircraft had landed without apparent difficulty had influenced John Paish's decision to give it a go.

CHAPTER EIGHT
WARMING UP

All is flux, nothing stays still . . . nothing endures but change.
Diogenes Laertius—Heraclitus

As the Karen rebellion worsened and Karen influence strengthened throughout the central and Delta districts, Government troops could do little to contain them. In no time they had severed all transport lines from Rangoon and completely infested the city, making themselves masters of the rich rice-bowl areas. But failing to appreciate the vital importance of communication, they left the airfield at Mingaladon almost intact. They wasted opportunities which might have given them control of it, and though they did actually capture it and hold it for a night, their sappers neglected the chance to devastate it so as to keep it out of commission, perhaps for months.

Rebel control of places elsewhere concerned the charter operators deeply, for flights would start from airfields that might no longer be Government controlled. Panel markings would be displayed at airports and, to fool the enemy, their positions frequently changed. But the Karens had been known to display the correct sequence of those ground signals, and the unwary aviator entered their spider-parlour like the unsuspecting fly. When Maymyo fell at the beginning of March this particular ploy had been used.

At this period we were holding a daily lottery, the prize going to the crew who counted the most bullet-holes in the airframe. The prize was a case of beer, a princely prize in those months of short supply. The crews were undoubtedly involved in a shooting war, but did not know what was really happening. The fact that their licences were granted by an overseas Government soon led to questions being asked. In Hong Kong A.J.R. Moss was communicating with the Colonial Secretary there, concerned not so much with crew safety as with aircraft nationality. Aircraft displaying the Colony's registration must not be suspected of being a part of the Burmese military operation. He felt the crews might even be suspected of being gun-runners.

Most of our charters were to bring food to beleaguered towns, payloads of onions, potatoes, rice and a foul-smelling clarified buffalo butter called ghee. Ed Berry, after loading his DC3 with the quantity on the manifest would add half-a-dozen bags of potatoes for himself, and with this sideline I don't think he ever had to use his salary.

Neither pay nor insurance cover had been adjusted to take the hazards of this dangerous operation into consideration. When the odd aircrew member broached the subject he was met with derision. One afternoon a group met in Bob Smith's hole-in-the-wall office to compose a letter to management setting out how the operations were approaching danger levels. Suddenly a 20 mm Oerlikon shell pushed its snout through the wall. Bob finished typing the letter in nothing flat and all present signed it, some with almost indecipherable signatures due to shaking hands, and they entrusted it to Ceddie Carlton who was returning to Hong Kong that day. When it really dawned on Bob that the shell was a dud he dug it out of the wall and used it as a doorstop for a long time.

Dick Hunt, as Operations Manager, answered the letter in person and loudly belittled the concern. On the morning of March 5 he arrived at Mingaladon to fly out with Captain John Riordan and see conditions for himself. He unceremoniously told John to 'hop into the right-hand seat' and they took off for Meiktila. All the way he lectured John on 'how bloody frightened you blokes have become, using every pretext to lever more money off a struggling impoverished company'. At Meiktila the airfield signals were correct, indicating that the place was still under Government control. As the engines stopped he said, 'Look John. Must be a VIP coming back with us. We've got a guard of honour.'

John looked and said, 'Yes, we have. And they look like Karens.'

'Bloody rot!' replied Hunt.

Riordan went down to open the cargo door and as it swung back he received a precise salute from a diminutive officer whose serious expression was replaced by a grin as he said, 'I am a Karen'.

'I thought so,' Riordan said, returning the salute. He returned to the cockpit with the good news.

Hunt, in a subdued whisper, asked what they should do.

'Just what they tell us,' Riordan said.

The Karens locked the crew in a room and their guard, speaking English with an Oxford accent, enquired if they would like anything special for dinner. Hunt said he wasn't hungry but would appreciate a beer. John, testing what the traffic would bear, asked for a woman. Neither request surprised the guard who soon returned with a case of beer and two women.

At dawn the officer came and casually told them his assignment for the day was to capture Maymyo, about 65 miles north-north-east of Meiktila on the other side of Mandalay. Hunt and Riordan, he said, had been given the honour of assisting. They would fly troops to the airfield at Anisakan whence his men would proceed to Maymyo five miles on. They would go at once.

'What if we refuse?' Hunt snarled. The still-smiling officer unholstered his revolver, blew down the barrel and said quietly,

'Now, Captain, I hope you are not going to be difficult.'

They flew two loads of Karens in to Anisakan that day and on the evening of the seventh Maymyo was firmly in rebel hands. The calm, almost casual way the Karens captured the airfield demonstrated their superiority to the Burmans. A few minutes after they landed at Anisakan they had the airfield firmly in their hands. A short time later an Airspeed Oxford of the Burmese Air Force touched down, and when it taxied to the verge, the crew was quietly captured. Under Karen persuasion they revealed that a Spitfire would land soon. The Karens made movements at the airstrip lazy and normal and soon had that pilot in their hands as well. Their capture of the important hill town of Maymyo was hardly more than an invigorating walk, the defenders departing the scene in complete confusion.

Hunt and Riordan were not called upon for other contributions; they spent two more days as honoured guests of the Karens and when they were released they found their DC3 had been cleaned inside and out and was shining like a new pin. The tiny officer autographed Riordan's logbook, plucked off the artillery badge he was wearing, pinned it to Riordan's jacket, and pinned Riordan's Cathay Pacific wings on his own breast, to the applause of his men.

'When we capture Rangoon we'll make you the first Marshal of the Karen Air Force,' he said.

Captain Hunt returned to Hong Kong and reported that the Burma operation did entail a certain amount of risk to the crews. They all got a 50 per cent pay rise and something like 30 rupees an hour danger money.

One vivid memory of this time concerns Captain C.F. Moore at Meiktila in Central Burma, whence Burmese troops were being rushed to Moulmein, where a heavy attack was then in progress. During the loading I saw Pat lying under the tail, puffing a disgusting pipe and peering at the tail-wheel strut. Experience had told him that by watching this strut shortening as the aircraft was loaded he could keep an unscrupulous traffic loader honest. On this occasion he wanted to take the weight of as many men as the old bus would carry, but not an ounce more.

The soldiers kept streaming aboard in full battle kit. Suddenly Pat shouted 'Enough', and going up to the transport officer instructed him to take off the last three men. Returning to his observation point he shouted to load one more man and with that was satisfied. He took off with 57 soldiers and a crew of two on that DC3, and although that was still way behind the 68 Captain Moon Chin of CNAC lifted out of Myitkyina just before the Japanese advance, this is my own story of how this aircraft type could be overloaded with no apparent fall-off in performance. I wonder whether Captain Moon Chin's passengers were carrying full battle packs. I think not. The incident endorses a then-current saying: 'Civilians taught the Army Air Force how to fly the DC3, and then the Army showed the civilians how to overload it.'

On Captain Moon Chin's flight he had the company of an old friend, a rather nondescript little bloke escaping from China after leading the bombing raid which became known as 'Thirty Seconds Over Tokyo'; the legendary Jimmy Doolittle. At the time of our flight Captain Moon Chin was yet to become involved in 'the battle of Kai Tak', the ownership squabble over some 71 CNAC and CATC aircraft which sought refuge in the Colony ahead of the advancing Communists.

Where his record-breaking flight had been a success, ours was not. True, we landed safely at Moulmein with bullets flying all around the place. Our courageous troops deplaned without waiting for the port engine to wind down and immediately were in the thick of the battle. We learned later that they were killed to a man within fifteen minues of our departure.

Our own troubles were not over. Before we had stopped Pat had issued me with strict instructions that the pins which safetied the undercarriage must not be put in. With bullets pinging all round I zealously guarded those wheels until Pat screamed out the window, 'Let's get the hell out of here!' After I slammed the rear door I struggled with difficulty up the aisle, battling against the forward momentum of his hurried takeoff. I plonked into my seat just as we crossed the treeline of the airfield. Pat gave the order for wheels-up, and to my horror they wouldn't budge. Someone had slipped the pins in the undercart in the few seconds it had taken me to scramble through the door. We flew back to Mingaladon with the wheels locked down, hoping fervently the engines would retain their harmonious note. Our walk-around after the landing showed we had not been struck by a single bullet, a stroke of almost unbelievable luck. Our own aircraft pins were still in their correct stowage, while those which had locked the gear down were the set held by the Moulmein ground crew. Some little traffic bloke at the height of a real battle had had the guts to follow standing instructions and pin those wheels. Perhaps this was taking good training a little too far.

Pat recently told David Bell, editor of Swire News, a story of another trip I made with him, this time to Sydney:

'Sometimes we brought back bags of Sydney rock-oysters. On one of those trips I had a co-pilot who was the most Irish Irishman I ever met, especially as he was a native of Melbourne and had never seen the Shamrock Isles. He was a great co-pilot.

'Anyhow, we had just left Sydney and this fella said he was going down the back, and I said all right. As soon as he was off the flight deck I thought what a mug I was. He'd curl up and have a good kip and I'd have to fly her for the next five hours myself.

'Well the next thing I know he's at my elbow wearing an apron, with a napkin over his arm and carrying a big plate of oysters. He said, "Would you care for an oyster, Captain?"

'A few days later Syd asked me how many oysters there were in a bag and I told him about 150 dozen.

' "That's what I thought," said the boss, "but there were only about 120 dozen in one of the bags you brought back. Must have shrunk, eh?" '

The oysters were about the only part of this story that was true. Indeed they were brought up to the flight-deck and served in the manner described, but the only Irishman aboard was himself, Pat begorrah! I was the first officer, as I said, and almost everybody in Cathay Pacific knows how much I loathe oysters. He had cleaned them up himself. David Bell, it was a nice story, but the ancient, oversized leprechaun flannelled you!

John Riordan was a character of characters. He joined the company on September 8, 1948, and much of the time I was his first officer, though the first time I flew with him was on April 7, 1949 in VR-HDA, a DC3. We left Kai Tak for Calcutta by way of Haiphong in Vietnam and Mingaladon. Over Dum Dum airfield at Calcutta we were in a holding pattern slap in the centre of one of the worst rainstorms I have experienced. The rain was so heavy it was running up the windshield. I was wondering how any engine which depends on a mixture of fuel and air could operate out there where there was less air than water, when first the port engine cut out and then the starboard. What a frightful silence it becomes—no engine noise.

Although there were only four hands on that flight deck there seemed many more. Hands were everywhere, pushing this, pulling that, but failing to get the donks going again. Then our powerless airliner nosed into a clear patch of sky. There below us were the lights of that vast sprawling metropolis and the easily identifiable runway at Dum Dum. With a shout of joy John turned towards that amber-lighted haven, but there was really no hurry, for suddenly both engines returned to full operating power with an ear-splitting roar.

We booked into a suite at Calcutta's palatial Grand Hotel, a magnificent edifice now run down and living on past glories. Ever mindful of the comfort of the crew John offered me the bedroom; he would rough it (as he said) in what might be best described as a reception room. We decided to have dinner late, and first I went to bed and dropped into the deep sleep of exhaustion—it had been a long day. I didn't sleep very long, dressed quickly for dinner, then bounded through the door which separated our two units. On the other side I found John and an Anglo-Indian girl doing what comes naturally. That caused me no concern but, as I was about to return to my room I saw that notwithstanding the intense effort she was putting into an enjoyable deed, she was also, with remarkable dexterity, using one hand to go through the pockets of John's discarded pants.

I walked over and gently slapped her wrist, and as I took the pants away I shook my index finger at her. Undismayed she gave me a broad wink and a wonderful white-toothed smile. She wasn't the slightest bit worried at having been caught rolling her client, and I took my hat off to her high standard of light-fingered expertise, no doubt developed over years of practice.

Some time later John staggered into my section and asked whether he had left his daks there. He displayed relief when he saw them hanging over a chair. He said he was off for something to eat—would I join him? I told him I'd be down a little later, and he said he hoped I wouldn't mind if he had a lady with him. When I arrived at his table he introduced me to the same nymph of the boudoir, now exquisitely sari-wrapped, and described her as an old member of the family. With a gracious acknowledgement accompanied by demure lowering of the eyelids she assured me she was charmed to meet me. As an old member of the family she had been going through John's pockets just like a wife. Had I been a little out of order? I dismissed the thought, especially as John was still holding my outstation allowance.

Riordan's reputation for the pursuit and conquest of the female of the species provoked some jealousy among us less successful operators. He wasn't of distinguished build in any way; he was about the same height as myself but there the resemblence ended. He had a strong face with lines between the brows which indicated an enquiring mind, and a deep weathered groove on either side of an aquiline nose. These grooves extended to the ends of a heavy moustache which fiercely bristled whenever a beauty hove in sight. Then he might be heard to mutter, 'It's time to give the ferret a run'. The casual undress of the barracks had revealed him to be more than usually well-endowed. There was more than a mere suspicion that he had got out of one of the Princely States of India just ahead of the flashing blade of the local Maharajah's chief knackerer having been discovered *in flagrante delicto* with the boss Maharanee. John, always the gentleman, defended the poor girl as having been ignored for weeks by her inconsiderate beast of a husband, who had been tied up with the younger members of the harem. Our hero saw himself, not as an interloper on another's preserve, but rather as a bringer of succour to the tyrannically oppressed. He believed his cause a worthy one.

The monsoon arrived on time that year, an important consideration. The year's worst period is prior to the break of the 'big wet'; everybody and everything gets unbelievably edgy and the domestic animals seem to suffer most. With the falling of the first rains a tremendous relief promotes well-being, although the initial violent downpour drives a vast horde of insects indoors until the walls are literally walking. I expect this invasion could be prevented, but few houses, even the more palatial, had been insect-protected in that land where windows and doors are habitually left open to trap any wayward breeze.

April 21 found John Riordan and me flying west from Mingaladon for the delta city of Bassein. We had been scheduled three return flights for the day, but we would complete only part of the very first one. We had flown the seventy-odd miles across at 500 feet and, other than meeting the occasional heavy squalls which battered themselves out in a few seconds, we had had a reasonable trip, with forward visibility quite acceptable. With no radio aids at Bassein, this was the best height to handle the flight.

As we crossed to the north of the strip we were struck by small-arms fire from the ground. The starboard engine stopped, flames billowed round my starboard sliding window, and the flight deck filled with acrid smoke which belched from the joints of the dural floor of the companionway. I grabbed a fire extinguisher and rushed into the cabin, but it was clear, and not being able to get at the seat of the fire, I returned to my post. As I was about to re-enter the flight deck, Bo Egan appeared from the smoky gloom like a ghost, and said he would monitor the rear door in case we had to force-land.

Back in my seat I found John losing the battle to get the starboard engine re-started, and having little success in maintaining height with only the port engine operating. The trees were now close enough to see them turning green. John yelled he would have to land straight ahead. I said if he did that we'd all be killed. Those innocent-looking paddy-fields were surrounded by great earthworks, some broad enough to take a bullock-cart. I said, 'Let's try for the strip'. It was appearing in and out of the rain squalls. I kept the engine speed up to regulate the airspeed while he did his best not to lose the strip.

Our combined efforts worked out splendidly. When we rolled the wheels on to that grassy strip our sighs of relief could be heard above the splashing of mud and grass divots the buoyant undercarriage was throwing against the flame-scarred fuselage. When the drama had ended both flames and smoke had abated. We did not know the reason until much later when Bob Smith was flown across in answer to our signal which John and I thought told everything, but which in fact told very little.

Bob's pilot was Paul Clevenger, flying a Norseman which Ken Begg later had to abandon south of Meiktila. Paul frightened our engineer to the degree at which Bob grabbed all his bits and pieces and told Paul to get lost; he preferred to take his chances with the Karen rebels. Although not much of a pilot, Paul was no fool. Assessing the flinty look in Bob's eyes he quickly swung his aircraft and belted off down the strip.

Our message had told Bob little more than that our starboard engine had stopped and the cockpit filled with smoke. He thought that was a bit weird and not knowing what he should take had piled a lot of junk into the Norseman. It took him a long time to find out what had happened. Then he saw a small hole in the leading edge of the wing. Getting on top of the wing he found a gaping hole where the bullet had come out. When he opened the access panel he found that the bullet had gone right through the centre of the fuel line so precisely that it had flared the line out. The line was about twice the diameter on either side of the hole. Luckily he had brought some hose and clamps, so he cut out a four-inch length comprising the damaged piece and put a piece of 'Hi-Pressure' flex hose on after bell-mouthing the ends of the pipe. The temporary repair would take the DC3 back to Mingaladon where he could change it for a proper union at his leisure.

'That's why your engine stopped,' he said. 'No fuel was being supplied. The only reason the fire went out was that the rush of fuel was too much to burn, and it actually smothered the flames.'

When he checked under the flight deck floor he found all the zinc chromate burnt brown and the protective grease on the control cables a mass of blisters.

From the time we had been shot down the gun-firing round the strip had been sporadic, but now a crescendo of small-arms fire was sending bullets pinging overhead, so without any run-up we got the hell out. Perhaps we need not have worried, for although the Karens had captured that Delta town on January 28 they had been quickly driven out again, and never repeated that success. Bassein was one of the few re-occupations achieved by Government troops at that time.

When we were drinking later at downtown Green's Hotel in Rangoon Riordan said, 'It was IFR [Instrument conditions of flight] outside, then the cockpit filled with smoke and it became IFR inside.'

In true music-hall fashion his audience, all together, asked, 'So what did you do?'

Quick as a flash came his answer: 'We broke the glass from the instruments and finished the flight on Braille.'

That very temporary repair was still in place many months later. The aircraft, VR-HDA was the one which hit the Macao reservoir wall on January 5, 1947, a beautifully appointed DC3 and the only one Cathay Pacific fitted with fuel-dump chutes. It was the last DC3 in the fleet and the company sold it on July 24, 1961.

Three days after this hairy episode at Bassein the Union of Burma Airways chartered Riordan and me to search for one of their Dove aircraft overdue after operating in this western Delta region. It had failed to land at Myaungmya, a town close to Bassein, and it may either have had engine trouble or merely run out of fuel, as the weather had been particularly bad.

We found it. It had made a forced landing on the only firm patch of grass for miles around. As we circled overhead a group of heavily-armed insurgents put it to the torch. The fate of the crew apparently deserved no mention in the Press, but the incident brought increased attacks from the media, which had been shoooting a lot of flak at UBA because of the type of aircraft this national carrier had chosen. Newapaper articles vigorously demanded the name of the person responsible and the amount of the rake-off. UBA directors said as little as possible.

Another Dove had failed to arrive at Moulmein a few weeks earlier. It had left the coastline about thirty miles east-south-east of Rangoon and was seen no more. Its captain was a lean Englishman whose name—Sparrow—was appropriate to the flying profession. It was assumed that he might have collided with a large bird, a number of which habitually cruised the area.

During my first tour in Burma I had met and become friendly with Kit Trimble, ex-RAF and, prior to the war, a London policeman. Now he offered me an immediate captaincy on Union of Burma Airways' De Haviland DH104 Doves, so during April I submitted the required month's notice to Cathay Pacific. With two days of the period still to run I was in Hong Kong and hurrying through the Peninsula Hotel lobby when F.A.P., Miguel stopped me. Miggie was our senior traffic officer at the time. In a bellicose, no-nonsense voice he said the company was looking for a co-pilot for a flight later that afternoon, and I was it, so I should get home and get ready.

I tried to reason with him. Not only was I tired, having returned from Manila that morning, but I had important business on the island. I suggested he forget he had seen me, but to no avail. His mind was made up and he ordered me to accept the assignment; otherwise he would report to the operations department that I had refused to accept a flight. Unfortunately my mind was not too receptive to that type of threat, so I told him to do his worst and pushed past him.

Later that day I was sitting in the United Services Recreation Club in Kowloon with Captain Pat Moore and his wife when who should hustle up and, in a loud voice, order me to report to Kai Tak for a flight immediately, but Dick Hunt. His belligerent attitude embarrassed everyone. When Pat tried to have him moderate his tone he told Pat to belt up—the matter did not concern him. His swinging on Pat at that point was to prove a Godsend when, some years later, I reapplied for a job with Cathay Pacific. Captain Moore was then the Operations Manager and immediately welcomed me back to the fold, notwithstanding the fact that Dick Hunt had succeeded in having Syd de Kantzow withdraw my resignation and issue a letter discharging me with immediate effect.

This was the only time in my life I had been sacked from any job. I had told Hunt to peel off (a term the Duke of Edinburgh uses and one I have come to prefer to my actual words at the time). I returned to my relaxation beside the United Services Recreation Club pool, concluding that, though Dick could dish it out, he could not take it.

I took up my duties with UBA on June 6 and fitted in so well with the environment it seemed I had been there for decades. I was comfortably ensconced in a large Colonial-type home on the Kokine Road. I had joined several worthwhile clubs—most expatriates feel this necessary to their existence. My savings account was showing a healthy increase, my employers were gentlemen of charm, and I was happy and contented.

The company had kept another side of the bargain and a shining new jeep was drawn up under the monsoon-protected driveway. Its smart appearance was not only the envy of all my friends, but it seemed to attract the attention of every dog for miles around. The appearance was misleading, for the jeep was forever requiring mechanical adjustments, so much so that administration took notice.

One day at Mingaladon I met the general manager U Taw in the parking compound. He greeted me in his usual courteous manner, then his eyes hardened as they lighted on the jeep. He gingerly approached the vehicle and after circling it warily, took his courage in both hands and aimed a kick at a wheel. Encouraged, he gave each wheel the same treatment, then leaned over and produced an extended blast from the horn. Then turning to me, he said,

'Really, Captain Eather, I don't know why you are continually complaining about this jeep. I know quite a lot about transport, and this car seems in absolutely first-class condition to me!'

He had been a big wheel in the Inland Water Transport Board, now defunct due to insurgent harassment. In the presence of such knowledge and experience what could I say?

I calculated the consumption of that fuel-drinking beast at gallons to the mile instead of miles to the gallon. It could not be locked in any way and frequently attracted the attention of the dacoits (robbers) who infested the area. Their attentions were so frequent I felt my own servants might be supplementing their salaries. At first, small items of equipment would disappear overnight, but when I awoke one morning to find a wheel gone, not the spare, mind you, I brought the police into the matter and for my pains was fined thirty rupees for allowing an envelope addressed to me to litter the outside gutter!!

Early that same afternoon I laid an electric wire from the closest power-point in the house. It terminated in a type of lightning-rod arrangement which I anchored in the concrete before driving the jeep against the rod. I assembled the servants and told them what I had done, suggesting they should tell all their friends. To give the current a better conductor I splashed buckets of water copiously round the object of my affection.

During the night an unearthly scream awakened me. Investigating I found my Indian watchman dancing round clutching his 'John Thomas' firmly in both hands. For some reason the one bloke I should have warned was the one I forgot. Nevertheless my experiment had solved the mystery of who had been peeing on my jeep.

CHAPTER NINE
BURMESE RUPEES

Cette rive, en malheurs trop feconde
Qui produit les tresors et les crimes du monde

Alzire . . . Voltaire

(This shore, too fertile in misfortune,
which produces the world's treasures and its crimes.)

A motley collection of air charter companies settled in Rangoon to vie for the Burmese Government's rupees. Some did their best to fulfil every obligation to their charterers; others were strictly fly-by-night adventurers whose interest went no further than the lining of their pockets. Some involved themselves in gold and dope running, bringing no credit to our profession. The volume of gold entering the country was of such immensity as to gravely concern the Government, for unauthorised flow of gold undermined the value of the local currency, and the Burmese rupee was weak and unwanted on the world market.

Many of these odious operators made little attempt to cover their movements; one of the most blatant, practically advertised on his letterhead that he was the designated agent for the insurgent movement in the Dutch East Indies, and that he was using Mingaladon as a staging-post for its gun-running. This did little to soften the hearts of the harassed Dutch to the equally harassed Burmese.

Some, perhaps most, were also changing their hire rates at a moment's notice, especially when they knew that the offered load was of vital importance, and that they had a tottering Government by the short and curlies. Unscrupulous greed shaped their policies.

The idea of establishing a Burmese national air charter company germinated in the ever agile brain of Millard Nasholds. Such a company would be free of the restrictive regulations that the expatriate companies in Burma had to follow, since they were imposed by whatever country registered their aircraft. When followed, they covered the country of registration against any accusation that they had engaged in military action.

Nash presented his scheme in detail to a Burmese citizen named Bo Setkya during a luncheon at Burma's Strand Hotel which fronted the Rangoon River. His guest, a capable businessman of 33 years, had vast interests in rice marketing, a nail factory, a vermicelli factory and several export and import concerns. He had been one of the 'thirty brave comrades' who had fought their way into Burma led by General Aung San. He had been Burmese Military Attache in Tokyo during the remaining war years, and had accompanied Aung San to the London conference with Clement Attlee which pre-dated the Union of Burma. To Bo Setkya

Captains Brian Legge; "Woody" Forte; "Jud" Judkins; John
Dalrymple and Radio Operators, Air Burma DCC3 Mingaladon
Airport, Rangoon, Burma, 1950

May 1949—Air Burma's first DC3 leaving Kai Tak enroute to Mingaladon.
L. to R: Captains John Moxham and Syd de Kantzow, U Shan and Mr Peccorini.

Captains "Nobby" Clarkson; Sid Smith; Frank Eretz;
"Woody" Forte; Mingaladon, Burma

UBA's chief pilot Capt. Kit Trimble and R/O Fred Braddel (who would join CPA as a
radio officer later that year, remuster as a pilot in 1960 and resign in 1972), checking
passengers on UBA's De Havilland Dove DH104 at Mergui, Burma.

the proposition Nash expounded was abundantly clear. Air Burma came into being on May 5, 1949. It worked closely with Cathay Pacific.

On June 1 de Kantzow scrawled his oversized signature on a document setting out new service conditions for captains, first officers and radio officers based in Burma. Salaries for both captains and first officers remained at $HK1610 a month, but the captains received in addition $HK24 bonus for every flying hour; first officers half that amount. The company guaranteed a minimum monthly salary plus pay bonus of 60 hours flying. Salary was to be paid in Hong Kong dollars, and since income tax there was only 15%, this was an additional incentive. Accommodation and messing was to be found for single aircrew who paid for it on a cost basis. Insurance protected aircrew 24 hours a day, in the air or on the ground, and included a War Risk and Civil Insurrection clause. The usual window-dressing phrases followed, and were followed in their turn by one which provided food for thought:

'Aircrew are being based in Rangoon primarily to operate Cathay Pacific aircraft. However, both aircraft and crews are under charter to Air Burma and are to be interchangeable with Air Burma crew, consequently the crew composition of Cathay Pacific and Air Burma will be at the discretion of the Rangoon Operations Manager, and may consist of the minimum crew of two persons.'

That was still not too one-sided, but section 11 put the cat among the pigeons:

'Cathay Pacific aircraft will normally operate civilian charters, but in view of their being chartered by Air Burma there is no longer a mandatory limitation, and aircraft belonging to both companies may carry loads of military troops, arms, ammunition, fuel and supplies on behalf of the Burmese Government. Air dropping may also be required to be carried out in peaceful areas, but military air drops will not be required of crews without recompense.

'It is therefore understood that aircraft of both companies will be expected to fly to whatever points are considered a reasonable operation by the company's technical management, and to operate in accordance with the company's directions.'

I thought this one-sided. I put the example of a man who had joined a Hong Kong-based airline to pursue a peaceful profession and then was required to sign another contract engaging him in a military operation in a foreign clime. Syd de Kantzow made little secret that he who did not sign should seek employment elsewhere. Several experienced men were not prepared to accept these hazards and others were sympathetic to the aspirations of the Karens, so the period was not one in which co-operation between management and aircrew was at its best.

When Air Burma began hiring its own personnel this unsatisfactory situation was eliminated. Many of the recruits were to migrate to Cathay Pacific when Air Burma's usefulness to the Government was at its end. One, Captain Dave Smith became the first Operations Manager to be honoured with a seat on the

1948
U. Sway Tin
General Manager Union of Burma Airways

Board of Directors. Another was Woody Forte, an American with significant charm, both in a group, which is exceptional, and alone, which is normal. He had once been selected as a strong prospect for representing his country in the Olympic swimming team, but his casual (if not lazy) nature persuaded him not to bother with the dedicated training his coach demanded. His marked ability had caught the eye of swimming movie-star Esther Williams and I understand he had played several silent roles in her films. When I met him his once athletic build was turning to what is politely called 'flesh'.

After Air Burma was liquidated his name cropped up in an article in the Hong Kong *Standard* headlined CAT PILOTS AT WORK. Many people believed CAT was a front for the Central Intelligence Agency. In Indo-China the CAT organisation (Civil Air Transport) had twenty-four volunteer pilots many of whom were former members of the wartime USAAF stationed in the China Theatre, and one was a veteran of the Flying Tigers. In March 1954, with other American pilots they were flying C119 'box-cars' based at Cat Bi, the airport of Haiphong in Indo-China. Two or three times every day these pilots brought sorely needed equipment to French and Vietnamese units in the front lines. Their planes were unarmed and the low altitudes to which they had to descend for a precise drop made them sitting ducks, so that they frequently returned with well-peppered fuselages. Woody had phenomenal luck but it finally deserted him: the last report was of his plane ploughing into a heavily wooded mountain to disappear in a searing sheet of flame.

The general manager of the Union of Burma Airways (not to be confused with Air Burma) was U Sway Tin, an admirable choice, both liked and respected. He controlled all air charter allotments to the foreign carriers. Today he is in exile in the United States and it seems doubtful whether he will ever return to his beloved Burma. He had been a technical officer of the pre-war Burma Civil Aviation Directorate, having received training from New Delhi's Air Training Centre in India. The principal and founder of that Centre, Captain Alan T. Eadon, became Burma's Director of Civil Aviation soon after U Sway Tin's return.

Just prior to Air Burma commencing operations, eight separate charter companies received trip allocations through Union of Burma Airways. Some of these had aircraft unsuitable for the type of work offering, but U Sway Tin made every effort to schedule business for them.

Under Captain Dallas Cederberg, Trans-Asiatic Airlines (Siam) operated five DC3s registered by Thai authorities. Captain Pete Holmes (who would join Cathay Pacific for a mere three months) was one of his pilots. Pete was an Englishman with a liking for evil-smelling cigars, made in Burma by the local women. He told me the cigars' exclusive flavour resulted from the women's practice of rolling them snugly in their groins. He always had one jammed in the corner of his mouth. One day as we walked to our respective aircraft I asked whether there was ever a time when his mouth was free of one. 'Only when I'm eating,' he said, and started my perhaps over-developed imagination conjuring up visions of Pete in various other situations.

Amphibian Airways operated four Catalina PBY5As. Roy Farrell owned

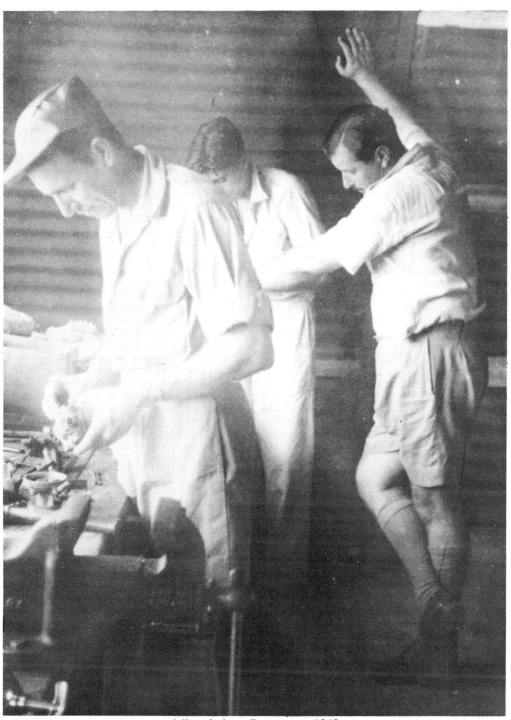

Mingaladon, Rangoon—1948
Wally Malmborg's Radio 'workshop'. Wally in
foreground with Capt. John Moxham giving advice to
local mechanic in the background.

these aircraft and operated them in Burma under the company's name, though his own name does not appear in the company's registration papers filed in the Philippines on May 21, 1947. He could have been operating under a later arrangement. He still retained a portion of the 10% shared by the American interest in Cathay Pacific, Cathay Holdings Ltd, but he had been quick to appraise the opportunity and had branched out on his own. He had gathered some good flying-boat men around him including Captains Don Teeters, Chet Brown and Larry Olsen. Olsen had had an association with MATCO which extended for four whole days during February 1949, flying their Catalina VR-HDH to and from Macao. He must have decided that fifty-mile trips were a little restricting, and sought a more enterprising life.

For his Operations Manager Farrell had brought in Captain James Atlee Phillips, who combined journalism with flying. Later he wrote a fictional book based on his time in Burma, using characters thinly veiled from the real people of the period. On the first printing this book was called *Moulmein Star*; with the next edition the name was changed to *Pagoda*, the dust-jacket showing the Shwe Dagon and an aircraft being shot down in flames. Radio technician Wally Malmborg is easily recognisable as the Wally Brittingham of the Phillips book.

Wally started with Cathay Pacific early in 1949 and as they had no immediate work for him filled in for a couple of weeks with PAMAS before being sent to Rangoon to keep radios serviceable on the single weekly flight Cathay Pacific was then operating there. Since he had little work to do, he was seconded to Amphibian Airways when Roy Farrell brought in the Catalinas. These were engaged to fly arms, ammunition and troops behind the Karen positions, a task for which they were admirably suited, for they could land on any reasonably good stretch of water.

'The reasons behind the Karen rebellion disturbed several of the expatriate airmen,' Wally recalls, 'and although some of the more outspoken made no secret of where their sympathies lay they were working against them. The dangling of "thirty pieces of silver" overcame scruples. Cathay Pacific had two sets of stencils they utilized on the aircraft fuselages. When they engaged in what I termed humane drops of salt, rice and flour, Cathay Pacific stencils were used, and I have seen incidents where the same aircraft was to carry ammo and troops on the very same afternoon, and a frantic work-bee would change the name from Cathay Pacific to Air Burma. For all this cunning shuffling, nobody thought to change the Hong Kong registration letters to Burmese ones. This would have paid lip service at least to an operation which must have been an insurance broker's nightmare.

'The conditions under which I worked were the worst imaginable, for my radio workshop was in a very inaccessible place near the old control tower. It was a bamboo structure with a thatched roof. My workbench was a couple of planks supported by two packing cases, and as the dirt floor was invariably under several inches of water I had to stand on a plank or a few housebricks. The power supply to run this "technical laboratory" was an old aircraft battery. Looking back now I wonder if anyone else would have stuck it out.

'At this time the Karens were at Insein, close to the end of our main runway. Karen intelligence had made them aware of the exact situation: Amphibian Airways had engine and airframe engineers in plenty but I was the only radio technician and consequently the weak link. The Karens decided to do something about this and took a couple of shots at me while I was walking across the airfield to my radio establishment. Naturally this didn't increase my enthusiasm and I complained bitterly about the one-sided contest to Captain Phillips who belittled my every argument. He seemed to take a delight in telling me that I was being paid to take risks—salary plus fifty per cent war-loading.

'I promptly reminded him that he was paid on the same basis and henceforth he would have the privilege of driving me across No-Man's-Land to my sumptuous laboratory, preferably at high speed. This didn't double him up with mirth, and had obviously fallen on deaf ears until he realised I had packed my spare spanner and was ready to resign. So he became my unwilling charioteer until my radio shop was moved to a safer location.'

Another character to whom Phillips gave fictional life in his book *Pagoda* is Dan Marino, a fellow of massive girth. He presents him as a repulsive barrel of lard, odious in every way, a disgrace to the human race. During the early days of Cathay Pacific's involvement in Burma it employed a big fellow who tipped the scales at a good 280 pounds. He was driving along the treacherous narrow road from Bangkok to the Don Muang airport when an encounter with a Cathay Pacific passenger bus caused him to lose control and roll into the ditch beside the carriageway. The car turned over and because of his great weight his would-be rescuers could not pull him free. He suffocated in the mud before their eyes. This was Cathay Pacific's handling agent, Dan Peccorini. It was Dan who once addressed a famous signal to Syd de Kantzow: 'Seeing we have a de Kantzow, a de Leuil, a Grabowksy, a Wolinsky and Peccorini I cannot resist hiring a Matlashewski.'

Roy Farrell's troubles did not finish when Air Burma eased him out. In his haste to get among the free-flowing rupees he had flown his Catalinas into the country without the necessary import documentation, and when he attempted to remove them the Government would not permit him to do so. His persuasive tongue eventually obtained the release of two of them. Radio officer Bo Egan told me of his involvement:

'One evening I got a phone call from Farrell who, in his most persuasive voice, asked me if I would like to go back to Hong Kong. I said, "Yes, yes, anyway at all." This proved to be a very foolish answer, for on arriving at Mingaladon the very next morning my happy mood was shattered when I enquired what service I was crewing. A little traffic bloke, showing quite uncharacteristic concern pointed, with a gulp, at an abandoned Catalina. As I looked at it I couldn't recall whether it had flown since the day I saw it make an astonishing landing. Larry Olsen, its pilot arrived in the circuit at Mingaladon and found he couldn't get its nose-wheel down. That didn't worry him unduly—all he had to do was raise the wheels and land it in the river, but then he found he couldn't raise the main wheels again either by hydraulic or mechanical means. He was flying an amphibian that couldn't safely come down on land or water.

'He was fortunate that day in carrying a group of well-disciplined troops. He told the officer of his plan and made his approach into Mingaladon. As the wheels skimmed the ground he bellowed 'Now!' and all the troops moved as far aft as possible. This kept the nose clear of the ground and actually dragged the tail skid. The Catalina came to a stop, the waiting ground personnel slipped a 44-gallon drum under the nose keel, and as the soldiers moved forward the nose quietly settled on the drum. Olsen did a remarkable job landing the aircraft with just a few scratches, and after the nose-wheel was forced out of its nacelle the Catalina was towed to the side of the old PSP runway, where it had remained since.

'While I stared at it, the skipper for the ferry flight to Hong Kong arrived. I had never seen him before and I can't recall his name. I made myself known to him but although he did return my greeting I got the impression he didn't really care who I was. As the starter engaged and the engines coughed into life I couldn't help but think 'what a miracle!', and when they had both settled down to a contented purr the eight Filipino ground engineers seemed relieved, and one or two actually forced a smile.

'Away we went, roughly in the direction of Kai Tak, but after about twenty minutes all the radio equipment went on the blink and a quick check proved that both voltage generators had packed up, with the result that we flew practically all the way to Hong Kong without any radio contact. Nobody seemed to miss us, or if they did, they appeared to be losing little sleep.

'Suddenly the skipper demanded my appearance on the flight deck and, without preamble, roared "Well. Where are we?"

'Trying to retain some semblence of friendliness I pointed out that I was a radio operator, not a navigator, in the hope that this might produce a smile, but it proved unsuccessful. His eyes merely bored through me with a flinty gleam and the silence which followed became even colder. Looking out, I said I thought I recognised certain types of fishing junks grouped below us and furthermore something about the purple-hazed reefs I could see to starboard was familiar, so I asked him for his map. That didn't save the situation in the slightest; he scowled even deeper and said he never carried such rubbish.

'Now thoroughly alarmed I suggested he turn to port to intercept the Chinese mainland, which without hesitation he did. This disturbed me even more, for my commander, who I expected to make the decisions, was anxious to follow the instructions of a lowly radio-man. Like many other serious situations this one solved itself and we made a good landfall a few miles to the west of Macao.

'We arrived over Kai Tak, still without radio communication and I managed to obtain landing instruction by pushing in the regulators with a pencil. This action had a high fire-risk, and although there were no actual flames the Catalina filled with smoke, so I had to abandon a landing listening watch. Our landing run occupied the entire length of the runway due to the fact that we had no braking capability, another small item our lackadaisical Yank had withheld from his crew. I just grabbed my bag and, dropping out of the blister, walked to the Customs area. Later I learned the Catalina was towed to the PAMAS hard-standing and to the best of my knowledge was never moved again.'

1948—The shrapnel scarred Mingaladon Hangar, Burma. Captain Cobley's
"Airways Burma" Avro Anson—the same type Cathay Pacific operated there
for a brief period.

1948
Mingaladon Airport, Rangoon, Burma.
The terminal building which contained Port Health, Immigration and Customs and 'The Palace
of Germs' Restaurant. Note the Avro Anson outside the shrapnel scarred hangar.

U Sway Tin reminded me of another of the small companies to be eliminated by Air Burma/Cathay Pacific co-operation. In early 1948, after returning from England, he became friends with Captain Cobley, an Australian pilot who used to fly round the country in an Auster spotter aircraft. Later Cobley formed a small air charter service which he called Airways Burma. He interested a couple of Burmese into backing him and bought an Avro-Anson, operating an air service to several places in the Delta—Bassein, Henzada, Akyab and Moulmein. When this single aircraft company could not earn enough to meet service and repair needs, let alone provide any financial return to his backers, Cobley just departed the scene, leaving the Anson to the backers to be sold for what it could fetch.

In August 1948 the Sydney *Daily Telegraph* carried a story that the Dutch Government accused the Indonesian Republic's Minister of Finance, Dr A. Maramis of conducting a large-scale opium racket in collusion with the Republic's Cabinet. He had already exported seventeen tons to Malaya with the object of building up foreign currency assets. At the time, Queen Juliana had not proclaimed an end to the 340 years of Dutch Colonial rule.

Dr Maramis was said to be using an Australian-registered Catalina crewed by Australians, but Air Marshal Williams, then the Director-General of Civil Aviation denied the existence of an Australian Catalina and crew 'wandering round up there'.

On December 29 the Australian Catalina and crew, that weren't there, attempted a takeoff on a single engine from a river at Djambi in Sumatra, where the Cat had lain for some days with engine trouble. The takeoff commenced just as Dutch troops who had been sent to capture the Catalina broke through the dense undergrowth bordering the river. They watched with horror as the amphibian gained speed and then slammed to the left, striking a partly-submerged boat, breaking up and sinking before their eyes. All aboard were instantly killed. The name of the Australian who had attempted the impossible was Cobley, the same captain as had pioneered the short-lived Airways Burma.

Air Carriers was another outfit eased out when Air Burma took over. However, its liquidation came about under pathetic circumstances. After withdrawal from the Burma scene it became Nan Yang Airways, based in Singapore. Its main task was to fly Aw Boon Haw's *Tiger Standard* newspaper daily to Ipoh, Kuala Lumpur and Penang. The company used Avro-Ansons for the run and provided a reliable service, accepted by everyone. Pilots were Paul Epperson, Bob Dyland and Englishman Nobby Clarkeson (ex-Air Burma). By this time both Eric Aylward and Bob Smith had also joined the operation. Eric wrote me how the liquidation of Nan Yang Airways came about:

'We still had this ex-Colonel USAF flying for us, Paul Epperson. He was a capable pilot, a very quiet bloke who didn't mix with the rest of us. He had no delusions of granduer and it was common to see him peddling round on a push-bike. One morning he was doing a run which took him along the Malay east coast towards the border with Thailand. The weather was bad and the usual procedure we adopted (for there were no radio aid) was to fly well out to sea, descend to water contact and then turn west until we intercepted the land.

Mingaladon Airport, Rangoon, Burma. June 1949.

'That day, instead of doing what he had done countless times in the past, he just put the nose down and crashed into a hill. I was on the search flight which found him sticking out of a hill like a dart. Later I was included in the land search to investigate the cause of the accident, but the jungle was too dense, we were continually harassed by bandits, and when they took a little time off, tigers and elephants had a turn. Finally we abandoned any hope of getting to the crash.

'Naturally, no fatal accident can be looked on with other than distress, but this particular one was heart-rending, for Aw Boon Haw's favourite son "Tiny" was aboard, and nothing is of greater urgency than at death a Chinese must be buried with his ancestors. Because of our inability to get to the wreck Aw Boon Haw just lost his will to continue with the operation and stopped the airline immediately.'

With all the wheeling and dealing of the charter operators the Government's green light for the Nasholds/Bo Setkya scheme came as no surprise. Barely one year later it was interesting to read in *The Nation* in June 1950 that only three foreign operators remained. They were Trans-Asiatic Airways with five aircraft, Indonesian Airways with two and Siamese with one. All were barely subsisting on the scraps which Air Burma disdained to handle.

The Karen advance had given them undisputed control of surface transport as well as the occupation of many important towns in Central Burma and the Irrawaddy delta, so that the foreign press was forecasting a total victory for them. They were almost at the doorstep of the capital city, holding the railway terminal at Insein, an outer suburb about ten miles from Rangoon. That proximity to the seat of government was of great concern, Insein even more so because its boundary was also that of the only remaining avenue of communication left: the international airport at Mingaladon.

Three runways were possible: the original pre-war strip directed 32 degrees from true north and now completely covered with perforated steel plate and reserved as an apron for parking and loading, the main runway running approximately southwest to northeast and directed towards Insein, mainly of concrete construction but with several sections where steel plate was used, and an unsealed strip running north to south dubbed the RAF or Air Force strip. Though the Karens had few heavy weapons they had positioned a deadly Oerlikon gun so that its arc of fire covered the latter runway. The Burmese Air Force made it a point never to use this runway; they never stretched their luck too far.

The Karens had also posted an exceptionally eagle-eyed sniper whose ambition was to make life as difficult as possible for everyone. From the top of one of the few elevations near Insein his field of fire covered not only the airport but two main bends in the vital Prome Road. His efficiency was responsible for closing the road after dark as he could pick up even the hooded headlights of transport using it. He pumped shots into U Sway Tin's station wagon a couple of times, and caused Wally Malmborg to dance a merry jig on more than one occasion. Before he was flushed out and eliminated he enjoyed himself immensely.

When we were forced to use the dangerously short Air Force runway payloads suffered. What annoyed us most was the Government's refusal to bulldoze away the written-off DC3 which occupied a position almost on the runway threshold at centre-line, reducing our landing distance even more.

Mingaladon's old-fashioned facilities were the bare minimum necessary for it to qualify as an international airport. It had one large shrapnel-scarred hangar for civil use, a long hangar west of this for the Air Force, and some concrete hard-standing where the BAF Airspeed Oxfords were parked. East from the hangar area the health, immigration and customs facilities shared premises with an eating-house. At the rear of the building a whitewashed stone blockhouse held the equipment of the International Aeradio organisation.

Moultrie's restaurant was an astonishing place and we doubted whether the proprietor had ever heard the word 'hygiene'. Its cockroaches appeared to answer to specific names and it was said an understanding government had issued them with identity passes to allow them unrestricted freedom after lights-out.

Big George Stephenson, an American ground engineer a.k.a. 'The Farmer' was a gigantic bloke who took no umbrage at what one called him, providing it was not late for dinner. He had an appetite proportional to his size, and although he knew he would suffer agonies after the meals he stowed away at Moultries, he just had to eat and hang the consequences. He claimed that a curry consumed at Moultries was the only meal known to science that could produce two different kinds of dysentery from the one intake. We called the establishment 'Moultrie's Palace of Germs'.

We had more merriment than instruction from watching the Burma Air Force about their duties. Three of their Airspeed Oxfords would scream off in formation, claw for altitude as though a banshee was nipping their tail-feathers, and cross Insein at 10,000 feet; then, with an ear-splitting roar of abused engine-power dive towards their target in Insein. Without exception they pulled out of their attack at never less than 5000 feet. Their efforts became so laughable that the defenders frequently didn't bother to return their fire and merely ignored them.

Air Control was sometimes less than efficient. Mum Louttit told me of arriving with Captain Vic Leslie at the height of the Karen confrontation. They were returning from Calcutta and Mum was furiously calling Rangoon Tower on 6440, but had no answer. They circled the aiport about six times while he attempted to make radio contact. Then he heard a faint but clear voice giving instructions to land on a certain runway. That runway did exist at Mingaladon, but it was loaded down with 44-gallon drums filled with concrete.

Vic turned to Mum Louttit and said, "Well, he okayed me to land, so that's what I'll do.'

They landed and didn't hit anything, which was amazing. It was difficult enough taxi-ing back; it was a real job avoiding the drums even when travelling slowly. What was really infuriating was that the moment their wheels touched down the Tower began screaming: Why had they landed? Couldn't they see the runway was obstructed and therefore closed?

'It showed the typical Rangoon attitude,' Mum said, 'We didn't bother to acknowledge.'

That was nearly Vic Leslie's last appearance. He sailed from Hong Kong on September 2, 1948 on the S.S. *Shansi*, the last of the three RAAF officers who had joined the Roy Farrell Export-Import Company. Neville Hemsworth and Pinky Wawn had left before him. Alan Marshall holds as an unforgettable memory the time he flew in with Vic and a team of divers, sent to clear the Rangoon River of the many bodies still entombed in wrecks that dated back to the Japanese advance.

One day a fussy, small and effervescent Frenchman landed at Mingaladon. He worked for Aigle Azure (Blue Eagle) Airlines and he had come from Nice. Bob Smith did some engine maintenance for him and as soon as the job was done he said he'd be off, pointing down towards the southern end of the runway. Bob told him not to go as lots of Karens with dozens of guns were down there. With an expressive shrug the Frenchman told him not to worry; he'd been in the war and a few guns didn't impress him. He taxied down, turned for his engine check and then began rolling for takeoff.

Suddenly one wing went down and he shuddered to a stop. His whole crew scrambled out of the door and gathered round the port wheel well. A couple more crumps started them all running back along the strip. The little captain was the last to start and the first to arrive where Bob stood watching.

He screamed, 'Zey ave don eet, zey ave don eet! Zee Oerlikon gun, boom! boom!'

Bob reminded him of his warning and he calmed down straightaway, saying 'Oui, zey are down zer all right.'

'Ave you ze olio?' he asked.

Bob lapsed into the language of the moment and replied, 'Oui, I ave zee olio, ze jack, I ave ze men, but zey no go down zer.'

They sounded like a couple of song and dance men but the Frenchman was a game little devil. Down he rushed, fired up his engines and brought the DC3 back with one flat tyre. That took a lot of guts. When Bob checked he found the tyre was the least of the Frenchman's worries and showed him a gaping ten-inch diameter hole in the starboard wing. The Oerlikon shell had gone through the mid-section, luckily missing the fuel-tanks, skidded off a spar cap and emerged on the upper surface of the wing.

Bob suggested he should check things a little more closely but the Frenchman waved that suggestion aside. So Bob suggested he would smooth out the edges of the hole and cover it by "cherry" rivetting a metal patch on it. The Frenchman thought that was going too far. He said, 'Get ze snips and ze fabric and ze dope. Zat will be okay.'

Bob said, 'Zat is a beeg 'ole.'

'Mais non,' said the Frenchman. 'In ze war I fly ze DC3 wiz ole in wing zis beeg!' he held his arms to indicate a three foot circle.

So Bob did as he said, gave the fabric a couple of hefty coats of dope, and off the little man went to France.

'He came back a month or two later,' Bob told me, 'and brought a big bottle of cognac. He presented it to me saying, 'For you, mon ami, ze ver best cognac.'

It was a smooth brew but I only got to drink half—someone swiped the rest.'

Bob had a nail-biting experience on the day the Karens surrounded Mingaladon and blocked the Prome Road so that the staff could not return to the mess. A little advance warning had enabled them to fly most of the aircraft out to Dan Muang airport at Bangkok, but Cathay Pacific still had one DC3 on the tarmac, needing an engine change. Johnnie Riordan had brought it in with a prop feathered, and it proved to have lost a master rod bearing. Bob Smith, Eric Aylward, a guy named Jacobs and a couple of others had stayed to work on it.

Despite an unearthly silence they knew the Karens were biding their time and would soon overrun the field, and consequently they made rapid progress. They estimated an end to the job soon after dark, when all they would have to do would be replace the cowls, make a quick run-up, get Riordan, who was in the RAF Mission headquarters across the strip, and take off for Bangkok. Smithy and Eric went across to the Palace of Germs to bring back something to eat, but all the staff there had scuttled off in advance of trouble. Food was on the table and, more importantly, the bar had been left wide open. They filled a big cardboard box with food and loaded a swag of grog into the buckets in which Moultrie kept his crushed ice. The group had something of a banquet under the aircraft wing and soon didn't give a damn when the Karens would come or how many.

They finished the job in the dark, slipping cardboard tubes over their electric torches to restrict the spread of light. They were making good progress when suddenly a barrage of shells whined overhead and crumped just to the rear of the civilian hangar. The barrage was repeated at ten-minute intervals, and with each explosion the racing hands would increase their tempo. Then a star-shell lit up the whole area as bright as day, finally floating to earth about ten yards from the DC3. They decided enough was enough and ran for the shelter of the paddy-fields across the runway. They had a front-row view of the bombardment from between the waving stalks of rice, and slept there that night. Eric Aylward wanted them to sneak back and fly the DC3 away. He didn't care about its having no cowls or having had no run-up; he just wanted to take it out. Smithy asked who would fly the thing and Eric said, 'Well, Smithy, you keep telling us you can fly, so you fly the bloody thing.' Smithy could fly, but he had never handled anything the size of the DC3, so they stayed where they were.

Just before dawn some Karens who had occupied the airfield under cover of the dark went over and knocked on the door of the Air Force hangar. Suddenly dozens of figures jumped from windows and dashed across the runway, changing uniforms to civvie clothes on the run. The Karens doubled up with laughter, and when the last courageous defender had disappeared they proceeded to smash the controls and bayonet the fuel tanks of the Airspeed Oxfords.

'It surprised me that they did not burn those Air Force aeroplanes,' Bob commented. 'Later, when they were repaired, they took part in the final defeat of the rebels. The VHF radio sets were all they removed, and with these they established a good communication network from their headquarters at Toungoo.'

Considering its extent the shelling did very little damage. It flattened the International Aeradio premises and added a few more shrapnel scars to Cathay

Pacific's already well-peppered hangar.

'The Aeradio fellows did a great job and it was a pity they had to lose everything,' Bob said. 'Those shells would have done a great service if they'd dropped a few yards short and eliminated the Palace of Germs.'

The ground engineers are my favourite people. They can handle the most unlikely situation. That a particular solution to a problem has never been used before means nothing to these efficient men whose ambition is to outsmart all the mechanical mischief which that inanimate collection of metal we call an aircraft can achieve.

An accident occured on the up-country airstrip at Bhamo near the Chinese border in Upper Burma. The date was June 5, 1949, the aircraft VR-HDB, the pilot Morrie Lothian and the cause, pilot error brought about by his pansophical attitude.

Standing instructions state that when a captain flies an aircraft without a first officer he must start the starboard engine first, and to fully observe the start he must occupy the right-hand pilot seat. When that engine is properly stabilized he resumes his normal seat and starts the port engine. These first-class procedures eliminate any problems arising during the start sequence.

Morrie had ignored these procedures, and when a worried radio officer tried to draw his attention to an abnormality—that he was choking from a vast volume of smoke which had invaded his small alcove just to the pilot's rear—Morrie told him to keep his advice to himself until it was sought.

Morrie then taxied the now merrily burning aircraft the full length of the runway, turned into wind, and presumably made the mandatory magneto check. Just as he was about to commence the takeoff run, the starbord engine fell off. The sequence of the repairs Eric Aylward carried out, with the capable assistance of Bob Smith was of such signal interest that it brought them some minor fame throughout the aircraft engineering industry. Ted Amor, chief technical officer of the Burma DCA, kept a wary eye on the operation.

The prime problem was transporting a replacement wing to Bhamo. It would have to be air-freighted for there was no surface transport, and once it was there, what could they do for the necessary installation equipmen? The burnt-out engine was no problem. A replacement could easily be ferried there in another aircraft, and, as with the spare wing, one was available in Rangoon. The nacelle which supported the engine was so seriously damaged Eric had to proceed to Cathay Pacific's aerodrome dump in Manila to procure a replacement.

Trans-Asiatic Airlines owned the Mingaladon wing which was still attached to the DC3 which Pete Holmes had ground-looped after a loss of hydraulic pressure, with such serious results that the aircraft had to be considered a write-off. It was Siamese registered, HS-TAI80, and Dallas Cederberg was directing the fortunes of Trans-Asiatic at that time. There was some poetic justice in the transaction in which de Kantzow bought the wing. Just a couple of months before Cederberg had needed a wing himself, and Syd had really hammered him over the price. Cederberg hammered Syd in his turn.

As Eric told me the story one of his main problems was devising a method of transporting the wing to Bhamo. 'This was time-consuming, and naturally Cathay Pacific had no intention of grounding one of its high-earning serviceable aircraft while I tried various methods of tie-down. I appreciated their attitude but when they kept at me to get that aircraft at Bhamo into a serviceable state I was in a quandary. Then I got the idea that by careful jacking I could get enough clearance on Cederberg's wreck to use it as my example for the required form-work. With Bob Smith, who is a first-class welder, we devised a sling and suitable brackets which we then transferred to VR-HEN, and soon had everything ready for the rescue operation.

'We were about to leave when Ted Amor arrived. He demanded to know our centre of gravity and when I replied that I hadn't a clue he nearly had a cardiac arrest. When he recovered his breath he told us we couldn't take off until we had found it. Bob is a wizard with figures, the written ones. He grabbed the form Ted Amor was waving in my face and quickly calculated a value which completely mystified Ted, but he grudgingly agreed that Bob had indeed found the elusive centre of gravity.

'The flight to Bhamo was without incident. Jimmy Harper of Douglas piloted and found the additional drag and consequent loss of speed almost non-existent. I think we lost about seven knots and needed only a little more elevator trim than usual.

'There was no crane at Bhamo, but they did have a thirty-ton gantry so powerful it could lift a house, no trouble, but it was quite unsuitable for the delicate operation of matching bolt-hole to bolt-hole at the wing and fuselage. The language problem also reared its head. When I realised I just wasn't getting anywhere I just threw up my hands in disgust and retired to an old shed at the edge of the strip. The way we were approaching the installation could only result in pushing the wing through the fuselage, or at least breaking this hard-won wing to pieces.

'Everything was pretty quiet at the aeroplane. I could hear some chattering and a bit of squeaking but nothing to tell me they were getting on with the job. Then the leading hand came round a corner and as I was about to tell him I hadn't thought out a solution he spoke up:

' "It's all right, master, the wing's on. It fits like a glove." '

This repair had a lot of similarities to the 'DC2½' repair made famous during the war years. During a Japanese air raid on Chungking a DC3 landed at a small outpost called Suifu. On their way back to base the Japanese passed over Suifu and, noting the aircraft, dropped bombs, blowing off one wing. No replacement was available, but there was a wing for a DC2 in Hong Kong and it was strapped beneath another DC3 and flown to Suifu. Despite the wisdom of experts who proved conclusively that a plane with such unmatched wings was an aerodynamic impossibility, a Polish-American engineer, Sol Soldinsky installed it. The aircraft, which now had one wing five feet shorter than the other, seemed to glory in its deformity, and became known in the trade as 'the DC2½'.

Ken Begg served two periods with Cathay Pacific, from December 1947 to February 1949 and again from September 1950 until October 1951. At no time

June 5, 1949 ... Bhamo, Burma
CPA's Douglas DC3 (C47A) VR-HDB showing damaged starboard engine.

did the management honour him with a command; I don't know why not, and the loss was probably theirs as I always found him a very earnest and a very competent operator. He was a Sydney-sider, 22 years old. Between these periods he was flying Norseman XY-ABB, a single-engined aircraft which constituted the entire fleet of Sky Freighters. This was the Norseman which had come to our rescue when Riordan and I were shot down by insurgents at Bassein.

On August 17, Ken was freighting a load of four 44-gallon drums of aviation fuel to Meiktila. His engineer and co-pilot was Don Laskey and they carried one passenger, an Indian, Mr. A.C. Aboo. Cruising at 7000 feet, with the Irrawaddy visible to port, they were about ten miles south of Taungdwingy when the engine began to splutter and to maintain cruising speed Ken began a gradual descent. This increased as the engine failed to produce much power. Laskey and Aboo made a valiant attempt to jettison the fuel drums but because of their weight were barely moving them. About three miles from Taungdwingy they were so dangerously low that Ken picked out the best spot he could see ahead and made an emergency landing—successfully, though later he learned he had skipped across at least two ditches hidden in the long grass. The only damage was a light dent in one of the wheel spats.

All they had to do was sit tight and wait for rescue, as Ken had managed to get out an SOS which had been acknowledged. But half an hour later a motley group of men in rough uniforms surrounded the Norseman and told its complement they were now the guests of the local Karen leader. While this was going on two aircraft flew low overhead, the crews waving frantically. The Karens took little notice of the first one, but were irritated by the second which flew much lower, and they began to blaze at it with abandon. They stopped when Ken protested that they were civil aircraft answering an SOS.

Taken by truck to Prome they were interrogated briefly and then shown to a small house in a compound surrounded by larger buildings where Karen officers were billeted. Here they met Bo Kun Zaw the Karen area commander, a humorous individual who made friends with them. He apologised for inconvenience caused and told them he would send them on their way once he had a clearance from his superiors. This could take time, as he was not sure where the Central Democratic Front Headquarters was actually located, except that it was in Upper Burma.

Bored with a period of inactivity Ken suggested to Bo Kun Zaw that he organise a deer hunt. Bo thought this a splendid idea and soon they were trekking through the neighbourhood looking for deer. He bagged a large stag, but the others had fisherman's luck—wet butts and no fish. Putting them on parole, Bo then gave them permission to return and work on the Norseman. It had been dragged under a nearby copse which afforded effective camouflage. They soon had the engine purring like a kitten. Their misfortunes had stemmed from water-contaminated fuel and a dirty carburettor. During the morning of September 2 Bo Kun Zaw waved them off and they returned by a variety of Karen-arranged transports, trucks, buses, trishaws, to Rangoon. The Norseman was never seen nor heard of again.

My first recollection of Ken was of his accepting a bet of $US200 that he wouldn't take off his pants in the Peninsula Hotel lounge (in Hong Kong), leave them in full view and walk around to his accommodation in the old Melbourne Private Hotel in Mody Road, Kowloon. Without hesitation he slipped off his daks, threw them over the ornate chandelier and walked to the Melbourne. On his way he threaded through the vast throng which frequents the area which never sleeps. It included the regular sprinkling of police, but not a soul questioned a European strolling in his underwear. I doubt whether anyone gave him a second glance.

The mid-morning of September 13, 1949 found me sitting in the basher-hut which passed for Operations Room, passenger check-in and restaurant at Anisakan airstrip. I was chewing the fat with Captain J Brown of Indonesian Airways and Johnny Riordan and his radio officer D.E. Smith, who constituted the crew of the Cathay Pacific DC3 that stood nearby with 'Air Burma' emblazoned on the fuselage. And I was drinking coffee, which shows that I was becoming acclimatized to a country where any unbottled fluid intake must be suspect—what an adventurous person I had become! My courage knew no bounds!

John and his radio officer left the group, and shortly I went out to 'drain the spuds', as the saying went. It was thus I missed seeing the accident which brought serious trouble to a respected pal. During my brief absence Riordan commenced the takeoff which terminated in a write-off for VR-HDW. By the time I returned the die had been cast, the dust was settling, the eye-witnesses had decided that the accident was being handled by experts and were drifting back to their seats in the restaurant. Soon after, John Riordan slunk in, and in a small, dejected voice announced that he had just smashed up an aeroplane.

His report to Captain Jim Harper, Cathay Pacific's Burma Operations Manager was without embellishment. To his credit John made no attempt to flannel himself out of the situation and merely gave the facts in his straightforward way.

Anisakan strip runs approximately north to south on a plateau of some 3500 feet above sea-level, and is subject to frequent wind shifts. For instance, the wind at takeoff could be showing a speed of 15 knots from the south, halfway into the run it could fall off to a dead calm, and then suddenly pick up to 15 knots again but this time from the north.

This occurred during John's takeoff. He was more than halfway into the run before he realised his aeroplane could never get airborne in the distance which remained ahead. He cut the power, stood on the brakes, and unfortunately just ran out of prepared strip, tearing the aircraft to pieces as he ploughed through some hefty tree-stumps which profusely dotted the clearway. His exit from Burma followed closely on this Anisakan accident, and thereafter he dropped from sight.

Jim Harper was another of the unlucky ones, but his misfortune was in an altogether different class. On the brilliantly beautiful morning of November 23 he was comfortably strapped into his seat listening contentedly to the smooth running of the R 1830/92 engines of his DC3. At 7000 feet he was about to pass over Thazi on his way to Anisakan. His euphoria fled with an agonizing stab of pain as a bullet entered the sole of his foot, a pain immediately augmented by the intolerable agony of another projectile entering his bowels. He slumped unconscious over his controls, in no way disturbing the operation of the automatic pilot. His aircraft continued on its steady path.

Consciousness returned briefly from time to time, and during one of his moments of rationality he instructed his radio offficer, who had miraculously escaped the insurgent ground fire, not to move him and to keep headed for Anisakan. At the time he issued those orders he had no idea what he would do when he arrived over his destination, but he summoned the will-power to land his aircraft safely. His radio officer had only to brake the aircraft to a halt. Jim made a complete recovery, but the pain of post-surgery must have taxed even his indomitable spirit to its limits.

CPA's Douglas C47B ... VR-HDW

Entered CX Service — 1947, taken over by B. & S. (CPA) Ltd., July 1, 1948 for HK$267,800. It was on charter to Air Burma and written off by Capt. John Riordan at Anisakan Airstrip, Burma, during a take-off accident. This was September 13, 1949.

CHAPTER TEN
BUDDAH RELICS

One race there is of men, one of gods,
but from one mother we both draw our breath.

Nemean Odes . . . Pindar

On March 4 and 6, 1950 I took part in a charter of grave responsibility. In addition to the Union of Burma Airways, Cathay Pacific and Air Burma were involved. My flights were on Dove DH 104 aircraft; the other companies used DC3s. Prime Minister Thakin Nu had convinced the Government of Ceylon that Burmese should have the opportunity to worship in the presence of the sacred relics of the Lord Buddha, which had not left Ceylon for more than 2000 years. These relics were then, and still are, housed in the famous Temple of the Tooth at Kandy, and are actually pieces of bone taken from Buddha's funeral pyre at Gaya in Northern India 2500 years ago.

Britain had made a cruiser available to transport the relics to Burma, and I was given the great honour of flying them from Rangoon to Mergui in the south, and then two days later back north as far as Tavoy. Cathay Pacific and Air Burma's part in this world-watched event was to transport a team of twenty Kandyan dancers and drummers who, each day at 11 a.m. performed the customary ceremonies of reverence which had been maintained for 2000 years, offering tokens of water and flowers. The dancers possessed such virility and grace that the great Anna Pavlova had rated Kandyan dancing more highly than anything else in the world.

At both Mergui and Tavoy the crush of worshippers who came to greet the sacred relics was outside anything in my experience, or my imagination. The reverence they displayed towards that golden-domed container was deep, pervasive, unbelievable and I, being its custodian, was looked upon with something akin to hero-worship and rapture. I felt the responsibility. I considered all manner of calamitous accidents. I shook for days afterwards, for much of the flight was across the restless Gulf of Martaban, and the loss of the aircraft would have entailed the loss, not only of the sacred relics which were beyond price, but also the co-operation and goodwill of millions of followers of Buddha.

The morning after found me arriving in the circuit at Myaungmya and pulling off one of the smoothest landings I have ever made in the Dove. The only fly in ointment was that I had forgotten to put down the undercarriage. True, I was tired, and hadn't felt well for days, but those excuses are not really valid, for I should not have been flying if I were not in top class condition. The only saving factor was that the undercarriage warning horn was later found to be unserviceable.

The company reprimanded me through official correspondence and demoted me half a bar from captain to junior captain. I thought this treatment more than generous, especially as I was a liar when I said I had indeed put the gear down. I knew I hadn't, and going to the hearing that morning I had intended to admit my fault, but on the way met an old pal from Air Burma, Captain Woody Forte, who told me to admit nothing. I wrongly allowed his advice to override my honesty.

It was at this time that I grew a RAAF handlebar moustache, which I hoped would disguise my feelings, if not my face. I was soon forgiven and restored to full rank, and realising that I had no further use for the disguise dispensed with it.

I had been off the line for slightly less than a month, but prior to being turned loose on an innocent, unsuspecting public, I was given a good check-out on all Dove procedures by Chief Pilot Kit Trimble. Kit returned to England soon after, and was replaced by a Frenchman of repulsive girth who soon gained the rather accurate appelation 'Mudguts'. Captain R.P. Tissandier was to hold the position of Chief Pilot/Operations Manager for probably the longest of all, packing up in August 1952.

To confirm their forgiveness of my transgression the company entrusted me in May 1950 with the task of bringing the President of the Union of Burma back to Rangoon from Anisakan, along with his lady and their five children. I found their faith in my ability somewhat strange as my recent non-wheel landing was not yet forgotten and my shares not yet on the rise. Further reflection even interposed the unwelcome thought that perchance an unscrupulous aspirate for the Presidency had hoped that under my care, there might be a chance for the office to be declared vacant sooner! But whatever the reason I must have impressed His Excellency with my capabilities, for two years later, on December 8, 1952, President Sao Shwe Thaik made a particular request that I should pilot him back from Mandalay. Each of these flights was without incident and the atmosphere in the Dove was casual and friendly. What impressed me most was the punctuality of an authentic VIP as compared with the upstart. The real one never keeps others waiting regardless of his station in life, and if his order of travel details a precise departure time he is always ready on the dot.

On the last day of March 1953 my duty took me to a narrow airstrip on the east bank of the Chindwin River. What passed for a landing strip was surrounded by a ramshackle collection of hovels, a poverty-striken village with the romantic name of Singkaling Hkamti. It is almost 600 miles north of Rangoon and barely thirty miles from the Indian border.

Aboard my DC3 was the Burmese Prime Minister U Thakin Nu, and as we left the aircraft my crew and I were requested to stand in line and be introduced to the Indian Prime Minister Jawaharlal Nehru. These two great statesmen were meeting at this remote point to discuss high-level politics. I must have impressed the Indian Prime Minister for he invited me to be an observer during the progress of the talks.

I rubbed my hands in anticipation of being in on the ground floor of such a momentous occasion, but decided later it was a waste of fuel and time. Nothing

March 1950
R/O Hla Pe and one of the Kandyan Dancers. At Tavoy, Burma, after I flew the
sacred relics of the Lord Buddha to that southern city

30th May 1950
Junior Captain Charles 'Chic' Eather hides behind the
RAAF handlebar moustache following 'finger trouble'
at Myaungmyu, Burma.

173

of any importance was discussed and the Prime Ministers seemed not to have pursued even an intelligent conversation. Each sat directly opposite the other and their fixed grins seemed to endanger their ears. Only these prevented the grins from going right round their heads. My main recollection of the whole event was that each had beautiful teeth and was a credit to his dentist.

The Sabbath is supposed to be a day of rest, but in the field of transport it is perhaps the busiest of the week, for some poor devils have to transport the masses pursuing their day of rest, or in a more recent cliche, their 'leisure time'. This accounts in part for the top salary a pilot draws, to the utter disgust of his fellow man. I think he earns it, for there can be few professions which made comparable demands. You find him at 30,000 feet encased in a giant shining metal canister, subject to the whims of nature not only through the night when others are comfortable in the pit, but on designated holidays on business as usual. He is subject to a probing search by medical examiners every six months, his technical knowledge is checked at least once a year to the same high standards as qualify the flight engineer, and his instrument rating (which possesses certain characteristics of the Spanish Inquisition) may come his way sometimes twice in thirteen months. Other professional people such as lawyers and doctors are never required to pass such recurrent checks on their ability once they have gained their licence to practice.

The pilot lives his life in a suitcase. His odd uncertain hours make it practically impossible to arrange a social life, he is separated from his family for long periods, he goes from the extreme of an ice-blanketed runway to one distorted by heat mirage all within a couple of hours, his system must be robust enough for him to eat and drink from questionable sources, and he is forced to sleep when his body is awake. With all this he must retain an understanding of his fellow man who, as a passenger in his quest to guzzle as much of the free grog as he possibly can in the shortest time he can, makes himself a damned nuisance to other passengers and useless to himself should an emergency arise.

The customs, immigration and health authorities do little to foster amity between themselves and the crew and thinly veil their belief that the crew is responsible for them not being at home in comfortable beds. All this makes a pretty formidable list.

Occasionally I would be given interesting charters which helped to break the monotony of regular schedule flying. Some were happy assignments; others not so pleasant. May 30, 1950 found me flying a sacred Bo-tree from Rangoon to Bassein. According to Buddhist tradition this was the type of tree under which the Buddha attained enlightenment. That original bodhi-tree grew at Uruvela on the bank of the Neranjara River near modern Gaya in India. The crowds which came to pay homage to this symbol of Buddhism were only slightly smaller than that which had come to meet the sacred relics I flew to Mergui and Tavoy two months before.

I still recall my roar of alarm when I found one particular group of passengers with faces beaming and hands industriously fanning a glowing charcoal brazier, preparing their afternoon meal in the aisle of my DC3. Their fire was

July 1950
General (later President) Thado Thiri Thudhamma Ne Win occupies the co-pilot seat of XY-ACK one of the DC3's taken over from Air Burma.

right above the centre section and hundreds of gallons of high-octane fuel.

In the forenoon of August 14 I was assigned a special flight taking several VIPs and a group of newspapermen to Moulmein to view the dead body of a Karen leader. The naked body was hung on a butcher's meathook. The photographers scuttled like rats round this disgusting exhibition of barbaric grandstanding, all bent on getting the best angle. There hung the mortal remains of Bo Kün Zaw, Ken Begg's flamboyant captor, once boisterous, co-operative and friendly.

Later that year radio officer Lewis and I searched all day for an overdue ship in the Sittang-Martaban area which is between Moulmein and the coast east of Rangoon, in effect covering the northern portion of the Gulf of Martaban. Nothing was ever heard of that ship again. Perhaps Burma can be credited with having its own Devils Triangle like the one off Bermuda.

An incident that took a life began with a DC3, a detachment of troops and a jeep. Pre-flight checks had indicated the jeep to be securely tied down in the cargo space with worn but serviceable ropes, but the weather worsened as the flight progressed and the lashings frayed and snapped.

Immediately in my cockpit I felt the aircraft begin porpoising and heard violent crashes in the cabin. I raced back to find the jeep slamming backwards and forwards and the soldiers doing their best to keep out of its careering path.
One man has not been fleet of foot, and now lay in a pool of blood which had gushed from his mouth. The jeep had crushed him against the rear bulkhead. I screamed to the men to steady the juggernaut which they managed to do while air was let out of one tyre. This stopped its rampage until it was once more fully secured.

Late in 1950 General Ne Win decided that his army had cleared the insurgents far enough from the 'three R's' (road, rail and river) to make them useable. Surface transport could do the job that had been performed by costly airfreight. Air Burma's proprietor, Bo Setkya, began winding up the show and asked Harry de Leuil to find a sale for his aircraft. Harry explained that this type of aircraft was becoming obsolete, that it could take a considerable time to find suitable buyers, and that those buyers would expect to name their own price.

'These statements made him quite unhappy,' Harry recalled recently, 'so I made him an alternative suggestion that he might like to approach the War Office with a blanket offer of all the aircraft and spares for a price he considered satisfactory.

'I reminded him that success or failure depended on convincing the General that it would boost his prestige as Supreme Commander of the Burmese Defence Forces if he could add a ready-made transport wing to his Air Force. This proved a relatively simply task, and as Ne Win was the real power behind the throne the Government readily acceded to the "suggestion". There followed a period of intense inspection and testing by the Burmese Air Force, and then in December Air Burma's equipment passed to Air Force control!'

Despite my love of the country and its people I resigned from the Union of Burma Airways towards the end of 1951, a move that had been necessitated by my wife's slow convalescence in Burma's unsuitable climate. Joyce's illness had been serious and for months she lay at death's door. There were no health benefits for the individual in Burma and all our savings were dissipated. On November 2 we caught a BOAC Argonaut out of Mingaladon, bound for Sydney.

Eric McIllree came to my aid the very next day, offering me a job with his Amphibious Airways, a New Guinea company which operated two Avro-Ansons and two Walrus amphibians. When I arrived in the country I found all personnel giving of their best, but there was a tendency to cut Civil Aviation corners.

Early one morning both Ansons departed Rabaul for Wewak, with technical landings planned for Hoskins, on the southeast coast of New Britain, and Madang. I was commanding one Anson with a full load of ten natives and a white plantation manager who occupied the right-hand pilot seat. The other aircraft, on paper, was under the command of a Dutchman named Jan Patcha, with Eric accompanying him ostensibly as a passenger but really in charge because of Jan's inexperience with the type. This was the first corner we were cutting, as Eric had no Commercial Licence. The next pruning was that we had stated that our intention was to land at Hoskins to pick up fuel from our private cache located there at high cost. We had decided we would not actually land there, and had prepared a series of erroneous position reports. To achieve this economy we left Rabaul overloaded with full fuel tanks.

As the flight progressed these things preyed on my conscience and I suddenly felt quite ill. I radioed Eric that I wasn't feeling well and intended landing at Hoskins. This we did, and after discussion decided that Jan would act as my co-pilot and Eric would take the other Anson on by himself. He realised he didn't have the required qualification but figured there was little chance he would be caught.

For some unaccountable reason two departmental officers were awaiting our arrival at Wewak, the upshot being that our licences were suspended: Eric's for flying for 'hire or reward' without licencing authority, and mine due to illness. My licence was subsequently revalidated after an interview with a well-known Sydney psychiatrist. Eric's was returned to him after a severe reprimand.

Eric died in September 1973, chief of the massive Avis Rent-a-Car empire. He was ever a good friend, and I appreciated the two short periods I worked for him.

Back in Sydney Joyce was still in a convalescent home, expenses were mounting at a greater rate than my earnings, so in March 1952 I returned to the Union of Burma Airways where I threw myself into my job with increased vigor. Union of Burma rosters for the next couple of years showed a fairly stabilised pilot contingent mainly of Englishmen. Of these, Captain Alex Hare had the most interesting experience. On June 26, 1954 the DC3 he was commanding was skyjacked by a trio of bomb- and pistol-packing dissidents who forced him to land on a beach on the Arakanese coast and there joyously relieved him of his custodial worries by removing 200,000 pounds sterling in currency. Their elevation to affluence was short-lived; for they themselves were almost immediately nobbled and murdered by another equally joyous band of brigands.

On my earlier tour I had become acquainted with Lance Rutherford when I was initiated into the Brotherhood of Free Masons in the Lodge Pegu, which operated under the English constitution in Burma and was numbered 3330. The date of my initiation was July 25, 1951. Lance was the general manager and major shareholder of the giant pharmacy empire of E.M. de Souza and Company Limited. He was a terribly reserved character and quite incapable of easy friendship, but for some unaccountable reason he and I clicked almost from our first handshake, and became close friends. He shared with me my interest in the occult, and during one of our early chats he calmly made a statement I have reason never to forget. Of that, more later. Like myself he adored Burma. He spent every leave he could arrange trekking through the most inaccessible terrain of its northern reaches.

On one such jaunt he teamed up with Frank and Jean Kingdon-Ward. Kingdon-Ward has written two books about the wilder reaches of Upper Burma, *Return to the Irrawaddy* and *Burma's Icy Mountains.* In the former he mentions Lance frequently throughout the first fifty pages, most of these references being disparaging—a great pity, for Lance held this man in the highest regard. On New Year's Day in 1953 Jean Kingdon-Ward and Lance boarded my DC3, XY-ACO of the UBA fleet at Myitkyina, and I flew them to Putao, which the British call Port Hertz. It snuggles in the most northerly reaches of Burma, peopled by a conglomeration of hill-dwellers, loosely termed Kachins. The operations department of UBA had given me strict instructions that I must not attempt the flight unless I could make it completely in the clear, and that I must abandon it if when I reached the hamlet of Sumprabum I could not see Putao. But that day the visibility throughout the brief 45-minute flight was more than a hundred miles, and we were treated to an astonishing panorama of 'Burma's Icy Mountains' with The Triangle so vividly clear I felt I could see a mosquito winking his eye.

The Burma political situation now began to disturb me. Although the country had a civilian democratic form of government the rumblings from General Ne Win's armed services, which he controlled with almost complete autocracy, became more audible. I discussed my fears with several colleagues, but was assured that in this land of waving palms, golden pagodas and happy folk, nothing of the sort could happen. I felt that so many well-informed and astute people could not be wrong and for a short while I put my fears behind me, but significant event followed significant event, and when Captain Pat Moore, then Operations Manager for Cathay Pacific, offered me a first officer position I grasped the opportunity with both hands and feet. In June 1953 I returned to the fold and there I stayed.

Though it took longer than I thought my native cunning proved more value to me than my well-informed advisors. On the morning of March 2, 1962 a young Karen nurse, hearing a rumble that rose in intensity, left the cool interior of the Prome Road Nursing Home at the 5½ mile mark on Kokine Lakes and joined her Matron, Sister Heather Ba Than. Together they watched as tank after tank roared past on their way to Rangoon to take over the country in a coup d'etat.

The palms continued to wave, the pagodas glowed golden, but the people smiled no more.

U Sway Tin, UBA's general manager, forwarded me a newspaper cutting which reported Lance Rutherford's death. He also wrote: 'It was a good thing in a way that Dr Rutherford did not live to see all that he had built up taken away in the mass nationalisation of business houses throughout the country.

'On the morning of March 19, 1964 there was unusual activity among the army personnel, but at that time there seemed little signifcance. A few minutes past noon the army convoys moved into the city and began dropping off small groups of uniformed men at each street corner. These men then paired off and marched into the surrounding shops and stores. A short time later officers arrived in well-kept army transports and called at each of the commercial houses, one after another. On being presented to the owner or manager the officer would announce that the firm or company had been nationalised.

'Dr Rutherford's company of De Souza was one of the first places visited. A couple of minutes after the officer had made his proclamation a truck rolled up and the soldiers from it erected a large green-coloured signboard bearing the words in Burmese: 'People's Shop Number 9999'. All the other shops and businesses were also placarded as being the property of the State, but each had a smaller number than the De Souza establishment.'

The terrifying statement that Lance had confided to me was that he knew the exact date he would die and how it would happen. He added, 'Although my death will be accepted as suicide, I will in fact be killed'. True to his forecast the Nation newspaper reported November 23, 1963 as the day he died 'a suspected suicide . . . The .22 bullet which ended his life pierced his right underarm and emerged from his mouth.' Suicide?

The most significant episode in my Burma experience began when I was scheduled for an early Bassein flight on December 22, 1950, and reached its climax on the grimy sidewalks of New York City almost 25 years later, as I approached my final year before retirement from Cathay Pacific. When I arrived at the airfield the despatcher told me the service was delayed indefinitely, and even if it had been on the ramp, the entire Irrawaddy delta was fogbound, with little improvement expected before early afternoon.

Having given me all this 'good news' the despatcher off-handedly mentioned I was to telephone Chief Pilot Tissandier. To reach the phone I had to pass round a corner of the operations room where I saw a Catholic priest gingerly nursing an object carefully wrapped in a blanket. As his eyes met mine they lit up and the worry creases on his brow ironed out. I thought to myself, 'What a friendly bloke!'

Captain Tissandier instructed me to leave at once on a special charter flight in DC XY-ACO for Bassein, and when I raised the question as to the extent of the fog coverage he airily told me 'Give it a go'. I collected my priest and his hand luggage and was soon on my way.

As we crossed the Schwelaung, a tributary of the Irrawaddy, wispy ribbons of fog began to thicken, and when our 45-minute flight brought us over Bassein, true to forecast the ground had disappeared beneath a smooth carpet of milky cotton-wool with only the topmost branches of occasional higher trees thrusting through. Noting that our 1500 foot altitude was clear of all fog I set the auto-pilot to take us on a wide unhurried circle, unbuckled my safety harness, instructed Van Kett, my radio officer, to keep his eyes peeled and went back to the cabin.

The priest was kneeling before a beautiful slender statue of Our Lady of Fatima. I caught my breath and successfully stifled a burst of racuous mirth which was not directed against the priest in supplication before his charge, but at the way he had braced her with pillows and circumposed her lovely outline with an incongruously worldly seat-belt. In a few moments he completed his devotions and I told him I thought a landing at the delta city would be out of the question for a few hours, but with a faint smile he replied that our landing would not be delayed.

I made my unhurried way back to my sanctum dwelling on his words with some derision. They reminded me of the Aussie's verbal placebo: 'She'll be all right mate!' Comfortable in my seat once more I looked down and saw some clearance with, at first, ghostly outlines. Then suddenly the landing strip was clear before my astonished eyes.

The northerly approach to Bassein was down a fairly steep gradient in a direction I had not used before, but the landing presented no problem. Taxi-ing back I turned the aircraft to face south for takeoff and cut the port engine. I then hurried back and fixed the steps for the priest and his charge. As I opened the door I heard the most etheral, melodious singing. Thousands of people were raising their voices in praise of the Most High.

As the priest negotiated those tricky steps his features were composed, but did I intercept a devilish twinkle in his eyes? They seemed to say, 'Didn't I tell you?' Giving the reception committee a few minutes to clear the area I restarted the port engine and took off for Mingaladon. As we paralleled the runway I saw with amazement that the fog had rolled in to cover the airstrip again, thicker than ever.

The Burmese *Sunday Nation* had of course no knowledge of my confused thoughts. Its report merely stated:

> 'Hovering over the town for half an hour, the special UBA plane carrying the statue of Our Lady of Fatima was unable to make an immediate landing owing to heavy fog which surrounded the airport and vicinity. When the pilot, seeing a lift in the fog, nosed the aircraft down on to the runway the unusually large crowd, including government and civil officials, in harmonious chorus sang a hymn to the accompaniement of a band.'

I found it a heart-warming experience, a demonstration of faith which seemed to be directed right at me, and I was impressed—but immediately thrust it to the back recesses of a mind programmed for more mundane matters. But years later, on another continent, a sequel to this long-forgotten incident stopped me in my tracks, and since then a day has rarely passed without my thoughts dwelling at least fleetingly on my greatest experience.

The small parish of Fatima in the Portuguese diocese of Leiria nestles in the foothills of the Sierra d'Aire, almost in the geographic centre of Portugal about eighty miles north of Lisbon. Legend tells us it derived its name from an Arab princess converted to Catholicism during the brutal Moorish wars. The Dominican friars had preached there with much success, and Portugal earned the title of Terra de Santa Maria—the Land of Mary—by its devotion to the Mother of God.

On May 13, 1917 three half-pint shepherds of Fatima were tending their parents' sheep in the Cova da Iria, about a mile from the village. At noon Lucia de Santos, aged ten, and her cousins Francisco and Jacinta Marto, brother and sister aged nine and seven, ate a scanty lunch. They were startled by a flash of lightning from a cloudless sky. A second flash followed, and then they saw a most beautiful lady, surrounded by a brilliant halo, hovering over a green oak a short distance to their right. Their first impulse was to flee, but the Lady beckoned, and in a sweet voice bade them approach, saying they would not be harmed. When they did, the Lady told them who she was and what she wanted them to do. What she told them has remained a closely guarded secret, but the site has become a place of pilgrimage.

July 29, 1974 was a bright, balmy day, and like thousands of others my wife Judy, son Edward and I were happy just to be alive. Our steps had taken us along New York's Seventh Avenue in the vicinity of Pennsylvania Station and Madison Square Garden. A chore for one of Judy's friends had brought us to that particular area, while our reason for being in the States was for me to ferry a Boeing 707 from Minneapolis to Hong Kong, Cathay Pacific's twelfth and final purchase from North West Airlines.

Our rubber-necking progress took in the bustle of mid-town Manhattan and included stops while I composed scenes for my 8 mm movie-camera. Suddenly a wizened old lady sidled up to me and, looking me straight in the eye, said, 'Our Lady of Fatima is gracing the altar at St John's Church just around the corner, and you should see her once more'. Judy was a witness to this exchange. She told me later that my face went completely white.

As kindly as possible we explained to this female leprechaun that we had a message to do for a friend, but we assured her that as soon as it was done we would certainly go along.

We completed our assignment, returned to the main street and were immediately joined by our guide, who convoyed us to the Roman Catholic Church in 30th Street. It was packed with people but we had an unobstructed view from perhaps forty feet away. As my eyes met those of Our Lady, a soft voice breathed in my ear, 'You do remember'. I turned my head to reply. No one was there.

CHAPTER ELEVEN
THE RED TIDE

They were going to look at war, the red animal—war,
the blood-swollen god.

The Red Badge of Courage—Stephen Crane

Charter operations of Cathay Pacific throughout 1949 were heavily influenced by the Communists' sweeping advance over mainland China. Hangchow, Shanghai, Canton, Chungking (the Nationalist capital) Cheng-tu (the temporary capital) and Kunming all fell to the Red advance between May and December, an incredibly short time considering the vast distances. In the terribly confused situation, the Generalissimo Chiang Kai-Shek would continue to establish headquarters further back. Practically all the charter companies in Southeast Asia were now to be found at Kai Tak, using the British Colony as a springboard to jump into the beleaguered Chinese cities on a variety of missions, mainly the evacuation of personnel.

On April 29, 1949 Bob Donovan made the first night arrival at Kai Tak since the war. He had been to Shanghai in connection with its evacuation and for his guidance fires were lit on the peaks and on a coastal landmark, as well as on the short approach to the runway. He landed without difficulty.

John Moxham and Ken Wolinski had left Shanghai before him. They encountered a severe line-squall near Foochow and turned inland to avoid it, while Donovan, coming soon after, had decided to press on. They were unsuccessful in getting out of the weather. As Ken Wolinski told it:

'A long way inland we still weren't getting anywhere. We finally just had to plough back through some of the worst stuff I've ever flown in. Suddenly, as from a bad dream, we were through, with a star-studded sky ahead and forked lightning behind. We couldn't see any gleam of horizon lights that would show us Kai Tak and our fuel gauges were the bare thickness of a needle from showing empty. We started to worry and were discussing our jettison priorities: first the passenger luggage, then the passengers, then the crew baggage and finally the crew, starting with me. This part didn't bring me on very much. Suddenly there were the lights of Hong Kong. We went through the southeast gap and thumped it on the deck.

'After we unloaded the passengers, Jackie Williams the ground engineer started up to taxi to the ground maintenance area and both engines cut out. We would never have got around again had there been a missed approach.

'It amuses me to look back from today, when we have every navigation aid on board and on the ground. I went up to Kunming for the evacuation there. All I had was a very old road map and an equally old DC3. The closer we got to Kunming the worse the weather got. The last half-hour I was getting iced up badly, but worse, the clouds were thickening and I had to have the cockpit panel lights on maximum though it was just past noon. There was no sign of a break in the overcast for us to get our bearings. About twenty miles before the estimated time of arrival on dead reckoning I heard a faint voice calling Kunming. It was Dave Lampard, of Hong Kong Airways. I called him up and said, "Dave, how the hell do you get into Kunming?" He gave me the let-down which went: "Go over the main beacon at 11,000 feet, then turn on 180 degrees and put down the gear and full flaps and descend as fast as you can. If, by 500 feet at the next beacon, near the runway, you don't see anything, climb like hell on such a bearing and pray." We got in by luck.'

The Kunming strip was at an altitude of 6,240 feet.

In November that year Bob flew the Chinese General Lee with his family to Jedda, probably the only Haj flight Cathay Pacific has ever made. Thirty years later he was flying Boeing 707's as Director of Flight Standard for Royal Jordanian Airways, 60 years old, and with 43 years of flying behind him.

'I believe I'm the only pre-war pilot still flying scheduled airlines, and possibly hold the record for most hours in that category,' he wrote me. 'My log-book total exceeds 31,000 hours—Jason Hazzard is the Australian leader with 37,000. I hope to be Number Two when I finish.'

Because the Nationalist troops were not being paid there were almost mass defections which the Generalissimo attempted to counter, again with the help of the charter companies. He airlifted boxes of silver Mexican dollars from Manila to Hong Kong, employing Cathay Pacific. From Hong Kong CATC trans-shipped them to various trouble spots. Woody Forte was the last pilot to fly into Cheng-tu on this mission, and by then the situation was highly dangerous, for the Communists were holding one side of the strip and firing blindly across the runway at the Kuomintang on the other side. Woody just had his loaders kick the boxes off and abandoned them at the side of the strip. As he tore off out of there he saw the Communists overrun the entire area. He managed to prevent another CATC aircraft, also loaded with silver coins, from putting down, and they both flew off to Kwangnan thirty miles to the northeast.

Kwangnan, the last important Nationalist air-base on the mainland, was itself swallowed by the Communist advance just three days after the fall of Cheng-tu, and more than eighty planes of CNAC and CATC based there were flown to Kai Tak, where they swelled the total of 'refugee' aircraft already scattered round the field's perimeter. Kai Tak was now literally bursting at the seams from the press of aircraft which arrived en masse during the first days of November.

Incidentally, another new arrival at this time was Cathay Pacific's first four-engined plane, a DC4 Skymaster it bought from KLM in September. In service with this Royal Dutch Airline it had been registered PH-TLO; on reaching Hong Kong it became VR-HEU. Captain John Presgrave, on loan from Australian National Airways and our own Chief Pilot Dick Hunt along with senior radio officer Mum Louttit constituted the very efficient ferry crew which brought it from Amsterdam. On Friday, September 23 it made its inaugural flight on the

Bangkok and Singapore route, carrying Frank Smith as second officer and Leo Callaghan flight engineer as well as the original ferry crew. On November 2, was the boss himself, Syd de Kantzow supplemented this star-studded crew, in inaugurating the Saigon route.

Throughout the flight Tom Bax, with most uncharacteristic control, merely sipped at his complementary drink and Frank Smith was heard to say the poor fellow must have been feeling poorly, but Tom possessed vital information that he had not shared with his colleagues, namely that Cathay Pacific's Saigon agents, Denis Freres d'Indo-Chine were hosting a cocktail reception that evening to celebrate the notable event, and if he overdid it too early he would miss out on an even better grade of grog at exactly the same price. The Skymaster carried 43 passengers with greater speed and comfort than the DC3's 28. This was the first of a planned two flights a week on Mondays and Fridays, with a stopover at Bangkok to permit the trans-shipment of passengers for Saigon.

On January 5, 1950 Cathay Pacific included in its schedule a route to Sandakan, in North Borneo, now called Sabah. It now reached from Hong Kong to cover Manila, Sandakan, Jesselton (now Kota Kinabalu) and Labuan, with the intention of extending to Kuching, the capital of Sarawak and the one-time home of the White Rajah Brooke and his famous family. Philip Blown was captain and his radio officer the indomitable but accident-prone John Fitzgerald.

The extensive press coverage on this route opening included one much-publicised picture of five loin-clothed, head-dressed Dyak chiefs against the incongruous background of the DC3. The chiefs were taken for a flight. Years later Fitz confided to me he had felt some uneasiness, particularly round the base of the skull, at having the Dyaks aboard, and the tingling sensation got worse as they circled the craggy, forbidden top of Borneo's highest mountain Kinabalu (13,455 feet), which is the home of the tapir, rhinoceros and orang-outang, and reputedly shelters the world's most exquisite orchids, alluringly beautiful and exasperatingly remote. The Dyaks were also agitated, no doubt because their ancestral homes had for centuries been sited on the slopes of that great mountain. The valuables treasured in each dwelling included the heads taken by their forefathers.

At this time the company was surviving something of a crisis caused primarily by the Colonial Office's vacillation in granting authorised schedule franchises. When these were granted in March 1950, nearly two years after the entry of the Butterfield and Swire interests, the company still had to acquire the direct Hong Kong to Singapore route. BOAC had been granted this but was doing precious little to exploit its potential; just the same it continued to resist its transfer to Cathay Pacific, apparently keeping it aside for a rainy day.

A minor trouble concerned the R2000-D7 Pratt and Whitney engines used on the Skymaster. They had been re-worked, using a batch of replacement parts subsequently found to be below manufacturer's specifications, and in the meantime hardly a trip was completed without cylinder failure in at least one engine.

The arrival of the refugee aircraft from China tossed a hot potato into the lap of the Hong Kong Government which teetered at the point of balance, trying

CPA Opens Service to Sandakan—5th January 1950—Captain Phil Blown in middle, R/O Fitzgerald behind him, Borneo Dyak Chiefs, with Syd de Kantow on extreme right.

1950
Kai Tak Airport showing some of the CNAC and CATC "refugee" aircraft. Curtis Commando, Skymaster and Dakotas are in evidence

to retain the respect and friendship of both the Communists at Peking and the Kuomintang, installed on the island of Formosa, rechristened Taiwan. The fate of twelve of these aircraft was resolved on November 9, when crews sympathetic to the Communist cause took ten of the CNAC planes and two of CATC's to Peking. At this point the airport authorities drained the fuel from the tanks of those remaining and took the unprecedented step of removing their wings as well, but the loss of twelve did very little to ease the airport congestion.

Claims and counterclaims to ownership, not only of the aircraft but also of buildings and other property now opened a period of extensive legal machination, providing princely sums for a small army of lawyers for some years to come. At this period, too, defectors who had assumed control of CATC's Kowloon office in the name of the Peking Government discharged Captain Moon Chin from his executive vice-presidency. All these factors forced the Hong Kong Government to assume responsibility for the mass of expensive equipment lying round and deteriorating.

Meantime the charter flights into China continued. Notable among those rescued were bank officials, who apparently put their monetary responsibilities before their personal safety, hanging on 'till the last moment. The Reds made an all-out attack on Chungking, the then National capital, and the city which had withstood the better-equipped Japanese during World War II fell with little resistance on November 30, 1949. The Communists now swung one of their armies towards Kunming in Yunnan province and sent the other hard on the heels of the fleeing enemy to Cheng-tu, where the Nationalists maintained a temporary capital for a short time.

With the fall of Chungking the Reds expected Nationalist forces to disintegrate, and when the Generalissimo fled to Formosa and set up his new capital at Taipei it seemed as if this dream would be realised immediately, but they still had to face four months of some of the most vicious fighting of the war before the Nationalists abandoned their final China foothold on Hainan Island.

Cathay Pacific and the other charter companies were thronging an almost continuous trail to Kunming. John Presgrave, on loan from ANA skippered the Skymaster there on November 27, with Dick Richmond in the starboard seat and Mum Louttit on radio. They had been chartered to fly out a portion of the Generalissimo's hoard of silver bullion. Each bar was about a foot long, three inches thick and six inches wide, and really heavy. They would fly the bars to Kai Tak whence they would go by DC3 to Manila. They had made a number of these flights. Sector time from Kai Tak to Kunming was about six hours, so they would stay overnight while the silver was loaded and then leave at first light.

On this particular morning when they arrived the silver had not been loaded, the Skymaster was surrounded by 44-gallon drums and a guard came warily to attention as they approached. As Presgrave got close to the Skymaster the guard yelled something at him. When the three crew took no notice—not knowing the language—he slammed a cartridge into the breach of his rifle and pointed it at Presgrove. Dick Richmond was carrying a heavy bronze rod used to dip the fuel tanks and he brought this down on the guard's gun. As it flew from his hand the three beat a hasty retreat. They found a transport officer and after a great deal of haggling, he released the aircraft. They returned to Kai Tak empty, but they had pulled out millions in silver on previous charters. Probably the troops were anticipating turning Red; a few loads of silver bars would help to appease their new masters.

Bo Egan was radio officer on five charters evacuating people from Kunming. At that time CATC had its main base at Kunming and part of their installation was a low-powered radio beacon. Their radio communication gear, however, was powerful, and fingered by some expert manual operators. Bo remembers the details very well.

'What intrigued me was the limited radio range of their normal airport area radio, which meant we were practically over the runway before we could establish contact, yet every time we arrived traffic personnel were awaiting us with crew bus and details of back-loading. We never had to wait a second, and this worried me until I got one of the head blokes to disclose the secret, which was that the company operated an illegal radio transceiver in Hong Kong with which they transmitted gold prices and so on. They had a contact at Kai Tak and he transmitted our estimated time of arrival.

'We stayed with CATC air-crews in an ancient walled house and got on splendidly with them. My first night there I was sitting on a sofa with a beer in my hand when the jowl of an enormous Alsatian appeared over my shoulder. He was one of two, and they answered to the names of Lupole and Asole. I don't know what happened to them but I hope they managed to eat a few Commies before they went down fighting.

'On our last flight there the country was falling apart. The Kuomintang troops had khaki uniforms of quilted jackets and head coverings like balaclavas. They would demonstrate a change of allegiance by putting the jacket on back to front, punching out the cap and doing the same with that. They were now accepted by the Communists as "turn-coats". CATC's manager was an American named Fogg. He had made a deal with the local governor that once it became clear that the troops were defecting *en masse* he would be given time to get his men and equipment out. The next morning the Governor himself defected, and as a Thai-registered Skymaster attempted to take off it was prevented by the very effective medium of an armed jeep which ran alongside the strip and stitched a bullet pattern in the fuselage with a .5 calibre mounted machine gun. The Skymaster, with a white-faced crew, quickly returned to the parking apron.

'Fogg immediately contacted the Governor and reminded him of his promise, and for reasons I shall never understand, that worthy gent agreed to give the aerial operators until noon to get out.

'All the serviceable aircraft now departed with aircrews racing in the rarefied atmosphere of the Kunming strip. As the deadline approached only three planes remained, two Curtis Commandos of CATC and a DC3 owned by a Philippine outfit. This last had engine trouble and the mechanics worked frantically to get it serviceable. Finally, one Commando got away with an engine backfiring but the other had a flat tyre and there were no spares. When Fogg departed on the first Commando he left instructions that this one should be destroyed. One of his pilots, a bloke named Bronksmeyer, made a deal that if he could get it out he should be entitled to half its worth, which was about $US60,000.

'Bronksmeyer chopped the flat tyre off with an axe and taxied out on the bare rim for takeoff. As the takeoff progressed the crew of the Philippine plane enjoyed a magnificent display of sparks, increasing as the Commando gathered speed on the strip which was surfaced with perforated steel plate. That takeoff has to go down in the records as an exceptional feat of airmanship. Just keeping the Commando straight was an accomplishment, while the thin air at that 6,240 feet altitude meant his ground run had to be longer. That brave man flew the Commando down to San Ya strip on the south coast of Hainan Island. I hope he collected the reward—he earned the money.

'The unserviceable DC3 did not share the same good fortune, for as the crew was cowling up a squadron of Mitchell bombers of the Kuomintang Air Force arrived overhead and blasted hell out of the place and destroyed it. The men actually walked out of China along the old Burma Road to Lashio.'

With the change in the National capital from Chungking to Cheng-tu, further north and west, Cathay Pacific had accepted charters, but as their equipment did not give the necessary range to a place where refuelling could be guaranteed, they farmed these out to the Catalinas of MATCO, which could do the seventeen-hour flight with fuel to spare. These were flights in which anything could and did happen, and Ian Fleming, author of *Diamonds are Forever, Dr. No, To Russia with Love* and a fistful of other suspense novels, persuaded Captain Leonard Cosgrove to write accounts of some of the incidents. Fleming would add the sex interest or whatever, and the backgrounds would be authentic. Cos wrote several of these, but Fleming had not got round to using them by the time he died. They are too good, I think, to fall into oblivion. In a story he called *The Two Airfields of Cheng-tu* he recounts what happened to Captain Ross Sanford Bohm on one of these charters:

'At this time, throughout the Far East, only two aircraft had the range to fly to Cheng-tu and return without refuelling. These were the Skymaster and the Catalina, and the nearest Skymaster was heavily engaged with other facets of the evacuation of China, naturally making a fortune for its owners in the process. So the Catalina was selected and MATCO's operations manager leapt to accept the assignment from Cathay Pacific. The choise of pilot fell on Bohm, as Cosgrove flatly refused to touch the operation. Co-pilot was Jim Kiernan, as there was no one else. A Chinese radio man who knew the area and spoke its dialect was hastily found and, with tanks filled to overflowing VR-HDS with a special dispensation carried out a night takeoff from Kai Tak and set out on her incredible journey.

'Cheng-tu lies almost 1000 miles northwest of Hong Kong on a high plateau marking the last great spur of the Himalayan thrust into China. The airfields were Kwangchow-wan and Cheng-tu, the first a small but adequate field on the plateau to the east of the city, the other a war-time monstrosity built for the fighting B17s on the bottom of a sheer-sided valley. Kwangchow-wan was Bohm's destination. He had been advised that a radio beacon of limited power was still operational, and the passengers he was to pick up would be ready for a quick turn around.

'Bohm planned to keep the very high ground well to port and to rendezvous with the beacon at the maximum height he could attain. His Chinese radioman indicated a safe let-down over the plateau, which consisted of one-minute legs to north and south of the beacon, and all being well, a safe descent to 500 feet above the plateau's height of 4000 feet would be a piece of cake. His early departure should bring him over the city of Cheng-tu after dawn with plenty of daylight.

'But as daylight grew the wisps of clouds below him thickened into a solid sheet and, uneasily aware of the rising ground below it, Bohm was forced to claw for yet more altitude. The outside air temperature fell rapidly as height increased and would fall even further as his flight took him northwest. He hoped that the front he was penetrating would prove narrow; that he would soon come out of it into the cold clear air of the monsoon blowing out of Siberia. He watched the thin ribbon of white forming at the bottom of the windscreen and hunched deeper into his flying jacket. Kiernan shifted uneasily and jabbed an expressive thumb towards the spreading white area on the side windows. VR-HDS could not be coaxed any higher; she was not fitted with any form of de-icing equipment, and Bohm remembered that ice was the salient factor which had led Cosgrove to refuse the flight.

'Kiernan made another expressive gesture, and this time his thumb indicated the direction of his thinking. Back to Honkers. Bohm shook his head, arguing that they were only an hour or two out and the beacon should come in loud and clear any time now. He promised he would return home if there were no improvement in weather conditions in an hour or so. Kiernan resumed his sombre contemplation of the zero visibility and found himself longing for a paper-run back in his beloved Perth.

'Some forty minutes later the wandering needle of the radio compass seized on a signal and wavered round a point some ten degrees to port. Swiftly Bohm tuned in the stand-by compass and that too spun leisurely to the same heading. The radio operator confirmed the Morse lettering from his notebook and the tension on the flight deck lessened. Bohm considered the situation. His Cat-boat was staggering at 12,000 feet, the bearing of the station now showed he was on the safe side of the plateau. He gently wound the nose down and then disengaging the auto-pilot he set himself the task of orientating his arrival over the beacon. Repeated calls by his radioman produced no sight of life; only the "KC . . . KC . . . KC . . ." on the frequency of the homing beacon proved that some devoted soul in the wilderness below was doing his best to assist the foreigners in the Catalina.

'At 9,000 feet he levelled out. The icing rapidly disappeared and, as his aerials became clear, so did the volume of the tiny station below build up in his headphones. The needles of his radio-compasses commenced to waver as he closed on the beacon until suddenly they swung through 180 degrees. This indicated that he had just crossed the station; Kiernan clicked the stopwatch, Bohm reduced power to set a rate of descent of 500 feet a minute. Kiernan called the check calls—"Forty . . . fifty . . . Go!" to Bohm who threw the Cat around on a reciprocal course, for this was no place for the orderly procedures laid down in the text books. Back to the friendly beacon . . . one minute on the southerly heading . . . round again to the north.

'The greyness which surrounded them started to lighten in texture and the tightness of the stomach which accompanies any descent through cloud in dangerous terrain was noticeable to both men. North over the beacon . . . stopwatch clicks . . . no room for mistakes . . . round in another tight turn to the south . . . again to the north . . . and this time—yes, it's breaking. The sheets of stratus are less dense. VR-HDS broke through between layers, and there, confronting their bulging eyes, was a sheer mountain wall where a level plateau should have been.

'Both pilots reacted immediately. Bohm flung the Catalina into a violent turn to port. Kiernan slammed both throttles and pit controls as far forward as they would go and the Catalina clawed in a desperate bid for altitude into a tight, too tight climbing corkscrew. Instruments toppled, and Bohm's only reference was the seat of his pants—which by now were unashamedly wet.

'With Kiernan's assistance he slowed the turn down, caged and uncaged the artificial horizon several times until it settled to its designed function, and continued the turn as long as the Catalina would climb. Neither man was prepared to proceed in any direction before reaching maximum height.

'At 13,000 feet with the aircraft in a gentle turn they held a council of war. Bohm, composure regained, was almost in favour of another attempt. Keirnan was equally prepared to do murder to prevent a repetition. The matter was taken from their hands when the direction aerial, weary of supporting its heavy load of glazed ice, broke away. They turned into the southeast towards Hong Kong.

'The same cold front which had obstructed their primary purpose brought them the blessing of a strong tail wind. They were conserving fuel, but as the darkness closed in they were disturbed for they were unsure of their exact location and with unserviceable direction-finding equipment they could not descend out of the icing level. The final miracle then occurred, for a strong English voice advised them that RAF Radar Control had them clear on their screen. The best-kept secret in Southeast Asia was made public. The radar controller brought them right to the threshold of Kai Tak runway lit by emergency flares, and Bohm brought his aircraft in for a smooth landing, 17 hours and 50 minutes after he had opened his throttles for Cheng-tu.

'MATCO's operations returned to normal in a few days. Other flights for evacuation were carried out as the debacle on the Chinese mainland drew to conclusion. The Catalinas rescued people from Hainan Island, from Mangtze, and a dozen other strips as the defenders threw the Sun badges away and pinned the Red Star to their caps.

'A Skymaster of Pacific Overseas Airlines (Siam) Limited, chartered to go once more to the rescue at Cheng-tu, solved the mystery. It flew in good weather in half the time taken by the lumbering Catalina. Its crew noticed that the signals from the beacon came not from the Kwangchow-wan airfield, but from the old B17 strip thirty miles to the southwest of Cheng-tu's forbidding valley, with mountains towering 9000 feet on either side of the runway. The approach of the Communists had caused an early withdrawal from the airstrip on the plateau, and some loyal souls, still determined to assist the pilots coming to their rescue, had transported the beacon by buffalo cart to the old abandoned wartime strip without giving a thought to the immense difference of using the other strip's descent pattern in an entirely different location. Had Ross Bohm erred for more than a few seconds in those tight one minute north and south legs of his descent another aircraft would have disappeared without trace.'

In December 1949 Cathay Pacific's sphere of operations extended to Hoi How, capital city of Hainan Island when for a brief spell there seemed some scope to expand from Hoi How to Bangkok and Singapore. The first charter to Hoi How was without incident but on the second our DC3 was hit by heavy machine-gun fire, and when the luggage was off-loaded at Kai Tak it proved to have taken the brunt of the assault, perhaps preventing the loss of the aircraft.

'Hoi How is the background for another story from Len Cosgrove:

'The Lieutenant-Governor of Hainan was in trouble. His wife had already left for Taiwan, but his most beautiful concubine, the Lady Ying was not accepted to the high circles of the Kuomintang and her entry to the haven of Formosa was denied. General Chin

191

sought an alternative and time was running out. Many of his soldiers had changed their allegiances and disappeared into the mountainous interior and he knew that when they re-appeared would be wearing the badge of the Red Star. As a last resort he appealed to Macao where several of his military colleagues had taken refuge, and through a process hard to fathom, the appeal, transmitted through Cathay Pacific, arrived on the desk of Captain James Ennis, operations manager of MATCO.

'By a strange coincidence the two busiest crews of the company were, in that month of April 1950, fully employed on the gold run, which left the ball in Ennis's court. The company had lately bought a third Catalina of indeterminate age and dubious flying qualities, VR-HEV, and Ennis had it prepared for the Hoi How flight. At this stage mainland China had been cleared of Nationalist troops except for a small area near Burma known as "The Golden Triangle", where the ragged troops of General Li Mi hung on to their opium-rich territory. Hainan itself was thinly garrisoned with rebellious and unpaid conscripts. The island was separated by Hainan Strait, which was trafficable on foot at low tide.

'Ennis mounted his rescue of the damsel in distress. There being no co-pilot available he simply dispensed with one and, accompanied by a mechanic and a radioman he actually shanghaied, he departed on his two and half hour flight. Only on impact with the runway did Ennis realise that the airfield was about to be abandoned. Potholes of terrifying size strewed the way and the few ragged soldiers in sight seemed unconcerned at the Cat's arrival. Of his beautiful passenger and her entourage there was no sign, and a lesser man would have about-faced without stopping engines, but Ennis was not easily discouraged when sober, and without a co-pilot he just had to be sober!

'His commanding appearances and the services of his mechanic as interpreter produced the intelligence that the lady had indeed been waiting several days for the aircraft, and was staying at a hotel in the city. After much haggling and flashing U.S. currency, a jeep appeared and whisked the captain off to a decrepit hotel in the decrepit city, where he was soon in the presence of the truly beautiful Lady Ying and her two small children.

'Ennis made it quite clear that he was anxious to be off, but the lady would have none of this and invited him to dinner that evening, deferring departure 'till the 'morrow. The gallant captain could do no less than concur, but took the precaution of removing the distributor cap from the jeep before retiring for a quick pre-dinner kip.

'One Chinese dinner is much like another, Ennis thought. The quality of the liquor available was the standard by which Ennis judged the dinner, and this one impressed him, for here, at the Kuomintang's last-ditch stand, flowed plenty of the best Scotch. The evening passed in a misty haze and endless rounds of toasts. Most of his dinner companions would be boarding his aircraft on the 'morrow and, with a total disregard of seats available, Ennis invited the rest. At the evening's end he did contemplate a discreet knock on a lady's door, but the muscular appearance of some of her entourage discouraged him.

'He seemed to have slept only a few minutes before he was shaken violently, and voices screamed for him to get up. He ignored them, but when a bucket of water was emptied over his head he bounded up with a great bellow of anger to confront his near hysterical mechanic.

' "The Reds have landed. They walked across the Straits at low water last night—you can hear the shooting." In truth the distant rattle of small-arms was unpleasantly familiar. He took the stairs two at a time, throwing the distributor cap to the mechanic. Outside the hotel the driver of an ancient bus was shoving off, leaving the vehicle unattended except for its load of passengers huddled beneath window level. Ennis dived behind its wheel and sent it rocketing down the road to the airport. He crashed through the wire that marked the strip's perimeter, and headed straight for his beautiful Catalina.

'The passengers needed no urging as they scrambled aboard. Ennis followed his mechanic through the hatch and as he slammed it shut he knew the mechanic was turning the propellors and all he had to do was flick the ignition switches which would bring them to life. Ennis peered over the nose to see all was clear, then slowly, with a sigh, he switched the ignition off again.

'Before the props had begun to wind down, the mechanic was out of his tower, eyebrows raised in mute enquiry. Not wasting words, Ennis jerked a thumb forward, indicating a group of uniformed men centred by two who trained a heavy Vickers machine-gun on the Catalina's cockpit window. Stomach muscles tightened still more when they noted that Red Stars had replaced the sun badges on the men's caps. Ennis ordered the mechanic to open the hatch and parley with the soldiers and, turning to the Lady Ying, he pointed through the window to the menacing machine-gun.

'No words were necessary. From the depths of the valise a servant guarded, she withdrew a small oblong package, and unwrapping it, Ennis drew a sharp breath, for there lay a dozen taels of gold. She handed them to him with a fleeting smile. He slammed open his sliding window and beckoned the leader of the group to ap-

Cathay Pacific's Ticket Office—Peninsula Hotel, Kowloon, August 1955.
L. to R: Miss Iris Stobart, Super. of Air Hostesses, Miss Lee, Philip Chen and
Captain Ken Steele.

MAY 1954
Captain C.F. (Pat) Moore, going on leave. Kai Tak, Hong Kong.
Cathay's then "flagship" DC4 . . . VR-HEU, just two months before
it was shot down by Communist China's fighters near Hainan Island.

proach. As the officer reached viewing distance Ennis lifted the corner of the wrapping and pointed meaningly at the machine-gun.

'The message got through. A barked command was sufficient to remove the gun, the parcel was tossed out and swiftly pocketed.

Within a few minutes the Catalina was on her way.'

Jim Macdougall, best-known and best-loved of the Sydney newspaper columinists of the era, spent some time in 1949 with Cathay Pacific on its operations and in Hong Kong, beginning a relationship which persists to this day, where he is the official Public Relations Manager, Sydney. That early relationship would also include the Peninsula Hotel, which itself has enjoyed a de facto relationship, or a warm one anyway, with the company since its establishment.

The hotel's history goes back to 1927 when James H. Taggart built it in a prominent position on the Kowloon Peninsula within easy reach of the docks and the railway station. When it was ready to receive guests the Government commandeered it to quarter troops rushed to Hong Kong at the outbreak of the Sino-Japanese hostilities, and the vandalism of these occupants was such that repair took nearly as long as the original construction. One of the more orthodox diversions had been hurling bayonets into the beautifully panelled doors.

For a while the Pen became the centre of life in the Colony, but its halcyon days were short, once again interrupted by the minions of Nippon. When it opened for post-war business after more repairs part of its clientele was the Cathay Pacific staff, and Syd's Pirates became regular habitues. It was an exciting spot to while away the time.

In 1947 a comfortable bar occupied the west wall where PAL and other airline offices now stand. Then, and now, the 'ladies of the evening' occupied tables west of the main entrance. The more upstanding locals frequenting the east side included a good sprinkling of 'ladies' who had advanced socially and donned mantles of respectability with their wedding rings. My wife and I remember explaining to Brenda Roberts and her mother that they were sitting at the 'pro's' end. Brenda was the wife of the Colony's Chief Secretary, Sir Denys. They went a little pale but saw the afternoon out where they were with British fortitude. Nevertheless they did not occupy that end again.

Li Bun, the telephone page, used to locate friends lost somewhere in the milling crowd by chalking the name on a small blackboard elevated on a broomstick, with a bicycle bell attached near his right thumb. We all had messages for him that were mostly quite reasonable but an overwrought management intercepted him on such occasions as when, for instance, his board bore a message for a "Miss Carriage'. During 1949 a Leopold Gaddi joined the staff, first as chef, and five years later, as manager. In the quarter-century he spent there he became great friends with the airline, and his name persists through Gaddi's, the internationally famous restaurant he inaugurated at Christmas, 1953.

In December 1949 Jim Macdougall had joined Syd de Kantzow, John Moxham and several others at that west bar, deep in grog and conversation. Called to the phone, Syd returned to say that he had accepted an immediate charter to Saigon. He nominated Moxham as skipper and himself as co-pilot. They needed a radio man and a hostess as there was a full load of passengers, and shortly an unlucky radioman was seen weaving an unsteady path through the lounge. Now only the hostess remained a problem.

Suddenly Moxham's florid moustachioed face became radiant and without another word he raced over to a beautiful Chinese girl sitting at a table wrapping herself round a gooey cake. A fork crammed with cake waved angrily in Moxham's face to punctuate the exchange that followed, but finally a smile spread over the girl's face and Mox the Ox raced back to announce they now had a full crew. He had decided to take the evening's entertainment on the flight. Finally Jim Macdougall was pressed into service as purser, to deal with the inevitable mass of paperwork which bugged cabin crews in those early days.

Some funny things happened in that lounge. One day Pinky Wawn flew in with a load of day-old chicks. The company had no place to store them so an understanding Pen manager allowed it to use a ground-floor room where they could stay 'till morning. After storing the last case Pinky and the others came through to the bar and set about reviving their flagging spirits. Then all hell broke loose as the lounge became inundated with squawking, agitated chicks. Women, young and old, were standing on chairs and holding their skirts up, screaming with alarm. The chicks invaded the kitchen, even the ladies' toilets, from which the occupants were running screaming to add to the lounge confusion. Everyone quickly got into the spirit of the hour, running hither and yon to round up the wayward chicks, but later it was reported on good authority that several dozen were still missing.

'This spread alarm and despondency over Syd's and Roy's brows for days,' Pinky said recently. 'Chicks probably graced the larders of waiters and room-boys for days to come. The great escape is supposed to have been triggered when an inquisitive room-boy, hearing the continuous squeaking, went into the room and somehow or other allowed them to escape. I have my doubts. It always did sound like a put-up job to me!'

Pinky also recalls an evening at the Peninsula when he and de Kantzow, Neville Hemsworth, Bob Wingrove and George Silk, the Time/Life photographer, were continuing a party from a room on the sixth floor, and feeling no pain. The room overlooked Nathan Road, and as George Silk left, he bet the others couldn't bomb him with beercans as he entered that road in a rickshaw. They lined up their ammunition on the window parapets and as he came into range they let fly, but in the strong wind the cans kept falling short. They didn't need George's taunting voice to realise they were missing him. The weight was the problem, and Syd switched to full cans, which soon were bursting pretty close.

'George was still screeching that we were missing him,' Pinky recalls, 'but now he was adding "YOU BASTARDS". The thoroughly terrified rickshaw puller was taking evasive action, and the last I remember of this childish prank was a weaving rickshaw disappearing past Middle Road going like the hobs of hell, and George's white featureless face staring up at us as he directed his puller to right or left while the cans continued to come.'

CHAPTER TWELVE
OUTSIDE THE LAW

Evil deeds do not prosper:
the slow man catches up with the swift
The Odyssey, Book VII—Homer

At 6.40 a.m. on December 15, 1950 Kai Tak logged the following radio signal:
'Hello Hong Kong approach. This is VR-HEV. My aircraft is sinking rapidly. Am being taken aboard Communist gun-boat. All crew
safe.'

The flying-boat's flight plan details showed that it had departed from
Chittagong in East Pakistan (now Bangladesh) at 2.28 p.m. (Hong Kong time) on a
direct flight to Hong Kong, expected to take thirteen hours. It carried fuel for 23
hours flying. In the early morning it had been heard circling over Hong Kong with
radio contact established. It then reported failure of the main radio transmitter, and
its radio officer, Bill James brought his auxiliary equipment into operation. Radio
contact ceased soon after, and the next message was the dramatic 6.40 transmission.

Just under two hours later an RAF Sunderland of the Search and Rescue
Unit took off to trace the wayward *fei gei*. It found an unidentified Chinese gun-
boat towing the Catalina into a small sheltered bay of Wang Kam Island in Communist water adjacent to the Portuguese Island of Colowan.

Background of the flight was that a Mr Sun Chung-liang had bought the
Catalina from MATCO, one of the batch previously purchased from Amphibian
Airways in Manila. The pilot was Ross Bohm, the radio officer William Michael
James, and the Catalina also carried a flight engineer and the owner from
Chittagong. A report in the *Sydney Morning Herald* declared that the crew had
agreed to make three flights for Mr Sun, and their pay, for what was said to be
checking fuel consumption graphs, would be in three amounts of $HK10,000,
$HK12,000 and $HK14,000. But that report came in two years later, on August
14, 1952. The pay seems more than adequate.

Chinese authorities took the crew from the gun-boat to Shekki, a town near
the Macao border, and placed them under house arrest. Certain Nationalist sym-
pathisers mounted a rescue bid, but the Communists got wind of it and transferred
the airmen closer to Canton.

An uncorroborated rumour circulated that the Catalina had landed in the
open sea. Conditions at that time were very rough, with a mountainous swell,
and the hull had been holed. Captain Bohm managed to get it airborne again
and sought the shelter of calmer waters in the lee of one of the many islands
close to Macao. Here the gun-boat picked them up, and as it bore down on them
some men fishing nearby saw, or reported that they saw, people on the Catalina
frantically dumping bags overboard.

197

The crew spent twenty months as guests of the Reds and were released only after signing statements, under duress, that they had been engaged in smuggling 40,000 taels (1260 kilograms) of opium which they had picked up from an abandoned wartime strip in Northern Burma. As they were pushed across the Hong Kong border at Lo Wu, Bill James was seen to turn and signal the Communist guards with that graceful two-finger gesture. But it was obvious to everyone that they were in bad physical shape, and they were taken to the Queen Mary Hospital where they spent several days before the authorities tossed them to the piranhas of the media.

They denied the opium charges, and of the many skillfully contrived theories that have surfaced, the next most likely is that they had been engaged in transporting Nationalist Chinese spies to a location from which they could find their way into Communist-controlled China, probably via the old Burma Road.

I tend to believe this, but I have been quite unable to determine the question. Captain Bohm met an early death during April 1978, the probable result of the privations he suffered under the benevolent care of his Chinese gaolers. Bill James, who suffers from terminal wanderlust, has not been heard of for years, and the flight engineer whom I did locate wants to keep his own counsel. The other person aboard that Catalina, who on paper at least seemed to be the owner, was variously reported as having been executed, and as living in far from impoverished circumstances in a South American country.

The incident underlined the unsatisfactory practice of interchanging aircrews between Cathay Pacific and MATCO, though in this instance it seems probable that the radio officer had sought permission. Even with this example the companies did not alter their policy, and records as late as 1956 show that MATCO's Captain Len Cosgrove was still doing first officer stints on Cathay Pacific's DC3s and Skymasters.

Noah Webster defines 'smuggling':'to import or export secretly contrary to law; to bring into or take out of a country merchandise, forbidden articles or persons contrary to law and with fraudulent intent; to import or export anything in violation of the customs law.'

Most of us are smugglers. It is a question of degree, the seriousness of the crime and the sentence depends on what is smuggled. The non-declaration of a watch or a ring, for example, can bring a fine of generally double the value, or the loss of the item. In many countries the importing of gold bars can bring a heavy fine and prison sentence. The heaviest punishments are properly reserved for those outside the human race who traffic in drugs.

I have been subjected to body-searches by customs officials of several countries throughout Southeast Asia but in the main I've had a fair deal from most of them. I have been asked to involve myself in smuggling activities by people respected throughout the community. They offered mouth-watering rewards, and there were times I could have used the money. The person who attempts to enlist an agent to smuggle is not easily discouraged; he is also an utter coward, for other than risking his investment, his welfare is never in jeopardy.

'Not easily discouraged' is an understatement. A straight-out refusal usually brings a demonstration of the latest creation in gold transportation. I have been shown a vest for this purpose which fitted the body so skillfully that only a body search would result in detection.

On one occasion I followed my first officer towards the customs section at Hanoi. He was a gum-chewing, casual type of man who never seemed discomforted, but on this occasion he was agitated, and puffing somewhat. I did not give this much thought until I saw how his knees were bending and his feet splayed; the ground was almost cracking as he made his way across the tarmac. He was carrying a massive load of the precious yellow metal but his figure gave no hint of this, due to the special vest he was, no doubt, wearing.

In earlier days, when the bars had to be carried, the smuggler was easy to detect, for bulges and misshapen pockets were obvious. One of our senior pilots was taken in Bangkok once, in something of a comedy of errors. As he pulled a handkerchief from his pocket out tumbled a gold bar which clattered to the floor, quite unseen by the customs man. The pilot, with presence of mind, gently kicked it away towards, as chance would have it, his first officer, but to his consternation it was toed back to him. The co-pilot was also carrying a load and had no desire to draw attention to himself. The captain was caught; the co-pilot was not.

A method much used if a carrier was not employed was to hide a few gold bars in a suitable recess in the aircraft. This, if found, would usually terminate any further search for a better-planted and more valuable hoard.

There were the born losers. Once a good friend of mine secreted several thousand US dollars in his plane. Foreign currency had been a prohibited import at this destination, but what he did not know was that the restrictions had been lifted a few days earlier. During the hours of darkness he crept out to the plane to withdraw his deposit and found the cupboard bare. One of the ground engineers had discovered his cache and, rationalising that his own needs were greater than those of the smuggler, had sequestered the loot.

On occasion a smuggler would plant his goods in a position on the aircraft so inaccessible he would foil his own attempt at recovery. Ground engineer Jack Williams discovered a hidden hoard of gold once when he removed a DC3 propellor-dome which had been snagged by an incoming crew unable to do a proper engine-feathering check. Jack's commission from the Customs Department was sufficient to buy him an Oldsmobile.

Language difficulty has bothered customs officials in many countries. Officials would have cards printed in several languages detailing prohibited imports. These cards covered almost everything imaginable, but I thought at first the Malayans were over-imaginative when I saw the word 'corpses' among their prohibitions. My own over-active imagination subsided when I realised this could designate a simple butterfly collection perhaps, or a well-stuffed bird, the feathered kind of course.

Throughout the years Cathay Pacific has had its share of smugglers and has made vigorous efforts to eradicate the menace, but the management realises it can do little to prevent an employee engaging in this misguided activity, provid-

Jardine Aircraft Maintenance Co. Ltd.—1949
JAMCO amalgamted with PAMAS in November 1950 and became HAECO

Captain Lawrie King ''HAECO staff positively bend over backwards to provide the service the customer requires''

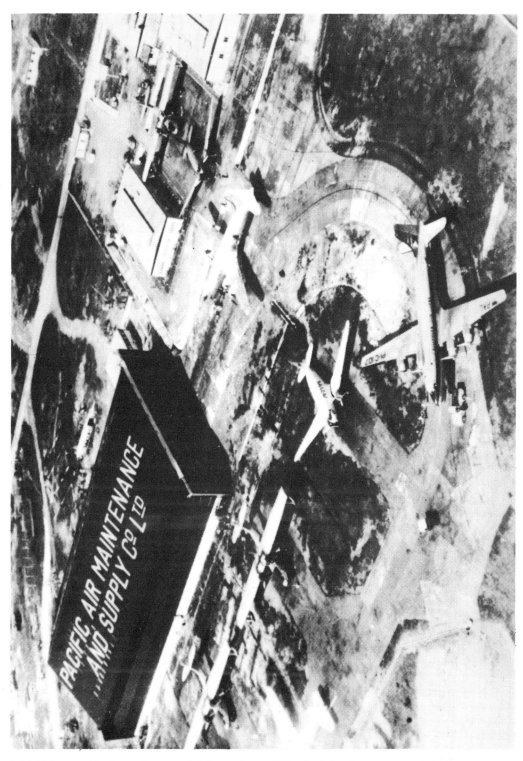

PAMAS was Registered on 4th November 1948—it joined with JAMCO and on 23rd November 1950 became HAECO. This photo taken during 1949.

1952
KAI TAK AIRPORT

ed he does not transgress the Eleventh Commandment by getting caught. On two occasions the Company was itself fined. The second was less serious than the first, but both left a slur on Cathay Pacific's reputation despite the fact that it was blameless. Others had used its aircraft for their underhanded work.

In July 1951 a revenue officer found two bags which did not appear on the Bangkok manifest. They contained 2305 taels of opium, 263 boxes of penicillin and 480 tins of Saridon tablets. In September the company was summoned before Mr. O.V. Cheung charged with importing unmanifested cargo and fined $HK5,000 although Tom Bax, prior to the plane's arrival had advised revenue Inspector Robertson that there was a strong suspicion of something wrong with the cargo on that incoming flight.

Then in April 1964 one of our aircraft was detained overnight at Manila for bringing in fifty cases of cigarettes labelled 'personal effects'. This was a dicey do, for President Marcos had issued an instruction that any aircraft bringing in prohibited goods should be held until a full enquiry had been completed. Indeed, the aircraft could have been confiscated.

Of the smugglers intercepted over the years, two operated in aircraft under my command. One was a purser who had brought in several wrist-watches. The contraband came to light when his Tokyo contact was involved in a car accident. Some blunt questioning disclosed my purser's part in the deal, and when we arrived at Osaka the next day he was removed from the plane.

The other was a good friend of mine. I had cleared customs at Calcutta and was waiting in the crew transport when I was recalled to the customs area and told that my first officer was being detained for importing gold without a permit. He went through a very rough time at their hands, and involved one or two other people in the company. One he named was also arrested at Dum Dum on a subsequent flight but satisfied all their questioning and was soon released. The investigation went on for many weeks and my friend was given more and more freedom of movement, until one night he was slipped aboard our Skymaster and hidden in the control cable 'hell-hole'. During the flight the skipper, who was not in the plot, kept commenting on the strange behaviour of the normally sedate aircraft. It was hardly surprising, for the smuggler (who was now being smuggled) had to keep moving in an effort to maintain his circulation, and it was no easy matter to avoid those dozens of sensitive control wires which festooned his temporary habitat.

A significant event on November 1, 1950 was the amalgamation of the two aircraft engineering companies that carried out repair work at Kai Tak: Jardine Aircraft Maintenance Company Limited (JAMCO) and Pacific Air Maintenance and Supply Company Limited (PAMAS). The move heralded one of the great success stories of the aircraft engineering industry for the new company, the Hong Kong Aircraft Engineering Company (HAECO) developed into one of the largest organisations of its kind in the world. H. Spencer Cooper became HAECO's manager and Tony Wakeford the chief engineer. Both had held these designations in the defunct JAMCO. Harold George Smith, ex-chief engineer of PAMAS became chief inspector in the new company.

"Workshop facilities" adjacent to Cathay Pacific's initial engineering Nissen Hut headquarters which stood just to the left of where the threshold of Runway "13" is now located. This picture was taken in 1948 and shows Bill ("Hokum") Harris's personnel, some of whom changed over to PAMAS when it was established. Leaning on the bike is Geoff Arnold, who is at present (1979) employed by the Main Road Department, Brisbane, Australia.

Prior to the amalgamation the JAMCO engine overhaul shop had been purchased *en bloc* in the United States and transported to the Colony with its crew of twelve Americans. In charge of the efficiently run department was Sol Soldinksy, the man who fitted the DC2 wing to the bomb-damaged DC3, creating the legendary DC2½.

'Those Yanks were a gregarious lot,' Harry Smith recalls. 'They were housed in the old Humphrey building in Kowloon, and they were always holding parties. Their propellor man was Eddie Walsh, a real good guy and an accomplished photographer, but neither a drinker nor a womanizer—in fact a most uncharacteristic serviceman. At one party his mates slipped him a Mickey Finn and he passed out. They undressed him, called in a girl, arranged them in a compromising position and photographed them. Next day Sol, who was in the scheme up to his eyebrows, called Eddie into his office, threw the pictures on the desk and gave him a stiff lecture on morality, concluding that if he didn't change his ways he would be shipped home. The words were prophetic, for it wasn't long before they all left the Colony.'

The engineering seed was sown at Kai Tak when Farrell and de Kantzow established a small aircraft parts store, a small iron-roofed blockhouse located slightly to the left of where the present runway threshold lies. Reginald William Harris, in charge, went under the name of Bill, or Hokum. Geoff Arnold remembers him well:

'Bill was an absolute necessity in those early days, for he seemed to possess the gifts of a magician, and with little effort could produce from some mysterious recess the necessary part to cure a sick aircraft. This was not easy, for Syd de Kantzow was not given to squandering money, no matter what the necessity. Bill's one small fetish was a Colony flag that had to fly by day on his castle's rampart. Woe betide the Chinese "master-at-arms" who was derelict in his duty of raising the colours at first light or striking them at night.'

Harris was chief to some very fine engineers, Geoff Arnold, Neil Norquay, Jack Williams and Charlie Rowe. It was Neil who christened Harris 'Hokum'. He was reading a book in which the senior slave-driver, himself a slave, had learned to weild a whip with such expertise that his master became a rich man and released him from bondage. This character's name in the book was Hokum and Neil saw some parallel.

Hokum's little kingdom had no hangar facilities and all work on the aircraft had to be performed outside on the hard-standing. The only luxury allowed the workers was a dirty tarpaulin slung between revetments that the Japanese had built to shelter their aircraft from bomb blast and sea spray. Though it was about a hundred yards to the water the salt spray was always giving trouble to delicate aircraft equipment. Hazards of open-air working are illustrated by one of Geoff Arnold's stories:

'I had been given the job of stripping the paint from the fuselage of VR-HDW. We had removed the wings as well as the tyres and had it sitting on its wheel rims to make it nice and low for the thirty Chinese labourers scraping off the paint with wooden chisels. Each man had two buckets, one containing a couple of inches of paint remover and the other about half full of aviation gasoline, and each was to cover an area between three rows of rivets. On this close hot day the air shimmered with the rising heat vapours. I got them all started, walked back to Hokum's office and was talking to Richard Chan, a licenced ground engineer when there was a terrific explosion.

'I looked back and every bucket of that highly inflammable fluid seemed to be burning. In just a second or two the labourers had scurried off the scaffolding and were running to all points of the field, and one well out in front had the seat of his pants burning merrily. Richard and I rushed over and were shovelling sand on the fires but we were losing the battle until the RAF arrived with their foam truck, and soon had things under control. I have never seen anyone enjoy themselves so much; they sprayed foam over everything and everyone within reach and seemed disappointed when their job was done. Only three men suffered burns, including the one with the toasted tail. These were sent to hospital, but they soon returned and Hokum sacked the three of them, which I thought was severe. The only damage to the aircraft was to the nose section, but as the company had recently bought an aircraft dump in Manila, this was soon replaced.'

That aircraft dump that Roy Farrell had purchased from the War Disposals Commission of the Philippines was a treasure trove, and PAMAS was really established with spares from this dump. It contained absolutely every type of part for our operation, including mint condition engines and even several aircraft, Commandos and DC3s, ready to fly. In addition there were also thousands of black snakes, one of which took particular umbrage towards me when I went there with Roy Farrell in January 1948. Even when I mingled with the others in the party it continued to single me out. Its attention only ended when one of the fellows who packed a .45 blew its head off.

The original PAMAS hangar was bought and remains to this day in the Run Run Shaw movie complex on Clear Water Bay Road in the New Territories, where it does sterling service as one of Asia's largest sound stages.

In April 1951 Cathay Pacific was still taking steps to consolidate its position, frustrated by Government red tape. Ivan Holyman of ANA even voiced the possibility of liquidation. He said, 'Cathay Pacific must speedily come to an arrangement where only one airline company operates out of Hong Kong. Possibly this could be achieved with Cathay Pacific and Hong Kong Airways in conjunction, but even this doesn't seem the best course for Cathay Pacific. The only alternative is to quit the airline operation and dispose of our assets while we can get a good price, and get out with very little loss, if any.'

In that same month de Kantzow resigned and sold his shares, half to ANA and half to John Swire and Sons Limited. Thereafter the share holdings of the company were held by ANA (39.69%), China Navigation Company (37.19%) and John Swire and Sons Limited (23.12%).

De Kantzow returned to Sydney. On November 16, 1957 he was travelling with two friends to Thredbo to build an additional ski-hut in their camp. 'Giner' (Ronald James) Mildren was driving, Pinky Wawn navigating from the front seat and de Kantzow installed in the back seat amongst the luggage. Six miles west

Run Run Shaw's Film Studio, Clearwater Bay, New Territories, Hong Kong. (This photo from "British Airways Executive" Magazine, March 1975).

View of Kai Tak Looking West
(Note: CATC and CNAC Aircraft without wings and wings in right foreground).

Kai Tak Airpot—1952
Shows the HAECO Installation

of Cooma on the Berridale Road the car went out of control on a slight curve. It veered sharply right and came to rest on its right side after tearing a fencepost out of the ground. They had entered the bend at 3.40 p.m., travelling at a reasonable sixty miles per hour, and within seconds Giner had gasped away his life, crumped across the forward undamaged wire of the fence. He had been hurled through the windscreen with the force of a projectile and sustained shocking injuries. Pinky was dazed and bleeding. De Kantzow was taken to Cooma Hospital in a matter of minutes, but failed to respond to treatment. Transferred to St. Vincent's in Sydney on November 20 he died the next day, having accomplished at the age of 43 more than most of his fellows. Under any management, Cathay Pacific remains a memorial to his enterprise, courage, ingenuity and single-mindedness.

General Claire Lee Chennault's Civil Air Transport, now located in Taipei, was by no means a spent force in 1951. On April 23 two of its Curtiss Commandos landed at Whenuapai, the airport of Auckland, and moved next morning to establish a temporary base at Paraparaumu, Wellington's major field. They had been indirectly chartered by a private company, Straits Air Freight Express Limited, on behalf of the industrially troubled New Zealand Government. Their mission was to maintain a flow of vital traffic across Cook Strait, which separates the two major islands. It had been halted by a waterfront strike which was bringing the country to its knees.

The strike lasted three months, a period in which the country was literally fed by the efforts of several charter companies. CAT's diminutive operations manager was Mrs Olive King, a petite, vivacious and energetic executive who managed the operations of several burly American six-footers. Her fleet, augmented by another Commando, made at least a hundred flights each week. Her husband Lawrie resigned from Cathay Pacific to join her in the operation, rejoining the company in August after settlement of the strike, to become Manager of Flight Training and to retire in 1977.

CAT's interest in the immobilized aircraft on Kai Tak intensified. Chennault maintained that he had purchased the Nationalist Chinese Government's interest in CNAC and CATC, and to prove his point introduced to the British legal arena a New York lawyer, Major-General William (Wild Bill) Donovan, wartime Chief of the Office of Strategic Services. The Hong Kong ruling in favour of Communist ownership (perhaps not uninfluenced by the military strength at the nearby border) was overturned by appeal to the Privy Council, and Kai Tak civil airport was closed to the public on the morning of July 29, 1952, when the local government took over full control of the 40 CATC aircraft awarded to the CAT company by the Privy Council decision. It remained closed to all except bona fide travellers until October, but during this period Chennault solved the problem of a counter appeal or more direct Communist intervention by bringing in an American LST with a big winch and simply hoisting aboard every aircraft he could get his hands on. Then he calmly sailed away to Taiwan.

That LST was one he had bought as war surplus from the Chinese Nationalist Government and converted into a floating workshop, complete with office

CPA Flight Hostesses and Purser in 1953
Rear: Jo Cheng; Anita Lee; Cecilia Cheng; Philip Chen; Rose Chan;
Judy Mao; Connie Rapp;
Front: Diana Cheng; Margaret Wheeldon; Iris Stobart (Hostess
Superintendent); Patsy Wong; Tilly O'Brien

CPA Air Hostesses qualify for St. John Ambulance Badges—15th
May 1953
L to R: Iris Stobart; Snr. F/H Judy Mao; Unknown; Patsy Wong;
Dr Carey-Hughes; Diane Cheng; Rose Chan; Margaret Wheeldon;
Cecelia Cheng; Anita Lee; Connie Rapp; Tilly O'Brien; Jo Cheng.

facilities. HMS *Amethyst* commanded world admiration by escaping down the Whangpoo River and sailing past Shanghai in July 1949. Chennault had master-minded a less dramatic but similar escape for his LST a couple of months earlier, for he had kept it in the Whangpoo River until the fall of Shanghai on May 25, 1949. Then he instructed his officers to fly his planes out and sailed his beloved SS *Chung* to Canton to reopen it for business.

His CAT airline had come into existence in October 1946, and kept operating until its liquidation following a crash on the night of Friday, February 16, 1968, when a CAT Boeing sank below safety height on the approach to Taipei. This crash made aviation history, for the Taiwan authorities charged both pilots with manslaughter through negligence. They were subsequently freed of the threat of gaol, but each paid a higher price, for Chief Pilot Stuart Dow lost an arm, and co-pilot Hugh Hicks his wife. Cat's days were numbered, but the General, the greatest Flying Tiger of them all, had died in July 1958 and was spared this final heartbreak.

DC4 Calcutta Inaugural Flight (VR-HEU)
23rd May 1953
Routing: Hong Kong—Bangkok—Rangoon—Calcutta
Front line: (l to r): R/O Ho Sai, F/O R.K. (Ken Parry), F/O J.H. (John) Warne.
Second Line: Capt. C.F. (Pat) Moore, Capt. A.B. (Pat) Armstrong, Capt. Phil Blown.
Back Line: F/H Margaret Wheeldon, R/O L.W. (Lyell) Louttit, S.F/H I.E. (Iris) Stobart, and F/P Marcel Lin.

CHAPTER THIRTEEN
VR-HEU'S MOMENT OF TRUTH

'No one can shorten my life by a minute,'
said Ghandi.
'It belongs to God.'

A breathless senior radio operator handed a message to Pip Pickering, the Kai Tak Duty Controller. It read: 'Mayday! Mayday! VR-HEU going down, engine on fire, engine . . .' The date was July 23, 1954. By the time the transcribed message was read Cathay Pacific's first Skymaster was committed to its total destruction, the victim of a murderous attack by Chinese Communist fighter planes operating from San Ya (now Yaxian) a strip on the southern extremity of Hainan Island.

Days before the actual attack the writing was on the wall, but its significance was overlooked. Captain Len Cosgrove had left Saigon's beleaguered airport of Tan Son Nhut after waiting for the morning fog to clear, in company with thirty-odd French Air Force pilots waiting to board their Corsairs and Martlets that stood in the dispersals, bombed up, with napalm cylinders slung under the wings, ready for another foray against the Viet Minh. The fog cleared on schedule, the circling Air Force Constellation from Paris made its delayed landing, and Cosgrove took off.

He had flown the coast of Indo-China so long that the chart he carried was almost a formality. The weather between Vietnam and China is benevolent, with sunny skies prevailing, except for seasonal typhoons. This July day was one of tranquility and typhoons were far from Cos's mind as his venerable Catalina droned on above a gentle sea: Height 9000 feet, airspeed 103 knots, outside air temperature eight degrees Centrigrade, fuel consumption 65 gallons an hour. Three and half hours to Hong Kong and a weekend's fishing ahead. Down on his port side was the brown mass of Hainan Island and the old strip of San Ya where the Catalina he was flying had landed in 1950 to lift the last of the war-lords to refuge in Macao.

Suddenly Cosgrove stiffened, for the strip, inch-long at this distance, looked very different. Concrete patches decorated each end of the bitumen runway.

'Oh boy! That means jets!' said Cosgrove. Closer inspection with field-glasses showed dispersal bays awaiting the arrival of their charges. It was the writing on the wall for sure, and Cosgrove realized that henceforth Hainan must be approached with extreme caution. After discussing the matter with co-pilot Jim Kiernan and flight engineer Winyard he pushed it to the back of his mind, but on landing he rang the most senior official of DCA and pointed out the implica-

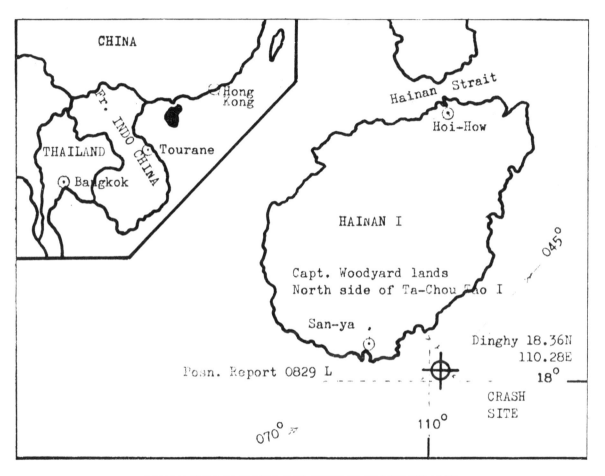

MAP 5: SKYMASTER LOSS OVER HAINAN ISLAND

tions of what he had seen. That official was not disturbed and the traffic lanes remained unaltered. No official warning was issued.

Captain Forgan-Smith, a senior skipper with Qantas, was flying his Constellation on the Sydney-Tokyo route which passed through Labuan, Hong Kong and Iwakuni. Approximately abeam of Hainan Island his first officer Arthur Whitmarsh suddenly threw his lunch-tray into the companionway and grabbed the controls. A dark-grey high-tailed jet zoomed up from underneath and disappeared almost vertically on the port side.

'It passed so close we could smell the kero-exhaust from it,' Forgie told me. He logged the position and on arrival at Kai Tak reported to the authorities, only to be told he must have been mistaken. Fighter jets could not operate that far from land, they said.

'The next morning,' Forgie said, 'I was walking with the Qantas agent when we overtook one of our onward passengers who wanted to know what was going on when the jet fighter nearly hit us. I was a little wary, so asked him to describe it. He said it was a black-looking high-tailed jet which came in from the right side, but by the time he put down his tray and raced to the left side it had disappeared. He thought it might have been an F86 or a "mig-Yak". He had seen similar aircraft in Korea where he had been a Lieutenant-Commander in the U.S. Navy.

'I immediately turned him round and we went to the airport flight-checking section where he repeated the whole story. The senior man now listened with greater attention than he had given my previous report and made all kinds of notes, but I don't think there was a follow-up.'

In Saigon, two days earlier than the Mayday message, Captain John Carrington on his pre-departure walk round the Skymaster noted that the port oleo strut needed additional air pressure, and as usual the equipment to provide this had to be brought out from the city. By the time the job was done insufficient daylight remained for the aircraft to be returned to Kai Tak before that airfield closed, for night flying was still not permitted there except under grave emergency. This meant that the Bangkok-Singapore service would have to be re-scheduled, but a flight that could arrive at Kai Tak at first light could ease some of the confusion. The crew spent a reasonable night bedded down in the Skymaster but when they went to submit flight clearance they were told the Viet Minh had raided during the night and they could not take off before an inspection had certified the runway clear of mines. Their landing at Kai Tak was shortly after 10 a.m.

From there Captain Philip Blown flew the first leg to Bangkok where he and his first officer Captain Cedric Carlton and radio officer Stephen Wong would overnight and pick up the service on its return from Singapore. The two hostesses, Esther Law and Rose Chen were to stay on duty the entire flight. Cathay Pacific's ground engineer George Cattanach was to join the return flight for discussions with DCA, with his name recorded on the passenger list rather than on the crew manifest. He had been associated with Hong Kong a long time, and in fact had been a crew member of the Catalina PBY5A which disintegrated while landing in Kowloon Bay years before. George was looking forward to the trip, for at the

Cathay Pacific Airways DC4 Skymaster VR-HEU
Hong Kong Island Forms the Background
1st July 1954

VR-HFF DC4 C54A in service August 1954. Livery slightly different
from VR-HEU which was shot down 23.7.54 off Hainan Island

other end was his fiancee Daisy Smith. She had an ill-defined job with Cathay Pacific, her duties including engineering drafting and associated art drawings. She was also Bob Smith's sister, which alone was sufficient for me to rate her as first class.

The Skymaster returned as anticipated, and Captain Blown was gratified that it had made up almost fifteen minutes, but the snag-book recorded a magneto drop in the Number Three engine which had to be fixed before departure. George Cattanach soon made the necessary rectification, but as he wrote off the snag he added a note that his work should be re-checked when the Skymaster got back to Kai Tak, for he suspected that the timing of the engine had slipped. All this was unnecessary, but he was not to know that he, the engine and the aeroplane would never reach Hong Kong.

The passengers loaded and Phil remarked to Ced that the time the other crew had made up had now been more than lost, and added that things could be worse. It was a prophetic statement, for when he tried to start the Number One engine the starter would not mesh. They had to disembark the passengers, make a three-engine takeoff, impulse start the engine in the air, and return.

Steve Wong transmitted his final normal position report from VR-HEU at 0829 hours local standard time. The Skymaster was then at 18 degrees north Lattitude and 110 East Longitude. Altitude was 9000 feet. At 0836 local standard time Phil Blown gently wound the auto-pilot knob to the left which changed the heading from 070 degrees to 045 and brought the airliner on a course which paralleled the east coast of Hainan Island some fifteen or twenty miles to port.

After about three minutes on this heading Cedric Carlton looked through his window, and then excitedly reported a cream-coloured low-wing aircraft with red markings closing in fast from slightly above. Phil Blown looked back through his window and saw another fighter in a similar position. He immediately disengaged the auto-pilot and as he did, both fighters opened up with machine-gun and cannon fire. The noise of the firing was terrific.

These initial bursts set Number One and Number Four engines on fire and ruptured the fuel tanks in the starboard wing, which immediately spouted flames. The skipper hurled the Skymaster into a dive, taking evasive action, first to port, then to starboard, but each incipient turn drew increased fire from the fighter on that side. For an undefended plane no evasion was possible.

Speed in the dive now exceeded 350 miles per hour, a full 100 miles an hour above the design speed for the wing. But Phil saw his only hope in attempting to outfly the fighters, and he prayed that the wings would remain attached to the fuselage—perhaps the speed would suck out much of the burning fuel from the gaping tanks, and just maybe the speed would also help to blow out the fire which enveloped the entire starboard wing.

'What a lot of hopes and maybes!' he thought.

Number Four engine now ran wild, its shrill declaration emphasising the general chaotic situation. Cedric managed to reduce the power to that at which he could safely feather the propellor and the terrifying sound abated. He pushed the CO_2 discharge button: the engine fire of Number Four was smothered, but

Captain Cedric "Ced" Carlton

there was no way he could fight the blaze in the wing.

The Communist murderers continued an unabated fire and some passengers had already died by bullet and shell blast. Both Phil and Cedric were subjected to a barrage of projectiles screaming up the main aisle, and boost gauges, fuel gauges and the engine instruments shattered before their eyes.

Other crew members pursued assigned duties with a calmness which reflected both dedication and first-class training. Steve Wong was upholding the highest traditions of the radio operator. The distress signal he had sent off had been acknowledged from Hong Kong but he kept transmitting although it is doubtful whether any of his messages were reaching the airways for, unknown to him, his aerials had been blasted away.

George Cattanach was assisting the hostesses to ready the cabin for a ditching which was only seconds away. About this time hostess Rose Chen was blasted into oblivion. Moments before, Ester Law had not fully grasped that the Skymaster was under attack and raced to the toilet to investigate a loud sucking noise: as she threw open the door she saw a great gaping hole in the roof. Most of the starboard wall was missing and the john had disappeared. She recalled saying to herself, 'Say, that doesn't look too good!' and hastily slammed the door shut again in the hope that if she could not see it perhaps it was all right.

Mr Peter S. Thatcher later told the *South China Morning Post* that the last he saw of his friend Leonard L Parrish was when he kissed his two sons, Laurence 4, and Phillip 2, as he gently laid his massive frame over them in protection.

The absence of panic and hysteria was marked.

At 5000 feet the rudder controls were shot away and the pedals became useless. At 3000 feet the starboard aileron control was shot off, but the gallant skipper still thought that all was not lost for his aircraft retained some control through the port aileron. That slight relief was short-lived for the aircraft was becoming more unmanageable and continued in a corkscrew turn to the right. He managed to control this by throttling back his two left engines and increasing his Number Three engine to maximum power output. By this time he had managed to reduce his speed to 160 miles an hour, but anything below this was causing his starboard wing to stall out, so he could go no slower in preparation for the impact on the water.

The Skymaster skimmed the crest of a wave and the starboard wing tore off between its two engines. The pilots knew that the next impact would decide death or survival. The cockpit ploughed into a fifteen-foot swell about a quarter of the way from the crest and the severe deceleration snapped their safety harnesses and hurled them against the rubber crash guards above the instrument panel. The water stove in the co-pilot's cabin window and the skipper's hinged clear-vision screen; a green turmoil of water flooded the cockpit. After several false moves the pilots managed to assist each other in a miraculous escape.

From the moment the airliner came under attack until it slammed into the ocean eleven miles south-southeast of Tinhosa Island a bare two minutes had elapsed; less time than it takes to read an account of it.

When he surfaced Cedric Carlton saw a few people in the water, the nearest,

Captain Blown. He swam around telling them to grab mail-bags and the like. A Mae West bobbed up right in front of him and he put it on, then swam to help Peter Thatcher support a woman. She had a deep gash in her throat. It was not bleeding and looked very grey. He could find no life in her, but got her into a Mae West before he left her and went to assist others. He had a moment of hope:

'It was then I noticed Mrs Thorburn hanging on to an object at the sight of which I joyously yelled. "You little beauty!", for it was a twenty-man dinghy. I was a bit concerned that if I inflated it too soon it might blow away before we could get aboard, so I gathered everyone round it and then pulled the inflation cord and we were all soon safely aboard.' His watch had not stopped at the time of impact as the skipper's had. It was 9.00 a.m. by the time they were all in the dinghy.

Captain Blown had surfaced in time to watch the burning wing slip slowly beneath the surface. The fuselage and tail followed it. He gathered five Mae Wests of the number that were floating round in their white canvas cases and inflated them. He saw Peter Thatcher hanging on to the woman's body and made his way towards him. On the way he saw three more bodies and identified them as Mrs Finlay, Miss Rose Chen and one of the Parrish boys. He felt all three, and could find no sign of life in any.

Cedric had by this time inflated the dinghy and was helping Mrs. Parrish aboard. Phil helped getting other survivors in. Of the nine of them, several had various types of injury; three had bullet and shrapnel wounds and one had a broken thigh.

Concerned lest the fighters return and strafe the survivors, the skipper told them to keep their Mae Wests inflated and be ready to jump into the water. Meantime they erected the weather awning, and all hid from view, to give the appearance of any empty raft.

At 11.25 two RAF Hornets flew over them at about 5000 feet but did not spot them. At 11.30 an RAF Valetta spotted them, commenced circling and recalled the Hornets. A Sunderland flying-boat turned up about an hour later but could not land owing to the high seas. Shortly after, an RAF York joined them, and then an Air Vietnam Skymaster and a French Privateer as well.

Other stations besides Kai Tak had intercepted the distress call. One was Mum Louttit, crew member of a Cathay Pacific DC3 bound for Labuan via Manila, Sandakan and Jesselton. He immediately called Hong Kong radio to confirm that they had received the SOS, and on being assured that action was in hand, made no further calls for he did not want to clutter that frequency. He kept a close listening watch, but by now Steve Wong was dead and the Skymaster beneath the water.

In Hong Kong Pip Pickering had calculated the wreck site from the information given at the Skymaster's last reporting point, and had scrambled the two RAF Hornets on call at that time for search and rescue duties. The position he gave the Hornets proved to be less than two miles in error.

The 31st Air Rescue Squadron at the U.S. Clarke Air Base, fifty miles north of Manila, received Pip's notification that a British airliner was reported near

Hainan with an engine on fire and losing altitude. They timed the message at 0835 Philippine Local Time (0935 Hong Kong time). Two SA-16 amphibious aircraft, Grumman Albatrosses were despatched. The first, AF1009, commanded by Captain Jack Thompson Woodyard was airborne 21 minutes after the Rescue Control Centre received the signal. The second, AF1018, under the command of Captain Dale R. Baker followed shortly. Woodyard's crew comprised co-pilot Captain Tommy B. Arnold, Navigator-Captain Albert F. Smith, Engineer Staff-sergeant Douglas F. Blair, Radio Operator Laurence E. Rodrigues and Aero-Medical Specialist Cecil R. Smith. Rodrigues and Smith were designated A/3C and A/2C respectively—but there were no second- or third-class airmen on that crew that day, rather first-class plus.

Smith had calculated a heading to bring the Albatross to a point midway between the last position and Hong Kong, but when Kai Tak radio advised no more messages had been received from the Skymaster he plotted a course that would take him fifty miles to the northeast of the last reported position. Woodyard instructed Rodrigues to advise Captain Baker, following in '2 Dumbo 46' the course alteration. A few minutes after he settled on the new course Hong Kong advised him that there were survivors in a dinghy, and that its position was fixed.

At 1300 Hong Kong time Rodrigues took a message from Hong Kong, relayed from the Chinese People's Government, requiring that no military aircraft were to approach the scene of the accident and were to remain well clear of Hainan Island. Woodyard told him merely to acknowledge the message.

About 75 miles from the raft Rodrigues established radio communication on 121.5 mc with a French Privateer aircraft which reported he had clear visual contact with the raft and that he had full rescue gear aboard. This Frenchman had received the distress call in Tourane, now Da Nang, and answered it.

Captain Woodyard now descended to 1500 feet to stay below a layer of broken cloud. At that height he could not spot the bobbing dinghy but the efficient Frenchman soon saw his dilemma and put a drift signal right beside the raft as a marker. The Albatross crew saw it from about four miles away.

The calculations Woodyard had to make before the touchdown were complex. The landing had to be so precise that the reversible propellors had to bring the Albatross to a complete stop by the time the next wave-crest arrived, and that day there were exactly 180 feet between crests. Captain Woodyard's report follows:

'The sea appeared fairly rough, being complicated by a ground-swell system running 60 to 70 degrees to the main flow as we approached Hainan. I estimated eight to ten foot seas were running and the wind was southerly at twelve to fifteen knots.

'We dropped two Mark Five drift signals at the raft's position and I prepared to land three miles north of the raft off the south-east coast at Tai Chou Tau Island just off the Hainan coast, where the ground-swell system was dampened. A normal rough water landing was made without difficulty on 240 degrees heading. The ground swell crests were barely touched before stalling on the swell crest. This eliminated any trouble from the ground swell. The sea condi-

DARING RESCUE IN THE SOUTH CHINA SEA
Captain Jack Thompson Woodyard's SA-16 Grumman Albatross AF 1009 churning through 10 to 12-foot swells towards the survival dinghy of Captain Phillip Blown's shot-down Skymaster off Hainan Island.   23rd July 1954

SA-16 Grumman Albatross

tions were approximately as evaluated, and after clearing the protection of the island taxi-ing was slowed considerably and on occasions the wing floats and pedestals were completely submerged. During periods of extreme roll when the props hit the water it was necessary to use idle reverse position to avoid straining or killing the engines.

'The French Privateer guided me to the raft, and on approaching it the engineer was posted in the bow with a throw-line and the radio operator and medic were stationed at the rear hatch with a throw-line and boathook. The raft was circled to check the condition of the survivors and to see whether they were able to assist during the pick-up. The first approach was successful, a single-engine approach, cutting the port engine before reaching the raft so the prop would stop and be properly positioned. Nine survivors were taken aboard.

'The captain of the downed Skymaster was among them and immediately came forward to the flight deck where he stated: "We were shot down. Watch out for yourself. There may be other fighters in the area." I immediately called Captain Baker in "2 Dumbo 46", told him of the number of survivors, and when he crossed to the rescue frequency I cautioned him to watch for "intruders".

'By this time I was taxi-ing back to the area where we had landed and Captain Arnold was being assisted by airman Rodrigues in an effort to hang the jato [jet-assisted take off] units. After a great deal of exertion they managed to get the port jato bottle into position but couldn't manage the bulky starboard one. Captain Arnold arrived at the flight deck and told me they were having trouble with the starboard bottle and would have to rest awhile from their exertions. About this time our cover aircraft reported a formation of unidentified aeroplanes approaching; this seemed to stimulate Captain Arnold and with an oath he rushed back and swung that bottle into place unassisted.

'As we approached the shoreline numerous natives could be seen running for their junk-type fishing boats which were tied up at anchor. We approached within a hundred yards to take full advantage of all the possible smoother water and the shoreline effect upon the sea. Takeoff was made without incident, turning approximately 110 degrees to port during the initial run. This allowed full effective power on both engines by the time the aircraft straightened out on heading. Control and altitude response was obtained before firing the jato units. During the final run the aircraft was nursed over three major crests and then stayed airborne. The approaching formation was identified as USN Skyraiders and as we completed our takeoff two of them broke formation and flew beside us. Needless to say we were greatly relieved. We set course for Hong

Kong.'

As the Albatross became airborne Captain Len Cosgrove arrived on the scene in a Catalina, accompanied by Captain Pat Armstrong. Pat had volunteered to help out for the only crew Cos could muster at short notice was Ambrose Tai, a young man who had not at that time been authorised to fly as co-pilot. Pat had been waiting at Kai Tak to take out the Skymaster when Phil Blown returned with it.

From the other Albatross Captain Baker advised Cos (along with all the other aircraft flying cover), of how the Skymaster had met its fate, and suggested that as there were no other survivors they should all get the hell out of there. The pilot of the French Privateer was the least understanding. At various stages the other commanders tried to reason with him but he had worked himself into a frenzy, at one time roaring across the air-waves that he wanted no suggestions or interferences from anybody. In suitable broken English he announced that he had sufficient armament aboard to shoot down the entire fornicating Communist Chinese Air Force, and only wanted the *pettite chance* to prove it. He became dejected when Captain Woodyard advised him that his offer of escort 'right to the ground' at Kai Tak was unnecessary, for all the aircraft which had been giving cover formed up round the rescue Albatross to take her home. With a good-humoured *au-revior* the Frenchman turned for his base at Tourane, but his desire for a fight was shared by others, for on July 26, just three days later, Washington released the news that two Communist fighters had been shot down near Hainan.

Precisely at 5.15 p.m. by Cedric Carlton's robust watch Captain Woodyard wheeled the Albatross down the Kai Tak runway. Their joy in safe arrival was tempered with sorrow for those who had lost their lives. Miss Rita Cheung had died within sight of Hong Kong and now lay in a tiny ragdoll bundle covered with the medic's flying jacket. Although Rodrigues had transmitted a list of survivors many in the vast throng gathered at the airport had not been told just who these were. The cries of anguish were terrible when all the survivors had disembarked and Captain Woodyard announced with a sob in his voice that there were no more.

A couples of hours earlier the Kowloon Hospital had received a directive to stand by for an emergency. Tired doctors who had worked throughout the night and all that morning tending the victims of a disastrous fire in Kowloon Tsai were called back to duty. Everyone was so weary it was late in the evening when Cedric Carlton complained to his visitor, Tom Bax, of a stinging pain under his right arm, and Tom discovered that a bullet had passed right through the fleshy portion. Cedric recalls with amusement that one of his wrists was carefully taped up to take care of a non-existent sprain while his ankle, swollen like a football was left unattended, and another survivor with a swollen wrist was receiving attention for a sprained ankle. When a weary matron asked him, 'Have you had a bowel movement today?' and Cedric answered 'Not voluntarily' she ordered him an enema. The bullet through his underarm was, he thought, the one which had killed George Cattanach, for as he turned to scramble back into the cockpit to assist Phil Blown with the damaged controls he heard George gasp and saw him fall to the side of the aisle.

At Labuan a group of his friends was holding a wake for him. Mum Louttit, having intercepted the initial message, stayed crouched over his radio until the moment he switched off on arrival. He had copied the list of survivors but Cedric's name had not appeared on it. When Rodrigues passed round a piece of paper for the survivors to record their names one of the Chinese had written both his name and his alias; Rodrigues had counted nine names and nine survivors and transmitted what he had.

Captain McKenzie, a close friend of Cedric's from their first flying days had met the DC3 at Labuan. When Mum told him that Cedric had been aboard the Skymaster and was not named among the survivors McKenzie organised a wake. It continued all night, becoming happier with each passing hour and producing some fragile heads next day. The company never knew their crew went straight from Cedric Carlton's wake to their DC3. Their condition did not make much difference to their performance, for several oil company passengers remarked they had never experienced landings so smooth before. In Hong Kong the crew was overjoyed to find that Cedric was hale and hearty, and that their wake had been all in vain.

Admiral Felix Stump told a news conference on July 27 that his fliers were under instructions to 'be quick on the trigger' if a hostile pass were made at them. A three-minute air battle twelve miles off the coast of Hainan resulted in two Chinese LA-7s being blasted to the waves by American Skyraiders. The first met its end under the guns of Lieutenant Roy Tatham and Ensign Richard Crooks, neither of whom had been in battle before. The second had been drawn into a real hornet's nest and fallen to the combined efforts of six other Skyraiders and one Corsair. Peking Radio announced that two American fighter planes 'had made piratical attacks on two Polish merchant ships and one Chinese escort vessel' but did not mention the loss of their two LA-7 fighter planes.

Mr Anthony Eden, the British Foreign Secretary, made some suitable criticism of 'the savage attack on an unarmed airliner belonging to Cathay Pacific Airways' and Mr Clement Attlee, Leader of the Labour Opposition was goaded into saying it was 'absolutely inexcusable'. He could not really go too far as he had planned a visit to Communist China for the following month. The politicians allowed themselves to be mollified by Peking's admission of responsibility for the attack which they described as entirely accidental. Peking expressed regret and sympathy and a willingness to consider payment of appropriate compensation for the loss of life and damage to property.

A British businessman who refused to be identified announced that the Peking apology would now allow him to reopen negotiations on a trade deal worth a quarter-million pounds, which he had cancelled the day before. He made the dubious statement that 'it would not have been moral to do business with people who shoot your planes down'. Sabre rattling gradually subsided, and soon the media were not mentioning the attack other than to report that BOAC had re-routed their aircraft flying between Singapore and Hong Kong further from the Hainan coastline.

Clarke Air Force Base, Philippine Islands
26th August 1954
Maj. Gen. John W. Sessumus Jr., pins the Distinguished Flying Cross on Captain
Jack T. Woodyard for his part in rescuing nine survivors from a Cathay Pacific
Airliner near Red-held Hainan Island on 23rd July, 1954. Gen. Sessum's aide, Capt.
Frank Rohan, looks on.

On 15th June 1955, His Excellency the Governor, Sir Alexander Grantham pinned the Badge of the Queen's Commendation For Valuable Service In The Air on Captains Phillip Blown and Cedric Windas Carlton.

L to R: Captain 'Ced' Carlton, His Excellency, Mrs 'Bunty' Blown, and Captain 'Phil' Blown.

In a comunique addressed on July 30 to Mr J.A. Blackwood, Cathay Pacific's Chairman, Mr Julian F. Harrington the American Consul-General in Hong Kong, expressed regret that so little had been said of the heroism of the airliner's crew and the skilful handling of the crippled plane by Captain Blown. 'Without the successful ditching,' he wrote, 'there would have been no survivors to rescue.'

The Governor, Sir Alexander W.G.H. Grantham GCMG was on leave, but forwarded a cable to Major-General John W. Sessumus Jnr., wherein he expressed the highest praise for the rescue crew. The Colonial Secretary Robert Brown Black GMG, OBE wrote similarly on behalf of the people of the Crown Colony. Paragraph three of Colonel E. Horras's Mission Report, dated August 4, to the Commander Air Sea Rescue Service, Orlando A.F.B., Florida, stated:

'In order to give personal recognition for a job well done, Captain Woodyard and his crew have been recommended for the Distinguished Flying Cross. Captain Baker and Captain Veith of the second crew have also been recommended for the DFC. The remainder of Captain Baker's crew have been recommended for the Air Medal.'

Cathay Pacific remembered Captain Woodyard at Christmas 1954 by presenting him with a salver engraved:

'To Captain Jack Thompson Woodyard, USAF. In grateful recognition of his gallantry in SA-16, No. AF1009 off Hainan Island, 23/7/54.'

Unbeknown to most of us, the company was assiduously trying to get recognition of the parts played by the Skymaster's crew. The wording of telegram No. 928 of November 4, 1954 must have helped, for in the following year, on June 15, 1955 the Governor Sir Alexander Grantham presented each pilot with the badge of the Queen's Commendation for Valuable Service in the Air, in the presence of a distinguished gathering.

Phil Blown had been born in Tientsin, China in 1913. During the war he saw service in New Guinea as a Flight Lieutenant in the RAAF. He joined Cathay Pacific in 1948 and held the position of Chief Pilot from December 1952 until he resigned ten years later.

Cedric Carlton, born in Brisbane in 1921, also served with the RAAF in New Guinea and on various stations throughout Australia, including Darwin, where his commanding officer was the almost legendary Bluey Truscott. He was with Cathay Pacific from 1948 to 1951 and again from 1953 to 1964, the hiatus occuring when the Hong Kong DCA withdrew his licence after a routine medical examination has assessed him unfit. Because this unfitness was a slight diabetic condition, the National and General Life Assurance Company of Teddington, London had refused to pay out $20,000 under a crew disablement insurance policy on the grounds that his diabetic condition was only mild, and that on a low carbohydrate diet he could still fly. He won his case in 1966.

From the time that VR-HEU entered service with the company in

September 1949 until its loss, she carried no less than 47,399 passengers during 15,279 flying hours. The J.K. Swire diarist recorded: 'We submitted a claim for 251,400 pounds to the Chinese Government, which paid this in full to Her Majesty's Government at the end of November 1954. We have so far been paid 175,000 pounds on account, but we look like having a stiff fight with the Claims Commission for the balance.' His fears proved correct, for not until August 1955 did the company receive a final cheque from the Foreign Office in payment of the claim, making a total of 268,560 pounds.

Of all the tributes to the rescuers, the one which stays in my mind was that paid by Mr John Thorburn, husband of a survivor. After giving the highest praise to Captain Blown and his crew he asked General Sessums to convey to Captain Woodyard and his men heartfelt thanks for all they had done 'to bring my wife back to me and her babies'.

Captain Phil Blown

CHAPTER FOURTEEN
MESSRS KAI AND TAK

'They dreamed not of a perishable home
who could thus build.'

... William Wordsworth

In the same month that the Communists shot down the Skymaster, the Hong Kong Legislative Council resolved '. . . that the development of Kai Tak airport, which is estimated to cost $HK96,750,000 based on the construction of a single runway and overrun 7500 feet long by 700 feet wide resting on a reclamation in Kowloon Bay be commenced.'

This was a modification of the original estimate of $HK135,000,000 for a 8,340 foot runway and saved nearly $HK40,000,000, but thirteen years later when the runway was lengthened to 10,280 feet at an astronomical cost it looked like a false economy. The Council had faced the alternative of the gradual stagnation of Hong Kong into an aviation backwater, off the world's major air routes and dependent on feeder-lines from Manila and Taipei.

The project involved removal of two million cubic yards of silt from Kowloon Bay and the procurement of eleven million cubic yards of fill from surrounding hills. Such an amount of fill, as Councillor Bowring advised his fellow-members, if dumped over the entire area of the Hong Kong Cricket Club ground, would form a pile 300 feet higher than the 1817 foot high Victoria Peak. Mr Bowring also noted ' . . . the unpleasant odour which arises during dry weather from the large nullah bordering Kai Tak originates from the densely populated areas surrounding the present airfield in which, except for a small developed section near Kowloon City, no piped drainage or sewerage system exists.'

His words did less than justice to the foulness of this odour. Most travellers to the Colony at that time will never forget it. It was told of one great comedian that he bounded out on the platform on top of the exit stairs from his arriving aircraft, took a great gulping breath, screwed up his face in disgust and asked a companion 'What is that terrible stench?' The companion whispered in his ear that it was plain ordinary shit. The comedian was terse: 'I realise that, man, but what have they done to it?'

Hong Kong's years of flight experience began in 1891, when a Captain Baldwin ascended in a balloon and, as advertised, descended by parachute. The launching was smooth and the descent uneventful. Other balloonists followed through the years and one, Senor Hernandez, had a narrow escape in 1911 when he attempted an ascent from North Point. As he stepped into his gondola the balloon exploded in a sheet of flame and the Senor emerged, according to reports,

Left to Right: W.C.G. (Bill) Knowles, A.J.R. Moss (Director of Civil Aviation H.K.) and Tom Bax (Cathay Pacific's Traffic Manager). 1951.

November 21st 1974. CPA's Balloon—Captain Geoff Green, Hong Kong Cricket Club, Central.

The most expensive playing field in the world.

Captain Geoff Green and F/E Ron Taffe preparing for the first free flight over Sekkong, Hong Kong, 1975. Sir Denis Roberts (The then Colonial Secretary) assists at right.

with a well-toasted posterior. He apologised to the crowd, which, in appreciation of his savoir-faire, took up a collection to buy him a new balloon.

This early ballooning was prophetic, for Cathay Pacific sponsors two of its aircrew, who have made a name for themselves in hot air ballooning, and their 'mounts' resplendent in the distinctive green livery of the company, have attracted thousands of dollars worth of free publicity in many countries of the world. On November 25, 1978 His Royal Highness Prince Charles presented the Medal of the Royal Aero Club to Geoff Green, a Captain of one of the company's Boeing 747s, for his world altitude record when he reached 30,500 feet in an AX-6 class balloon.

In 1924 a private group later to be known as the Hong Kong Flying Club gave fixed-wing flying its first real toehold in the Colony by developing a grass area about 300 yards by 400 to serve as flying school and aero club. The venture attracted more scepticism than support, but then two businessmen, Mr Ho Kai and Mr Au Tak formed a firm they called 'Kai Tak Investment Company'; its object the reclamation of part of Kowloon Bay for building purposes. The Club rented a portion of the land so reclaimed and it became known as Kai Tak.

The sceptics' assessment of the future of flying appeared confirmed at the inauguration ceremony on Chinese New Year's Day 1925, when a parachutist featured in the ceremony jumped from an aeroplane and drowned in the harbour. Kai Tak's growth was almost imperceptible and so retarded by lack of commercial interest that, to further public awareness, the Government in 1930 voted a grant of money and an annual subsidy, at the same time taking over the airfield's upkeep and creating a post of aerodrome superintendent within the Harbour Department, this forming the nucleus of an Air Service Department.

The man they chose was Mr Albert James Robert Moss. He had gained experience in the RAF and took over his appointment in August 1930. The Japanese interned him on Christmas Day 1941. When he resumed his duties after the war the Government separated flying activities from the Harbour Department and appointed him Director of Air Services, replacing Mr. G.F. Hole who had held that title from 1930 to 1940. In May 1946 the title was changed to Director of Civil Aviation. The first to hold that title, Mr Moss departed the Colony on pre-retirement leave in 1952. He died on April 16, 1979.

His Assistant Superintendent of Aerodrome, Maxwell Norman Oxford was appointed in 1938. Mobilised, he served with the RAF through the war and on return became Deputy Director of Civil Aviation and Airport Manager. Late in 1950 he was transferred and became Director-General of Civil Aviation, Malaya.

Another dedicated administrator was Owen Fitzwilliam Hamilton, MBE. An ex-Merchant Navy Captain, Hammie became Kai Tak's Marine supervisor in 1938, when Kai Tak's main function was servicing the flying-boat base. Like Moss, Hamilton was interned and suffered severe privations. He resumed his job after the war and on April 1, 1958 his title was changed to Airport Commandant. He went on pre-retirement leave in 1962 and died in Middlesex in September 1973.

The Japanese occupation advanced the development of the aerodrome, ex-

KAI TAK AIRPORT, KOWLOON, HONG KONG 1950
The black spots surrounding the HAECO premises and also to the North and South of Runway
"07" represent the CNAC and CATC "sanctuary" aeroplanes flow in when China fell under
Communist domination.

Proposed 13/31 Runway looking towards S.E. gap.

Aerodrome Development at Hong Kong (Kai Tak) Airport June 1951

This is an ultra-rare photograph for it shows the Surveyor's markings of the proposed new Kai Tak runway.

Notes: 1. The hills at Kowloon which were removed. 2. The Wall of the old Chinese Walled City also demolished. 3. The centreline of the new runway running right through the hangar of the Far East Flying Training School; 4. The existing (then) "07" runway threshold just in front of the training school hangar; and 5. The Sacred Hill which just overlaps the starboard side of the perimeter of the new runway.

This Hill to be removed

3 FLATS TO BE MOVED

HILLS TO BE CLEARED TO THIS LINE.

R/W E

R/W E

S-0498-0

Aerodrome Development at Hong Kong (Kai Tak) Airport June 1951
This is another ultra-rare photograph as it shows the Surveyor's notations of the portions of the surrounding terrain and buildings which had to be cleared to abide with an unobstructed approach.

236

panding it from a 171-acre grass field without runways to 376 acres with two concrete runways. Here Tony Weller and Geoff Sloss worked as prisoners of war under the harsh discipline of the Japanese, at first just fetching and carrying, cutting grass and moving bricks from one place to another. About July 1942 work began in earnest on the runway, and the whole camp became involved from predawn until after dark.

'An old Star Ferry picked us up from Sham Shui Po and took us direct to Kai Tak,' Tony told me. 'I think we completely levelled a hill at San Po Kong. Very hard work, it went on 'till the early months of 1943. During this time we put down Kai Tak's first concrete runway with a compass direction of 31/13, and it wasn't very good. We put in mainly sand and a mere touch of concrete and it fell apart quite frequently.'

For some post-war years the airport remained unimproved. The Port Health, Customs, and Immigration authorities shared the inadequate accommodation of Transport Command, located a few yards off the turning pan of Runway 25. Such sharing which, as Police Inspector Buckingham recalls, included the Police Post, made use of a single table, affectionately dubbed 'the office' and standing under the building's verandah.

After returning to the Cathay Pacific fold in June 1953 as first officer, I had my first command on February 26, 1954, captaining DC3 VR-HDA. My first officer was Lou Mose, who was to meet his death in October 1961, crashing into high ground near Croglin Fell, in the English County of Cumberland. My Chinese radio officer was S.Y. Ho, the air hostess Diane Cheng and the flight engineer Raymond 'Rascal' Racela, a Filipino. We were on the Labuan run—Hong Kong, Manila, Sandakan, Jesselton and Labuan, a pretty hefty day's work. The first day's flying time was nine hours 53 minutes, which entailed a total duty time of thirteen hours.

The service was unable to return to Kai Tak before failing light closed the airport, consequently we stayed overnight at Manila where we became almost family to the management of the Shellborne Hotel, a drab building overlooking Manila Bay. It had acquired the reputation of being haunted by the spirits of those tortured and exterminated by the Kempei Tai, the dreaded Japanese counterpart of the German Gestapo. I never proved that it was haunted, but it became a recongised procedure to inform a new, impressionable air-hostess of this phenomenon with the well-based expectation that she, after checking into her room, would soon appear at the door of the bravest member of the flight-deck to be protected and comforted through the long, dark night.

An Indian hostess named Shanta Mansukani told me that on a flight which carried two hostesses they were determined to find out about the spectral visits. They left one dim light burning and demanded loudly that the ghost should show itself. A great horned goat appeared before their terrified eyes and asked what they wanted; they ran screaming from the room. Shanta assured me she would never enter it again. I wonder how that particular crew managed it. After a while some of the older hostesses caught the ear of the management and the accommodation was changed to another establishment not far away.

Problems in plenty beset some of our runs. The political situation in and around the Red River Delta in North Vietnam continued to add to the problems of Operations Manager Captain Moore, for by flying the big dog-leg round Hainan Island, we had a five-hour flight to Hanoi or Haiphong instead of three and a half, a big increase in fuel operating costs. When he made allowance, as he had to, for the possible use of our friendliest diversion airport, at Manila, he had an operations nightmare.

I had been diverted to Taipei a couple of times, but there we were unwelcome guests with a standing just better than that of rogues, while our passengers were treated only just above the level of contempt. Each time I had been forced to leave passengers aboard during refuelling while our hosts bullied us in their efforts to get rid of us as quickly as possible. The worst insult was the boarding of the aircraft by military guards. They pulled all the curtains and woe betide anyone misguided enough to take a quick peek outside. This may have been reasonable enough, for we were carrying passengers from a Communist-infested area, and their political leanings were anybody's guess. At that time the island of Taiwan was on a full war footing. Later, as things settled down we found our first impressions of the local authorities were completely wrong, and over the years we established a very friendly rapport.

M. Dehase, of Denis Freres d'Indo-Chine, our Haiphong handling agents kept emphasising that there was little war risk in the Hanoi-Haiphong area and that the Viet Minh had no anti-aircraft equipment there. He then concluded with:

> 'But there is always an appreciable risk of war sabotage during any night-stop at Hanoi and Haiphong. You are certainly aware of the latest incidents which happened on March 4 at Gialam [Hanoi] and Cat-Bi [Haiphong] when several aircraft were destroyed by time-bombs and we think this must be taken seriously into consideration for your future services.'

He was having a bet each way. He threw the onus right back at the company.

His indefinite approach led the company to request my view on local conditions, for on March 16, 1954 I skippered VR-HDB to Haiphong. The Haiphong airfield was grossly overworked, with the main runway being repaired along one whole side. We had to hold for fifty minutes while the American 'packets' took off and then twenty fighter-bombers landed. The rebels had infiltrated the whole area but were expected to be routed out when clear weather returned. Sabotage after dark was a real possibility but we were parked adjacent to their fighter aircraft line which was lit and well patrolled. Hanoi was little better and some days the Hanoi-Haiphong highway was closed for twenty-one hours a day. It was no surprise when the company terminated our Red River Delta schedules the following month.

Our Skymaster underwent major overhaul between February and April, and while it was off the line its schedules were operated by a similar type on a dry lease from Korean National Airways. A 'dry lease' meant that Cathay Pacific merely leased the aircraft and manned it with its own crews; in a 'wet lease' the owner's crew came too. I first flew that Skymaster (HL-108) during April 1957, and all went well until April 27, when I had to feather Number Three engine. As I was only 180 miles from Dum Dum, Calcutta I continued on. Next day I was faced with a three-engined ferry flight of 5 hours 49 minutes to Bangkok, and after a night's sleep continued on another seven hours to Hong Kong.

By that time I had had enough of that garlic-permeated Korean aircraft. It was a great relief when our own Skymaster returned from overhaul. 2,180 miles on three engines did little to soothe my liver. My spell had included two three-engine takeoffs and three landings. Never again!

The Hong Kong *Standard* of April 5, 1954 published a report headed: CPA PILOT SHOWS SKILL AT MANILA. The 'skill' so described had been called on during the takeoff. Just after I got the tailwheel off the ground the starboard tyre burst and the DC3 slewed towards the terminal building, where I could see people abandoning its precincts in the most undignified ways, with the strong male of the species leading the evacuation as usual. I followed emergency procedures with terrified thoroughness, and managed to bring the wayward plane, which apparently had a drink problem, to a stop just before it mounted a stool in the departure lounge bar.

An incident on the Labuan run demonstrated how close-knit was the Cathay Pacific family of that era. A Mr. H.G. Rice contributed an article to the magazine *Flight* in 1954, from which I quote a small extract:

'At Labuan in British North Borneo a DC3 of Cathay Pacific was delayed some months ago for lack of a certain engine spare. The captain sent an urgent AOG signal to the company's base at Hong Kong. About midnight that evening a Chinese radio operator employed by Cathay Pacific, on returning home from the cinema and idly tuning his own ham radio station picked up the Cable and Wireless frequency. He found himself listening to the text of the AOG telegram which he scribbled down on an envelope and then telephoned the chief pilot's home. The chief pilot rose from his bed and drove to Kai Tak airport where he sorted out the parts needed and put them on a Qantas service which left at 8 a.m. for Labuan. At nine o'clock the original telegram was delivered at the Cathay office. What team spirit!!'

One of the world's most beautiful women joined the Skymaster flight from Hong Kong to Singapore in December 1954. Miss Ava Gardner had spent a week in the Colony publicising her new picture *Barefoot Contessa* . As Captain Dave Smith approached Kallang Airport at Singapore one of the worst rainstorms in years was dumping fourteen inches of water over it and had flooded it, forcing him to divert to the RAF station at Butterworth, 500 miles to the north.

At the 6 a.m. departure from Hong Kong traffic manager Tommy Bax had arrived to meet Miss Gardner. Tom was fond enough of the grape himself, but when the lady refused his offer of a cup of tea in favour of a glass of champagne his face blanched, according to Mum Louttit, who was flying as radio officer. But if that was what she wanted at six in the morning, that was what she would

Cathay Pacific's Douglas DC6 VR-HFG—Miami, USA, March 1955.
L to R: Ken Steele, Bill Sparkman (Pan Am Grace), Jack Williams, Dave Smith, Vera Williams, Jack Gething, Jimmy Harper (Douglas), and Phil Blown.

get. The company had curtained off the forward compartment of the Skymaster and Miss Gardner was seated there in splendour accompanied by her sister and two male publicity managers. By the time they arrived at Butterworth they had consumed ten bottles.

Installed in the Station Commander's quarters, Miss Gardner discovered that someone had stolen her shoes, and sent her sister to the plane for another pair. Dave Smith detailed Mum to accompany her.

'She must have checked through a dozen cases before we found the required pair,' Mum said, 'but in order to make sure we took back about a dozen pair, for the sister told me that Ava changed her mind pretty often.' It seemed an exorbitant number of shoes for one who was at that moment making a fortune by her portrayal of a girl who refused to don footwear.

During 1953 Cathay Pacific had approached ANA with a request that they lend one of their senior captains to check and train crews. ANA seconded Captain Kenneth Williams Steele for these duties, and what began as a temporary assignment soon became substantive. Ken was another pioneer airman, and when he left Cathay Pacific in 1963 he had notched his thirty-second year in the air and on the ground dealing with aircraft. Though he had been 'flying a desk' during many of his later years he had still managed to log a substantial total of 17,000 hours aloft.

The boy Ken had focussed his attention on planes and like other youngsters of his generation fiddled with crystal radio-sets and home-modified hot-rods. He had a spell trying to sell radios in New York and was picking up a little extra money with casual announcing jobs at a radio station. One evening he meant to announce the next record as 'Charlie Kunz and a handful of keys', but it did not come out quite like that. His employer, an elderly gentleman perhaps suffering from a lapse of memory, decided that Ken's mind was not on the job and suggested that he seek his fortune in a different environment.

Back in Australia he joined the RAAF and became a pilot in 1931. From there he migrated to commercial flying but there were too many pilots for too few jobs so he turned to barnstorming, for which he purchased his own plane, a 'Spartan' for the princely sum of 150 pounds. The going rate for joyrides was five shillings for a quick circuit, ten shillings if anyone were foolish enough to ask for a loop. He made no money but he had no intention of giving up the thing that kept him poor. The Spartan was to have an interesting future for it was eventually sold to Eddie Connellan who used it as the pioneer craft for Connellan Airways.

In the mid-thirties Steele instructed for the Royal Victorian Aero Club and later moved to the RAC Western Australia, where he stayed until he joined ANA in 1937. The following year ANA transferred him to Guinea Airways, where he soon rose from senior captain to flight superintendent. His work in New Guinea was primarily to carry gold-mining equipment and supplies between Lae and Salamaua in three-engined Junkers and Ford transports.

With the entry of Australia to the war Ken Steele returned to the Air Force and became Liaison Officer with the US Fifth Air Force. As the war ground to

June 1955
Section of Cathay Pacific 'Fleet'
L to R: Douglas DC6 VR-HFG; Douglas DC4 VR-HFF; Douglas DC3 VR-HDB.

an end he was flying a courier run from Brisbane to Biak and Hollandia in DC3s and Commandos. When ANA took over Guinea Airways in 1945 the management posted Ken to Perth as the company's senior route captain, Western Australia. During that time he enjoyed a 'rest' flying the Pacific Ocean from Sydney to Vancouver on Skymasters. This portion of the Holyman empire was soon taken over by British Commonwealth Pacific Airways.

Captain Holyman, asked to set flying standards for Cathay Pacific, sent Ken Steele to check on the abilities of its pilot contingent. In January 1955 when Cathay Pacific bought its first DC6 Captain Steele was appointed Flight Superintendent. He left an enviable record and a legacy with Cathay Pacific where his son Bill, an accomplished jet pilot, carries on the family name. Asked how he came to follow a flying career, Ken put it very simply: 'Because I couldn't sell those bloody wireless sets in New York, back in the thirties.'

The DC6 was a low winged, medium range aircraft specifically built for the transport of 58 passengers and a small quantity of freight. The main cabin, the flight deck and the lower fuselage compartment were pressurized. It had a cruising speed of 285 miles an hour and a top speed of 345; its maximum gross takeoff weight was 92,500 pounds. The power was from four Pratt and Whitney Double Wasp 18-cylinder engines driving Hamilton Standard reversible-pitch propellors, and this particular aeroplane was one of only three straight DC6s with auto-feathering, and had been fitted so as to allow takeoff from Mexico City where the airport elevation is 7,347 feet above sea-level.

The cost of this aircraft was an impressive $US1,225,000 ($HK5,699,663). Included were all spares, two additional built-up Double Wasp engines and the cost of conversion training of four pilots. Pan American-Grace Airways also gave the aircraft a comprehensive overhaul to the standard required by Hong Kong DCA and allowed Cathay Pacific's chief engineer Mr Gething to supervise all the check sequences. Jack Gething was joined during the latter part of the overhaul of HAECO's chief maintenance engineer Jack Williams. The aircraft was entered in the Hong Kong register as VR-HFG and commenced schedule service in April 1955.

During June several newspapers reported that since its re-organisation in 1948 Cathay Pacific had carried more than 101,000 passengers, flown 8,500,000 miles and that since the DC6 had entered service it had transported two-thirds of the passenger traffic on the Singapore-Bangkok-Hong Kong run.

In October the company instituted a DC6 direct service between Hong Kong and Singapore, departing the Colony every Tuesday just before dusk and leaving Singapore just before midnight the same day. It arrived at Kai Tak around first light on the Wednesday morning. This 'Midnight Special' was a boon to the businessman who saved ten per cent on the normal excursion fare and could book a sleeping berth if his deals had culminated in the usual banquet. The flying time of 5 hours 55 minutes was two and a half hours less than the twice-weekly Hong Kong-Bangkok-Singapore service.

But the operating crews soon dubbed this service the 'Midnight Horror' because of the absence of even elementary navigational aids throughout the flight.

This changed to some degree with the next acquisition—a brand new DC6B with its radar—but in the meantime the surprise of entering undetected cloud banks would continue to provide a terrifying rock-and-roll progress, replaced by some astonishment at seeing the Malayan landfall of Mersing, with its confirmation that we were still in the right hemisphere.

On August 6, 1955 the company sold the first aircraft ever owned by the Roy Farrell Export-Import Company, the DC3 VR-HDB. When Butterfield and Swire entered the business in 1948 they paid $HK159,000 for this plane, and when they sold it (to W.R. Carpenter and Company) it realised $HK320,000. Its registration changed to VH-MAL, the initials of Carpenter's Mandated Air Lines it served mainly in New Guinea. It was certainly rugged: as late as April 1978 it was still in full service with Bush Pilots Airways at Cairns, having completed 36 years of flying since the USAAF took it on charge at Mobile, Alabama in June 1942. It is probably still going.

Our patterns of crew-slipping now gave us a great deal of time in Bangkok, on what we blithely called a 'double-header'. This constituted two return flights to Calcutta via Rangoon as operative crew. We then returned to Hong Kong as deadhead crew, the sequence taking five days. It came up about once a fortnight. Intrigued with Bangkok I made of course the usual pilgrimages to the dawn Floating Market, the Snake Farm, the National Museum, and innumerable temples, and was impressed with each, but my most vivid recall is of the Thai girls, astonishingly beautiful, soft and very gentle.

The contacts developed when I befriended two local youths Andrew and Kwan who by day served Cathay Pacific as traffic assistants and by night pursued the female of the species with a single-minded determination. They knew haunts normally closed to the expatriate and I would be accepted there and given *carte blanche* with suitable advice from my guides. I found this very exciting until a friend told me he had been escorted to a spyhole where he could watch the antics of a companion. He told the madam that this was hardly cricket, which naturally meant nothing to her, but after they assured him his own friend had used the spyhole while he was in its focus—and had in fact expressed some criticism of his aptitude—his scruples disappeared.

In one evil establishment the lovely Thai girls would dance around the room and when they approached a table with a tical note on the edge would quickly flick up their dresses to, as it were, absorb it. The light was not too bright, but some customers brought electric torches. This type of innocent entertainment would go on for hours until the star performer made her entrance. As one the patrons would rise in joyous acclamation, for not only was she the most gorgeous of all the girls, but she possessed an astonishing muscular dexterity. I saw her act several times, and never could believe my eyes!

From July 1954 when the 17th Parallel Agreement became effective Hanoi had been under Communist control, but on the morning of April 3, 1957 the company accepted a charter there to bring out Peter Noble, a young diplomat who had contracted a paralytic sickness and was being supported in an iron lung. His death was certain unless he received advanced medical treatment. The necessary permission to land at Hanoi had not been granted, but the 27-year-old diplomat was sinking so rapidly that on that morning Captain Ken Steele took a chance by starting off in the hope that permission would be forwarded in flight. He captained the DC3 himself, with Captain Pat Armstrong acting as first officer and Mum Louttit on radio, and carrying a group of medical personnel.

As he approached the southeast coast of Hainan Island permission still had not been given and he had to change course for Tourane, there to await it. It had to come from Saigon, and what was so infuriating was that Saigon seemed to be doing nothing about it.

On the ground Steele kept the engines running and Louttit co-ordinated the transmissions, first to Hong Kong, then to Saigon. An aircraft is a poor plat-form for radio communication until it is airborne, but they overcame this by turn-ing first in one direction to receive Hong Kong, then in another for Saigon. It took a long time and burnt a great deal of fuel, but that was considered a necessary expenditure, since this was a mercy flight. With permission granted they landed at Hanoi at last at 4.30 in the afternoon.

An ambulance awaited them with the patient, but doctors advised a depar-ture at first light, since the young man had sunk so low that the likelihood was he would not survive the flight. They returned him to the local hospital where he gained some strength during the night as he realised his transportation had actually arrived.

What interested Mum Louttit was that the traffic personnel at the airport consisted of the same individuals Cathay Pacific had employed when their services were running there. They wanted to know when the company would be coming back on schedule flights, and he told them jokingly we would not be coming 'because you are all Commies now'.

'But nobody was put out by this. They thought it was a good joke,' Mum said. 'On our way into the city red flags flew everywhere and at about two hundred yard intervals loudspeakers blared forth martial music. Our driver had been detail-ed a designated route and told if he diverted even a few yards from it, regardless of the reason, he would be shot.

'The patient stood up to the flight far better than was expected. We landed at Kai Tak with one of the smoothest touch-downs I have ever experienced, and it was quite a long time before I realised we were on the ground. Pat Armstrong, flying that sector, had really excelled himself out of regard for the sick man.'

Throughout the flight Dr Thomas Taylor, Mr F. Miles and the crew had taken it in turns to pump the iron lung. The patient must have served the shortest period of foreign service in the U.K. Diplomatic Corps, for he had been in the Far East for only three weeks before posting to Saigon, and then two more weeks in Hanoi where he became ill. With the passing of time he made a full recovery.

During the early months of 1957 I was allotted a flat in the block at 130-132 Argyle Street which the company supported and which was just opposite the casualty entrance of the old Kowloon Hospital. For the first time I found my rent proportionate to my salary. Phil Blown had the top floor unit and Pat Moore the ground floor, with a minute lawn and garden. A keen gardener, Pat had con-

Captain Alex Wales, Captain John Carrington, Captain Bill
Bridgemans (Chief Test Pilot, Douglas Aircraft Co.) F/E Bob Smith,
F/E Leo Brennan—1958

structed a compost heap removed as far as possible from the actual building, but nowhere near far enough, for it was really on the nose. Pat maintained that that compost, strengthened with a few buckets of night-soil, would grow flesh on a wooden leg.

As the year 1957 ended, so did the aviation career of Pat Moore. Time took from us a valued friend and an understanding administrator. Fortunately he was replaced as Operations Manager by Ken Steele, and Captain Dave Smith became flight superintendent.

On Friday, June 13 1958 Cathay Pacific's brand-new radar-equipped DC6B landed smoothly at Kai Tak after a delivery flight from Los Angeles of 54 hours at an average cruising speed of 295 miles an hour. It arrived under the command of Captain Alex Wales, with John Carrington co-pilot, Bob Smith and Leo Brennan engineers, and F. Saleeby navigator. Saleeby had navigated our DC6 ferry flight. Also aboard were chief engineer Jack Gething, and a renowned aviator Captain Bill Bridgman, the Douglas Aircraft Company's test pilot.

Aged 42, Bridgman had been flying for 21 years. He had become world-famous when in 1951 he broke all previous speed and altitude records by a large margin while attempting to fly at double the speed of sound in a research rocket aircraft, named 'Skyrocket'. Besides this he had tested the X3, and the new interceptor the F4D, which climbed to 50,000 feet in two and a half minutes.

The DC6B began scheduled services on June 22, but five days earlier 63 guests on a courtesy flight very nearly enjoyed a free trip to the Philippines when a sudden deterioration in the weather prevented the landing, and a half-hour jaunt became a three and a half hour city-circling marathon. Restricted visibility aborted a landing approach three times. On a fourth approach, with an improvement in the weather, Captain Wales brought her in. The radar equipment had already proved its worth.

I found and maintained an ever-absorbing interest in Kai Tak's new runway, particularly its seawall border. About 16,500 feet in length it grew about eighty feet a day. Two-ton blocks formed the seaward side; smaller blocks of about a ton were used on the wall which faced the harbour. Nearly 80,000 stone blocks were needed for the entire job and the daily delivery was between 350 and 400. Most of these came from the Kowloon Hills, but some were quarried at the Sacred Hill.

This hill featured an historic boulder weighing 1000 tons. It posed a problem for it was close to the centre-line of the airport development scheme and had to be removed. A strong public resistance to this was based on its historic association. On one face the characters 'Sung Wong Toi' were inscribed, literally 'Terrace of the Sung Dynasty Emperor'. The last Emperor of that dynasty had taken refuge here when fleeing from the Mongols. Preservation and removal of the entire boulder would have been too costly, so the part bearing the characters was split off, dressed, and re-erected in a specially built garden just to the southwest of the airfield.

Kai Tak developed as a modern airport in 1958. In August a temporary control tower constructed at great cost was handed over to airport authorities.

FEBRUARY 1956
Access road from Kowloon Hills for the new Kai Tak Runway construction. Looking west along Nga Tsin Wai Road with filler-truck freeway passing in front of Kowloon City Market— note humped back crossing of Hau Wong Road.

The Sacred Stone—1000 tons Characters "Sung Wong Toi"
('Terrace of the Sung Dynasty Emporer')

1957
Senior Captain "Chic" Eather.
DC6 VR-HFG

Opening of new Runway, Kai Tak—12th September, 1958
HE The Governor's Helicopter breaks the ribbon

Senior Staff—Department of Civil Aviation, Hong Kong
1st February 1957.
Far East Flying Training School, Kai Tak — Airspeed Oxford VR-HFC
L to R: Bert Clifford (A.R.B. Surveyor), George Cannon (Chief Signals Officer), Ralph
Winship (Deputy D.C.A.), M.J. Muspratt-Williams (D.C.A.), Ben Hewson (Chief Air Traffic
Control Officer), and Fred Lillywhite (A.T.C.O. i/e).

VR-HFK DC/6B
KAI TAK AIRPORT 1958

Everything was ready for opening the new runway in September, but Hong Kong's aviation history turned a new page fifteen hours ahead of schedule when a U.S. Air Force Skymaster from Okinawa undershot the threshold of Runway 31, hit the seawall with its starboard undercarriage and skidded 500 yards with its right wing down, setting the wheel well area on fire. Seconds before the entire plane exploded and became a flaming holocaust on the intersection of Runways 31 and 07 the five crew members were seen to scramble out of the most unlikely exits, each trying to break the four-minute mile. Interviewed later, Staff Sergeant James A. Austin, the 24-year-old radio operator, was asked whether there had been any panic aboard. With a catching grin and tongue in cheek he replied, 'No panic at all. We are all U.S. Air Force men.'

His Excellency the Governor, Sir Robert Black KCGC, OBE formally opened the new Kai Tak on September 12, a seeming anti-climax for most of us who had been using it for weeks. Fifty thousand people packed the airport perimeter, the surrounding streets and rooftops. All eyes turned upward as a helicopter flew in over the runway from Kowloon Bay and a loudspeaker announced it as the Governor's. It was the wrong one, and another announcement advised that the *Governor's* helicopter was approaching from the other direction. Struggling against thirty-knot gusts its pilot inched it forward between two red, white and blue poles and nosed into a ribbon, breaking it cleanly before swerving away. The two ends of the ribbon flapped wildly in the wind, and three ten-foot lengths of fire-crackers exploded for more than two minutes.

The Director of Civil Aviation, Mervyn Muspratt-Williams greeted Sir Robert, his wife and their two daughters and led them to the dais. Organisers with fingers tightly crossed kept glancing at the sky's threatening low clouds, but the rain held off while Sir Robert made his speech and declared the runway open. At that moment a rainbow bloomed from the clouds, arching at the further end of the runway, and with this emblem of good fortune the crowd relaxed.

Two green flares signalled the pilots of three waiting RAF Venoms, and as they roared down the strip the rain pelted down and the official party scurried for the shelter of the airport's fire station. But the squall was short; as nine civil aircraft taxied to join the fly-past it stopped. The Tiger Moth which was to have led was scratched on account of the boisterous wind. A Cathay Pacific DC3 took the lead instead, followed by Super 'G' Constellations of Qantas and Air India, a Viscount 760 of Hong Kong Airways, then a Britannia 314 of Canadian Pacific. This was the first time that Hong Kong had seen that new version of the Bristol Brit, but the star of the show was BOAC's giant Comet 4 pure jet airliner, which had a cruising speed of 520 miles an hour. Captain John 'Cat's Eyes' Cunningham, de Havilland's chief test pilot, had flown it to the Colony especially for the occasion.

One section of the community was happier than most with the assurance that with the opening of the new runway the old 07 strip need never again be used. In times of restricted visibility we would line up with Argyle Street and follow it until this strip hove in sight. This was no problem while we were operating the small DC3s, but it became more exciting when the DC4 and 6 series

KAI TAK AIRPORT
A good view of both the old and new installations
(Note: The high ground on approach to Runway 31 and the rugged terrain on the end of
Runway 13).

KAI TAK AIRPORT, KOWLOON, HONG KONG 1966
Prior to the South-East extension which commenced during October 1970.

arrived, for with their greater weight that short runway meant we had to combine our direction with a reasonable rate of descent so that we could arrive at the threshold at the proper height, for there was a steep mountain at the end.

One captain we had at the time was getting on in years and fairly haughty, not an endearing combination. He had developed the habit of decreasing height early and then pulling his plane in with excessive power, much to the consternation of the inhabitants below and the police at the Kowloon station. The wash amahs at the station must have obtained a schedule from Cathay Pacific's Booking Office, for it became normal procedure to remove their handiwork from the drying lines on the roof shortly before our aircraft were due, otherwise the laundry would be covered with engine soot.

One day they were a little tardy and our hero, a little lower than usual, collected most of the clothing in his aircraft's undercarriage. This was the signal for a particularly irate police inspector to jump on his motor-bike and arrive at the terminal at the same time as our hero switched off his engines.

The inspector began to berate the skipper in language which would have brought a blush of shame to a tugboat captain. The pilot listened from the safety of his sliding window, far too cunning to leave his plane just then. When he managed to get a word in he assured the inspector with hand on heart that he was innocent and without blame. Thereupon the policeman stalked beneath the wing and emerged brandishing several pairs of expensive smalls, now in a hopelessly ragged mess, and without another word shook them in the skipper's guilty face. The elderly aviator and the angry police inspector later became the best of friends. There cannot be many friendships which have thus developed.

CHAPTER FIFTEEN
THE HONG CONSOLIDATES

An efficient and successful administration
manifests itself equally in small as in great matters.

. . . Winston Churchill

Shortly after noon on April 14, 1959 Captain Dave Smith wheeled our first Electra, VR-HFO to a beautiful landing at Kai Tak, completing an 8500-mile flight from Burbank, California via Honolulu, Wake Island and Tokyo in just under 26 hours. This was well under the published airspeed of 400 miles an hour but it had lost time in severe head winds. Powered by four 3750 h.p. Allison engines it had a top speed of more than 450 miles an hour, a gross weight of 113,000 to 116,000 pounds and a 104.5 foot fuselage with an inside diameter of 10.5 feet giving 632 cubic feet of luggage and cargo space. Its smooth-running turbines were quiet and, with 350,000 pre-service hours of engine experience, dependable. Lockheed had designed it to carry 99 passengers on a high-density configuration or 66 as a luxury service; Cathay Pacific carried 66 standard and twelve de luxe, the latter in fully reclining sleeper seats.

My main interest centred on the twelve Lockheed men aboard who were to train us in the Electra's finer points and capabilities. Our prime instructor, Frank Lutomski, a gifted fellow of Polish and French-Canadian ancestry led us through the maze of various systems and left me with a good working knowledge transmitted in a rhetoric all his own. A device vaguely resembling a musical instrument became 'de piccolo toobe'. One day I left the class for a short time to check something with Daisy Smith at the operations department, and while there I could hear Frank's voice reverberating through the whole building. He was advising the class (and everyone else for miles around) that the particular fan he was describing had only one function, 'to remove de farts'. Daisy visibly blanched. She told me later she was becoming hardened to the language of the admirable Lutomski and when his descriptive comparisons became a little two bawdy she 'went off the air'. Daisy wore a hearing aid.

Other good instructors supported Lutomski. This was the first time I had taken a part in a comprehensive technical programme and when I got on the line I was more than ready to handle anything that might arise. I had never had this composed feeling before, as previous courses had been somewhat disjointed. Once I was perched on the edge of my pilot seat in a DC6 just waiting for something to happen when suddenly a fearful clatter behind me nearly put me into orbit. It turned out that Mum Louttit was bashing a salt-shaker against the bulkhead behind me, trying to make its damp contents flow.

On July 1, 1959 Hong Kong Airways was merged into the Cathay Pacific

CPA's Douglas Fleet
1st July, 1958
DC4 VR-HFF . . . DC6 VR-HFG . . . DC6/B VR-HFX
Kai Tak Airport, Hong Kong

One of CPA's Electra aircraft VR-HFO in flight over Repulse Bay
Taken 14.4.1959.

operation and the company lost little time in promoting the northern routes thus acquired. Three days later the DC6B VR-HFK flew the Taipei sector and the very next day inaugurated the Hong Kong-Taipei-Tokyo route. That same day Phil Blown flew into Kai Tak in command of the delivery flight of our second Electra (VR-HFN) from the United States. On July 12 a Cathay Pacific DC3 left Kai Tak at 8.30 p.m., checking all the airport lighting installations. I had to wait for my 'night endorsement' until the next night, but I felt a little superior to former colleagues for I had done my check-ride not on an old DC3 but on the modern Electra L188.

A new chapter in Hong Kong aviation history opened on the night of July 17 when the DC3 VR-HDA made the flight which officially opened Kai Tak for night operations, but on June 29 a Pan-American Stratocruiser on a special flight to Phnom Penh had already used the lighting to depart at 4 a.m.

On July 16 the Lockheed Electra departed on the 4,300 nautical mile proving flight to Sydney, via Manila and Darwin. VR-HFN was the second L188 built at Burbank, and had the serial number 1002. Aboard were newspaper representatives and other invited guests including the lovely 18-year-old Chinese film actress Miss Ting Hung, the Hon. and Mrs J.D. Clague, Mr Jock Sloan the Colony's television programme controller, Doctor and Mrs Herbert Kai-Chee Wong, and many other identities of the local business community. The Electra also carried a large crew contingent, for management was giving a route familiarisation to as many as possible. The hostess supervisor Josephine Cheng came to glean information to pass along to the 51 cabin attendants she controlled.

They got away in a blaze of flash-bulbs at 8 p.m. and a little more than two hours later were in Manila. A brief publicity conference there delayed them for an hour, but soon Captain Pat Armstrong had them in the air again, heading for Darwin. Then a generator began to play up, he lost an essential electrical bus and had to return to Manila. They were well above landing weight so he had to dump fuel. Pat went through the whole fuel-dumping exercise, announcing his intention to the passengers, exhibiting the 'No Smoking' sign, the whole song and dance so that even Ben Hewson, the DCA rep, seemed impressed. Bob Smith soon isolated and repaired the trouble and they were off again.

'That delay was more than enough for Dr Herbie Wong,' Pat told me. 'He got stuck into the booze and was feeling no pain. At the top of the climb Dave Smith wandered back to check the cabin and found Herbie enjoying himself to the point at which the other passengers were giving him the fish-eye, whereupon Dave asked Mrs Wong to tell her husband to behave himself.

' "What husband? I divorced him in Manila!" the lady replied. Then Herbie realized his brand of humour was being wasted, and dropped off to sleep.

'When we arrived in Sydney, off he bounded, his shoulders festooned with transistor radios and cameras galore, his spectacles perched on the very tip of his nose. Without hesitation he planted himself first in line at the Australian passport holders' counter. This annoyed a fussy little immigration man who told him to go over and join the Oriental line. Thereupon the doctor, still feeling little or no pain from his 18,000 foot celebrations, asserted in a voice which was clearly

Adrian (now Sir Adrian) climbing aboard his private Spitfire at
Leavesden, Hertfordshire, U.K.
1969

audible in Martin Place that he was Melbourne-born, a Dinkum Aussie, much more so than the obviously New Australian objector, who retired to lick his wounds.'

That flight cut 7 hours, 32 minutes from the previous record of 23 hours 25 minutes held by a Super Constellation. The Electra had made the trip in 15 hours 53 minutes, with a flight time of 13 hours and 14 minutes.

August 7 brought the Electra on to the direct Hong Kong to Tokyo run, covering the 1656 nautical miles in a block time of 5 hours 9 minutes. 'Block time' is recorded from the moment the aircraft leaves the ramp until engines are switched off again. This is in contrast to 'flight time' which is from commencement of the takeoff until the landing run is completed.

The next day our DC6B was brought on to the Hong Kong to Calcutta service, with Jim Hargraves as Captain. The flight called at Bangkok on the way out, Rangoon on the return. Following that, Cathay Pacific withdrew the Skymaster from the Hong Kong to Phnom Penh direct route and replaced it with the DC6, and again Jim Hargraves had the honour of upgrading an existing service.

With the modern prop-jet Electras giving full satisfaction (a situation that was not to last, for the type was soon to be involved in a series of structural failures causing fatalities) the DC6 was being underworked and had hours available. The Company therefore sought opportunities in the charter market, and three of these are worthy of recall, if only for the distances involved. The first was to Amsterdam, the next two to the United Kingdom. Under the command of Alex Wales the Amsterdam charter left Hong Kong on October 14 and returned on October 18. On November 26 Bob Howell lifted its wheels off Kai Tak runway and 49 seamen settled back in comfort for the long haul to London.

A United Kingdom trip in December was a happy event for all except Captain Jim Hargraves, for his gout became worse and he had to remove a shoe and prop the pain-wracked extremity up on the central pedestal. This gave only slight ease, but he was determined to finish the charter. First officer Ron Hardwick seemed to find more occasions than usual on which to adjust the heading with the auto-pilot knob, and as that control was just beside Jim's gout-ridden foot an unearthly scream would shiver the air with each adjustment.

Adrian Swire (now Sir Adrian) and some others from the Group's London office trooped along to Gatwick to welcome the long-distance charter.

'We felt so proud when the smart-looking DC6 taxied in,' he reported. 'The surprise and contrast was, however, quite considerable when Captain Hargraves appeared at the door of our symbol of modern technology and hobbled down to the tarmac supported by two sticks and wearing his bedrom slippers. It was quite a funny scene for all except Captain Hargraves, who was in considerable pain.'

Captain B.C. Hargraves was a product of pre-war aviation in Australia, but my first contact with him dated back only to my Burma days, when he was with Air Burma. He joined Cathay Pacific in March 1954 and retired in July 1965. He was popular. My main recollection of him was the anger he vented on the head-sets when he couldn't establish a radio link with a ground station. He would

HAECO INSTALLATION KAI TAK
"Ma" Saunders Canteen and Catering Supply Establishment is at left middle of picture.

Some early Cathay Pacific Personnel.
Rosemary Sun's Party—Peninsula Hotel 1950.
Front Row (L. to R):Jo Cheng, Margaret Wheeldon, Rosemary Sun,
Marcel Lin, Irene Hsu, Marie Bok.
Back Row (L. to R): Patricia Wong, Delores Silva, Lorna Salisbury,
Cecelia Cheng, Dorothy Coates, Connie Rapp, Tilly O'Brien, Eleanor Wong,
"Ma" Saunders and Alma O'Hoy.

NOVEMBER 1959
CPA's new composite Operations/Stores/Canteen
Kai Tak Airport
(Note runway 31/13 in foreground)

hurl them across the flight deck and barely stop short of trampling them underfoot. Bill Forgan-Smith knew him from Qantas days, and tells an affectionate story of when they messed together in New Guinea:

'He was a very funny man with a good-natured sense of humour. We called him Bert, but later he became Jungle Jim, which became plain Jim by the time he joined Cathay Pacific. One night in the mess he received a telephone call, but before he left the dinner table he removed his dentures and placed them in his mashed potatoes, telling them to get a little practice 'till he returned. He started away, then on an afterthought swung back and told the teeth to make sure nobody touched his dinner while he was on the phone.'

Agreement with the Government for a lease of land at Kai Tak enabled the company to complete a new operations/stores/canteen building on the east side of the old 13/31 runway in August 1959. It was of three storeys and a lift was installed much later. We now possessed an Operations Department of some consequence and not only felt grown-up but were anxious to face whatever 1960 had in store. A fortunate attitude—that year brought accidents to State-side Electras which necessitated comprehensive structural modifications, and involved Lockheed in losses of millions of dollars.

During its formative years Cathay Pacific catering had been prepared in a long wooden hut-like structure, one of the buildings used by HMS *Flycatcher* when Naval aircraft were based at Kai Tak. The building formed part of the HAECO complex and was affectionately called the canteen. Undisputed queen of the establishment, Mrs A.K.A. Saunders answered only to the sobriquet of 'Ma'.

She did a first-class job on a minimal budget, but as the years passed she tended to become a little forgetful of how much liquor she had added to the dessert. Much of the meal she would leave to her assistants, but her wine trifle she trusted to no one else. However, she was never quite certain that she had wined the trifle; she always maintained that too much was preferable to too little, and by the time she brought the object of her attention to perfection it was as dangerous as sweating dynamite.

It became quite interesting to see some of the crew who had never eaten dessert clamouring for more, and unremarkable to find a captain pulling rank and without shame removing the dessert from the first officer's tray, assuring the youth, of course, that the action was for his own good. Perhaps this was the first time in British aviation that consumption of alcohol on the flight deck of a commercial airliner appeared to be condoned. No wonder Ma had such a vast following among the elder aircrew members: she was without blemish.

An improved service to Borneo began in January 1960, when the DC6 replaced the Skymaster, offering a faster and more luxurious flight also to Kuching and Labuan. Then the inaugural flight Kyoto-Osaka-Kobe began on April 1, when Captain Norm Marsh flew the DC6B to Japan.

Norm had joined the RAAF as a clerk but was remustered and commenced training with the Empire Air Training scheme in Canada. He graduated as Sergeant-pilot in 1942, but unlike most of his course was posted to the RCAF

15th April, 1959
Cathay Pacific's 400 mph 78 passenger seat, Lockheed Electra L188 aircraft
VR-HFO cruising over outlying islands of the British Crown Colony of Hong
Kong.

VR-HFN at Mascot, Sydney 1960

August 1960
CPA's first Lockheed Electra VR-HFO, arrived in the colony April 14, 1959.
(Taken over H.K.'s central district)

Exterior markings approved 25.4.1959

Flying School for Instructor training on the Harvard and the skis-equipped Fleet Finch. 1944 brought him to Operational training on Hurricanes and Spitfires and he was attached to Squadron 453 in the European theatre. In March 1945 he was in a dive-bombing sortie off the Dutch coast. It went sour, and he had to bail out of his Spit. He spent a day and a half in a dinghy while several unsuccessful attempts were made to rescue him. Wind and tide carried him ashore, where he was made prisoner. The Russians liberated him from Stalag Luft 1, a camp on the Baltic coast, and he was back in the UK a bare two months after his capture. Discharged in December he was flying co-pilot on DC3s and Skymasters with ANA by the following March. In 1953 he held a command with my old company, the Union of Burma Airways and joined Cathay Pacific the next year.

Norm decided on an early retirement which became effective in November 1973 after he had reached the pinnacle of his career with a seat on the Board from December 1971, the second Cathay Pacific pilot to be addressed as Operations Director. Currently he is an examiner of airmen with the Australian Department of Transport, based in Melbourne.

In June 1960 Indonesia imposed an airspace restriction following Dutch moves to strengthen West New Guinea defences. It necessitated a 315-mile detour and added 55 minutes to flight time between Manila and Darwin. It was soon lifted but then Indonesia narrowed the width of the air corridor in that sector from 30 to 20 miles and raised the minimum height to 13,000 feet.

During the later months of 1960 our aircrews slept at the Cathay's Ocean Park Hotel in Singapore and the Shiba Park Hotel in Tokyo. I remember each with affection. Ocean Park, the friendliest of establishments, boasted the largest cockroaches I ever saw. It was rumoured that when management insisted on them carrying guests' luggage they demanded uniforms. My fondest memory of the Shiba Park features an irate American. Prevented from taking his night's entertainment to his room he was berating the night clerk, thumping the counter and insisting loudly that 'No Nip is going to do me out of my piece of ass!' While the clerk was telling me how repulsive were some of the guests the American and his selected entertainment sidled in the side door and with a wink so broad I wondered that the clerk did not hear it, crept up the stairs immediately behind him.

In October that year Chittagong, the steamy river port of East Pakistan was hit by a tidal wave which, by the official count, killed 4000 people. Other observers maintained the death toll was ten times as large. The Pakistan military administration was so secretive it refused an American offer of a helicopter from Karachi and granted a strictly limited turn-around at Chittagong's Patenga airport to six giant Hercules C-130 transports that had brought about eight tons of blankets, medicines and other relief from bases in Germany.

On October 31 Bernie Smith left Kai Tak in the veteran Skymaster VR-HFF to pick up a ship's crew at Chittagong. Headed for the same destination was a cyclone with winds exceeding 120 miles an hour, and a catastrophic tidal bore of twelve feet rising to twenty. There may have been an accompanying earthquake which a local seer had predicted, but this could not be substantiated as the seismograph was destroyed with the building that housed it. But cracks in brick walls seemed to confirm it.

Not surprisingly Bernie's recollections were detailed:

'The weather as we approached Patenga airport was very overcast with driving rain—none of this had been forecast. We wasted no time and got right on with refuelling for a quick turn-around, and we noted that the wind was increasing in velocity. The refuellers were doing a good job and one wing was soon completed. However, as the chief Shell refueller was moving to the next wing he walked into one of our propellors and sustained a deep head-gash. This stopped further progress while we called the airport ambulance which took him to hospital.

'About this time the meteorology office at Chittagong was alerted by a ship fifty miles off the port that they were being buffeted by winds in excess of sixty knots. This was the first indication that there could be a cylcone in the area. Naturally we were anxious to get away, but with the unbalanced fuel load a takeoff was out of the question, so we made preparations to tie the Skymaster down to weather the elements.

'I taxied over to an ex-wartime blister type hangar, but after an inspection I was not impressed with this structure and decided to tie the plane down some fifty-odd yards from the hangar at some tie-down points in the hard-standing. This we did and to give additional protection we tied several concrete blocks around the main wheels and another at the tail-skid.

'As the cyclone hit the wind rose unbelievably quickly accompanied by torrential rain squalls. The aircraft's port main wheels and nose-wheel were lifted almost six inches off the ground, with co-pilot Bob Crockett, flight engineer Brian Lewis, a Pakistan International Airlines engineer and myself pulling the plane down at the nose strut while at the same time another PIA engineer tightened the lashings. The hangar roof then started to peel off and sheets of corrugated iron began flying through the air like playing cards. Suddenly the whole hangar reared up vertically and the entire front structure collapsed in a mass of twisted girders.

'Now followed an unearthly calm, for the "eye" of the cyclone was upon us, so we took this brief respite to get over to the terminal building where we grabbed our purser C.C. Pak and hostess Cathy Lam and rushed to the control tower.

'We had been in this safer location a short time only, when the wind blew even harder from the opposite direction and we could see our Skymaster rearing and pitching all over the place. Suddenly wind and rain ceased and we looked out to see a massive wall of water tearing in from the sea. Within seconds the terminal building was practically submerged and the water was gushing just a few feet from the roof of the tower where we had scrambled, in company with the civil aviation staff on duty.

'After some time we heard cries from the water and pulled a four-year-old boy on to the roof. He was crying bitterly and didn't know what had happened to his parents. During the night we pulled out several other people. Tragically, many others were just out of our reach as they tore past on tree-trunks or anything else that would float. The following morning we heard more cries and we managed to pull up a man and a woman who turned out to be the parents of the boy we had rescued the previous night. The expression on the boy's face was something I shall always remember.

'As the daylight strengthened the flood waters receded, and I have never seen such carnage. Bodies of both humans and animals lay around, and as we made our way out to our aircraft we passed the terminal building, and were surprised to see no people there. The reason soon became obvious as we entered the lounge area and were subjected to the baleful glares of the scores of snakes that had taken possession of the many chairs.

'Our Skymaster was in fairly good shape considering what it had been through, and after a full day of checking it, Brian Lewis announced that all was well. We departed on November 2, but as the runway was still covered by about three inches of silt it was quite an interesting takeoff.'

The city and surrounding country suffered disastrously. Steel freight cars were overturned on railway tracks, metal telephone poles were twisted into knots and some had been slanted so that they resembled lances—a fit description, for several had human bodies skewered on them. One carried three bodies transfixed in this way.

More than a dozen ships were aground, several a couple of miles from where they had started to drag their anchors. The master of the British *Clan MacAlpine* took a sounding as his ship, torn from her moorings, ran aground. The reading was 18 feet. When the water receded *Clan MacAlpine*, on her final voyage to a Japanese breaker's yard, lay high and dry on what were formerly rice-fields. That the owners worried over this is doubtful, for her insurance would be more valuable than the Japanese offer for scrap.

The year was one of problems for Electra aircraft, as I noted earlier. I had heard rumours of trouble, and towards the end of March General Elwood L. Quesada, Administrator of the Federal Aviation Agency issued an instruction that all Electras must restrict speeds to 275 knots at or below 15,000 feet, and to 260 knots above. He advised Lockheed by telegram that this was a safety precaution measure, for the crash at Tell City, Indiana in which 63 people died on March 7 seemed to have sufficient similarity to another crash of the same aircraft type the previous year to warrant such speed restrictions. Thirty-four had died at Buffalo in the crash of an Electra operated by Braniff International.

In the States Senator Vance Hartke charged that the General had rejected the Civil Aeronautics Board proposal that all uninspected Electras should be grounded. He said, 'When a type of plane flies only ten per cent of the total hours and accounts for 76 per cent of the deaths its safety record is not good.'

General Quesada resisted a grounding of the type. He ordered a further reduction in speed to 225 knots and the disconnection of the auto-pilot pending modifications, because certain malfunctions had resulted in oscillations (porpoising) of noticeable magnitude. He was waiting the findings of three separate investigations then in session. One of these centered round the testing to destruction of a new Electra worth about $US1,750,000.

The *Daily Telegraph* of May 5 reported that the Civil Aeronautics Board enquiry seemed to lay the blame on 'clear air turbulence', a phenomenon found near jet streams and in regions where hot and cold air masses meet. This is possibly the most serious weather condition the aviator can encounter, for it can neither be seen nor detected by radar. The only warning is a sudden change of temperature, and by the time the pilot realises this he has no time to reduce airspeed, the only safe procedure in turbulence.

The same newspaper reported that 'a strange harmonic vibration' might have caused the crashes, that the outboard engines of the Electra set up an unusual wing vibration at certain speeds.

Lockheed would spend $US25,000,000 improving Electras, paying a major share of modifications. At the time Lockheed's Vice-President announced the offer, only two of the thirteen airlines using the type had agreed to share the cost. The defect to be remedied was a weakness in the mounts which held the engines in their nacelles. Investigations showed that a hard landing or extreme turbulence could damage these mounts sufficiently to cause the engine to shift. At a certain speed vibration caused more strain on the mounts and a chain reaction transmitted engine movements to the wing. The culmination of this reaction was a flutter so violent that the wing separated from the fuselage.

Modifications would add 1400 pounds of metal reinforcement to key areas. It was also suggested that flight recorders (the black box) be installed. Previous FAA regulations had required these for aircraft which operated above 25,000 feet, and therefore applied to pure jets.

Cathay Pacific's problems were the same as those of other operators, but also routine inspections had found an extensive organic fungus growth in fuel tanks and associated filters and pumps. Now this spore was also found adhering to the wing inner skin and planks, and was causing severe corrosion. Not all operators were experiencing this. The company's Electras operated in hot, humid climates, and local thought also blamed sea-water condensation.

On December 4 Captain Blown flew Electra VR-HFN to Burbank via Tokyo, Wake Island and Honolulu. VR-HFO followed three days later under command of Pat Armstrong. Our part in the modification programme was ended on Saturday, February 4 1961 when both our Electra touched down at Kai Tak within a few minutes of each other. During their absence day to day services were flown by a Bristol Britannia wet-leased from BOAC. It operated 79 round trips, sixteen of them on the Hong Kong to Sydney route. Electras never again gave the company cause to regret having chosen them.

Pilots considered the Electra a wonderful aeroplane. It was devoid of mischievous surprises and most pilot mistakes brought no retribution, for it practically flew itself. The modifications had returned the type to its full speed potential and they were a credit to the family name of Lockheed. True, there were minor lapses such as can happen in even the best of families, but the Electra rebuilt its somewhat tarnished reputation to one of maximum reliability.

I experienced one minor incident when I had to feather Number One engine over Mount Isa, en route from Darwin to Sydney. We merely reduced altitude a couple of thousand feet and she flew like a homing pigeon. My confidence in

Lockheed Electra 10B—1960
Showing extent of corrosion in fuel tanks

B.O.A.C's (now B.A.) Bristol Britannia 102 G-ANBO at Kingsford-Smith Airport, Sydney, during the period C.P.A.'s Lockheed Electra fleet was out of service—between December 1960 and February 1961.

VR-HFF DC4

J.K. Swire, Miss Gillian Swire and H.J.C. Browne insepct VR-HFX
upon delivery from Viasa. November 1965.

the type was comforting when on August 6 the Netherland Royal Dutch Mail line entrusted 120 of their seamen to my care, sixty each way between Singapore and Calcutta. As the flight progressed any lingering thoughts I may have had that the type was gremlin-bugged were eliminated, for the weather was frightful, with moderate to severe turbulence throughout.

Captain Lawrie King's feelings were similar when his Electra encountered a violent electrical storm in February. For the first ninety minutes out of Sydney he was in moderate turbulence and picking up some light rime icing. Then a severe lightning stroke hit the radome in front of the co-pilot and left the aircraft near the Number Two engine. Radar was in use at the time but after the strike the radar antenna started to jam. Lawrie overcame that by increasing the angle of tilt and thus managed to keep the scanner working. The flight continued normally until during descent into Darwin the entire radome collapsed. His airspeed at the time was 300 knots and altitude 11,000 feet. He experienced considerable vibration but as he reduced speed below 200 knots the roughness ceased.

During 1961 Qantas introduced the wonderful Boeing 707 on the Sydney to Hong Kong route and Cathay Pacific, aware that its older equipment would be less competitive, decided to withdraw from the route. They arranged a lease with BOAC of their hard-won rights. Thus on November 1963 the final Electra service departed from Sydney. It was under my command.

J.K. Swire's arrival in the Colony in August settled the whole question of whether to buy a jet, and if so, what type to buy and how it should be financed. Just before his arrival the General Dynamics Corporation and the General Electric Company had made a very tempting offer of a Convair 880; and shortly afterwards occurred a fortunate opportunity to inspect a Boeing 707, a Boeing 720B and a Convair 880 all at Kai Tak at the same time.

The 707 was too big for our then-current needs, while the 880 possessed ancillary advantages so overwhelming that the decision to purchase was unanimous. A pool of Convair spares was held in Japan which would simplify and cheapen replacement parts. HAECO and Air Asia in Taiwan were already tooled up for the GEC engines. Furthermore, General Dynamics had recently had a number of Convairs returned by the bankrupt Capital Air Lines, and this would allow a quick start. The clincher was that General Dynamics was prepared to accept payment over four years in sixteen quarterly instalments at seven per cent per annum, the spare engines being paid for over five years in twenty instalments. This was all too good to miss, and Cathay Pacific was able to persuade the Hong Kong Bank to guarantee all payments and finance us with a running overdraft.

In the month before that a 'sold' notice was hung from the captain's sliding window of beloved DC3 VR-HDA. This was the company's second DC3 but its first 'plush job', which meant she was fitted with cushioned passenger seats. The adventures she had been through were legion. She was the first plane I flew with Cathay Pacific and the one from which I nearly tumbled to my death over the Southern Philippines; John Riordan and I were 'shot down in flames' in her over Bassein while helping the Burmese Government in their fight against insurgents;

July 24, 1961
VR-HDA (C47B) Sold to Societe Royal Air Laos, Vientianne.

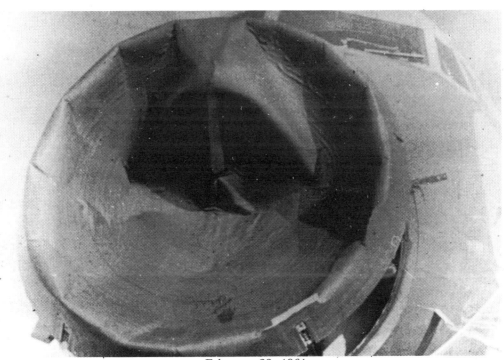
February 28, 1961
Collapsed radome on CX-012 from Sydney to Darwin. Lockheed Electra L188.

she carried Johnnie Ray, the crying singer, on a special charter to Tokyo; aboard her Ken Steele brought our Mr Peter Noble of the UK Consulate in an iron lung. She was concerned in dozens of other incidents.

Her 'birth' is something of a mystery. All available records show that de Kantzow and Farrell bought her in Australia, at which time she bore the temporary registration of VH-ASJ, but inspection of the DCA records in Melbourne show that registration as having been issued to a Tiger Moth in September 1946 as its initial user. Whatever her history she performed sterling service, and when we retired her she immediately began a new career with Societe Royal Air Laos based in Vientiane.

Charles Edward Michael Terry CBE became manager of operations staff and administration in December 1961. Well known and highly respected, his association with the Colony spanned forty years. Born in Ireland, educated in England he served with the British Army during the 1914-18 War and arrived in Hong Kong after demobilisation to join the Police Force. Once his contract finished there he joined the Hong Kong and Kowloon Wharf and Ferry Co. Ltd., and by 1954 had become their General Manager and also General Manager of the Star Ferry Company. From his wartime internment quarters he with others planned the re-occupation and when the Port Committee was formed became a foundation member. He was appointed to the Urban Council in 1947, served on the Legislative Council from 1950 to 1959 and the Executive Council from 1956 to 1961. His was the driving force which formed the Hong Kong Home for the Blind. He also formed the Civil Defence Corps and remained its Commissioner until March 16, 1968.

On the Osaka run we stayed at the Oriental Hotel in Kobe. This was a comfortable establishment but the road journey between Osaka and Kobe was an exercise in survival and each trip a hair-raising adventure, for this was before the completion of the rapid transit roads. Later the crews were accommodated in Osaka City itself, but most of us preferred the seaport of Kobe for more of its population spoke English, the night-life catered more for the foreign visitor and the commercial parts of the city were more centralised.

Interesting memories centre round the Club Tammy, in the Fukuhara blue light district. Tammy was always addressed as 'the mama-san', which seems quite normal until you learn that Tammy's hostesses were males whom the coarse and unsympathetic described as trimmed and shimmed. Tammy's star performer was blithely named 'Pinko-san'. A first officer colleague who preferred the company of the 'gay' boy was one of Tammy's most loyal and regular customers. On one flight to Osaka I must have ingratiated myself with him by taking my courage in both hands and giving him the entire flight. This included two interesting takeoffs and two astonishing landings. On arrival at the Oriental Hotel he sidled up to me and offered to introduce me to a bar somewhat out of the ordinary. This was indeed an honour, for he had the reputation of being secretive, sharing little of his private life—and certainly none of its sexual interests—with others in the company.

We were greeted as honoured guests at Tammy's , and as it was something

5th November, 1965.
"Pinko-San"—Principal gay-boy
of the Club Tammy in the
Fukuhara blue light district, Kobe,
Japan.

of an off-night my worldly f/o soon arranged for Pinko-San (whom he described as the Principal Boy) to perform a strip-tease for my benefit, in the course of which everything was removed except for a small beaded fringe. Pinko-San's figure was absolutely magnificent and I found it well-nigh impossible to believe that it had been surgically built up and trimmed again where necessary. My mentor assured me that this was a fact, and to prove it was willing to take second choice—obviously a great sacrifice. I did not have the desire or courage to embark on such a voyage of discovery and as courteously as possible I declined, much, I might add, to his obvious relief and delight.

On February 8 Bernie Smith received takeoff instructions from the Kai Tak controller, but as he waved the wheel chocks away from his Seoul-bound DC6 he was directed to hold position and shut down engines. The stairs were hastily moved to the loading door, and as it slammed open custodians of the law, Hercules size, bounded into the cabin and soon emerged frog-marching a struggling man off to the local bastille.

It seems that one Jack Collins had left an envelope for safe-keeping with his hotel receptionist. It contained $3,400. Later, a European arrived at the reception counter and asked to be allowed to add something to the envelope. The unbelievably naive receptionist handed it over, watched the man add something to it and put it away again. When Mr Collins opened it later he found a sheaf of neatly cut newspaper and a note which said, 'Jack, I've received it, John'. It revealed a good sense of humour, enough, I trust, to sustain the felon during his residence as a guest of her Majesty.

On Monday April 2, VR-HFS, our first Convair 880-22B touched down at Kai Tak with Flight Superintendent Dave Smith at the controls. Aboard was 2500 pounds of wood-working machinery for Hong Kong's self-help programme called 'Care': a complete workshop, the gift of the American people carried free by Cathay Pacific. Also on board were Captain Ulysses Sherman Johnson and flight engineer Charles J. Falkenthul, each a magnificent character, expert in his own particular field. But it is strange how trivia remains in one's mind to the exclusion of matters more important. Of Sherm I remember him listening attentively to a youthful first officer bewailing the choice he had made of a beautiful companion for the evening. The lady's performance, it seemed had not matched her good looks; he had found it a total loss. In a dry voice Sherm said, 'The worst performer I ever had was still excellent'.

During his time with us Chuck received a cable informing him that he had become a grandfather, and we could not understand his lack of enthusiasm until he admitted that the event really thrilled him except for making him feel so very old. All he had to look forward to on return was that he would be sleeping with a grandmother. To him it was a fearful thought.

My time to join the Convair fleet soon rolled round and from June 1 to July 5 1962 I became a temporary resident of beautiful San Diego. We were a happy group, booked in at the Outrigger Motel. Roger Chaney, our Convair instructor kept us busy, but he was so efficient I found additional study at home unnecessary. So I could accept the P&O Company's invitation to celebrate the

Captain K.W. Steele, Operations Manager of Cathay Pacific Airways,
surrounded by the 1961 class of new flight hostesses and flight
Pursers who had recently graduated from a special training class held at
Cathay Pacific's headquarters, Kai Tak, Hong Kong.

Cathay Pacific's latest cabin crew graduates photographed with
a Cathay DC4 in the background— now a
stand-by in the Cathay Pacific fleet.

15th March 1962

Cathay Pacific's First Convair 880-22M VR-HFS at the General Dynamics Division, San Diego, USA

L to R (starting from front row): F/O Peter Stockell, Capt. Geoff Leslie, Capt. Pat Armstrong, F/E Len Weston, F/O Chris Bushe, F/E Jack White, F/E Stan Pain, Capt. Lawrie King, F/E Bob Smith, F/E Don Brown, Capt. Phil Blown, F/O Julian Greenwood, F/E Bruce Holyman, Capt. John Carrington, Capt. Dave Smith, F/O Ron Hardwick, F/O Stuart McQuilkin, and Capt, Norm Marsh.

DC6. VR-HFG Kai Tak, 1962

CATHAY PACIFIC Lockheed Electra II

VR-HFN 1962

Cathay Pacific group photo taken before the new Convair 880-22M jet left California.

Back Row L to R: Captain D. Smith; Mr Tom Laughlin (navigator on the ferry flight); Mr Edward Sullivan, Cathay Pacific's active Sales Representative in the USA; F/E W.B.A. Holyman, Snr. F/O J.H.S. Greenwood; Snr. F/O R.C. Hardwick, Chief F/E R.J. Smith and Mr D.S. Delaney, Assistant Chief Engineer.

Front Row L to R: Captain A.B. Armstrong, Mr. D. Kemphaus, CPA's San Francisco Salesman, a token CARE package, Captain Norman Marsh, and Snr. F/O C.K. Bushe

SS *Himalaya's* first call to San Diego, and most weekends we trekked the few miles south to the Mexican border town of Tijuana. I saw my first bull-fight there, attended others, but could raise no enthusiasm for this so-called sport.

As a den of vice Tijuana was wholly without peer. As a commentary on the place, when I took a sore throat to the surgery of the doctor across the road from the Outrigger, the beautiful blonde nurse took my particulars with the remark that it was quite a novelty to treat a patient with an orthodox complaint.

We returned to the Colony to find the Convair gaining popularity with the travelling public, and it seemed reasonable to expect an increase in the fleet soon, but our next Convair did not go into service until November 14, 1964. A quite understandable delay: this one cost $HK22,762,194.

An item of good news made the local papers when NBC cameraman Grant Wolfkill was released by the Communist Pathet Laos. He had been captured in April 1961 after a helicopter in which he had been riding crashed behind Lao Communist lines. He spent fifteen months existing on a diet of beetles, dogs and grass, living in a tiny dark room watched by gun-toting trigger-happy guards. He had become a close friend of many of the Cathay Pacific crews and was well liked.

Another who survived imprisonment, at least temporarily, was a gargantuan pilot Captain J.B. McGovern. Most of us knew this charming American who travelled frequently on our aircraft between Kai Tak and Hanoi, a trip necessitated by his own R and R requirements. Besides female company, these predilections included steak meals at 'Gingles', a restaurant along lower Nathan Road of which the proprietor, a retired American sailor, specialised in them. Gingles's dimensions were similar to McGovern's, and McGovern was known widely as 'Earthquake McGoon'. Bo Egan tells his story:

'Earthquake McGoon had flown with Chennault's Flying Tigers, but the first time I saw him I just could not believe he could ever have got into the cockpit of the P-40 Warhawk they flew those days. Later he flew with CAT, and on one of these flights engine failure forced him to land on a river sand-bank behind Communist lines. He spent a long time being publicly exhibited all over China until, as he told me, "The message finally got through, and waking up to myself I asked to read the manuals of Mao Tse-Tung and such-like—I kept telling everyone I was now a lovely Communist."

'Someone must have agreed, for he was pushed across the border into Hong Kong and his once twenty-stone figure was reduced to a scrawny ten. The Commies had extracted a promise that he would never fly against them again, anywhere in the Far East. He returned to his homeland for about six months and came back flying C-119 Flying Box-cars, throughout internal Indo-China.

'He came to an unfortunate end. He was engaged in CAT's famous airlift to Dien Bien Phu, making parachute drops of essential supplies. The North Vietnamese announced on their radio broadcasts that they were aware of his return. They reminded him that he had broken his promise and he could expect extermination at an early moment. Soon after that a flight of C-119s commenced their drop approach to the French fortress. Not a shot was fired until it came to the McGoon's turn to make the pass and then every possible weapon was brought to bear on his aircraft. Earthquake McGoon was last seen trailing flames which only ended as his plane dashed itself to pieces, screaming into a nearby river.'

The 985 millibar cyclone Wanda brought eight hours of terror to Hong Kong on September 1, accompanied by fires, tidal waves, widespread floods and winds rising to 170 miles an hour. It made 20,000 people homeless, leaving destruction such as the Colony had not suffered since 1937 when a typhoon caused 11,000 deaths. Wanda killed 42 and injured 397, for the Colony was fully prepared, as it had not been in 1937. Kai Tak suffered only superficial damage. Hundreds of oil drums broke their lashings from the depot at Kun Tong and swept across the harbour to be deposited on the runway. The seawall became the graveyard of dozens of ferries and small craft.

Death remained close to us for the next couple of months, in which a respected first officer, Jim Couper-Johnston died in Melbourne, and John James Williams suffered a fatal heart attack on October 11, in the company's Kai Tak canteen. Jack was one of the engineers who helped pull me back into the plane on my first flight with Cathay Pacific. I had over-balanced while dumping cargo in an effort to maintain height on our engine-out DC3.

Cathay Pacific hostesses commanded the admiration of the traveller to the Orient, and throughout Asia hardly a newspaper or a woman's magazine failed to feature our beautiful girls. They featured also in a fashion parade arranged to pay for a well at St Christopher's Orphanage, which had a newly constructed wing for babies and could not use it because of water restrictions. Six of our girls showed off the *haute couture* to perfection, but when they paraded in their respective national dresses guests rose in acclamation.

Soon the administrators sank their well and moved the babies into the new wing. Shortly afterwards an exchange programme of *Hostesses de l'air* with Canadian Pacific Airways brought immense publicity to the company but took my wife-to-be, Judy Yuen-Ching Hui away from Hong Kong for what seemed an eternity. Judy and Rose Tam were our representatives, and Helen Phillips and Margaret Shumski came in exchange in the care of two mountainous Royal Canadian Mounted Police.

In October the 86-seat jetliner Trident arrived on a 100,000 mile demonstration and proving flight under the command of the same John Cunningham as flew the Comet at the opening of the Kai Tak runway in 1958. This was his first sight of the newly completed Terminal Building. Cunningham noted another addition to the Kai Tak skyline: the massive HAECO hangar which came into operation on December 15 that year, and now was humming with activity.

At the International airports of Manila, Tokyo and Osaka Cathay Pacific introduced and publicised their revised in-flight meals. The guests, predominantly from the local Press corps, were seated so that all the food could be served from trolleys in typical aircraft style, an inspiration of Maurice Hofstein, 'Chef of Kings and Queens' and our newly appointed passenger service superintendent. Mrs K.L. Hodson in charge of the flight kitchen was now preparing 3000 meals a week for ourselves, our pooled partners and several other transiting carriers. Impressive for those days, the figure is now overwhelmed by the output of the multi-million

"Hostesses De L'Air" March 1963
Judy Hui and Rose Tam (right) enroute to Kai Tak for their fortnight exchange and promotional programme on CP Air's domestic routes in Canada.

Lockheed Electra

subsidiary Air Caterers Limited, which by 1968 prepared 5000 meals a day—a far cry from Ma Saunders and the days when an air hostess had to stay behind after her flight to count each piece of cutlery and the salt-shakers, in the knowledge that any missing would be deducted from her salary.

Phnom Penh was the only port at which The Ambassador personally met every flight. He did not miss an arrival for more than twelve months and his actions demonstrated in the clearest way his appreciation of our tasty in-flight meals. Unfortunately he did little to publicise their excellence, for he was the friendly airport dog. Throughout our network other animal friends were also willing to consume our leftover culinary delights.

One incident this year was blown up into quite astonishing proportions before it was sorted out. Flight Engineer Ron Huckstepp was walking back to our plane at Dum Dum airport, Calcutta. Without warning Huck, who possessed a foghorn type of voice, screamed: 'Get off there, you two black bastards!' Thereupon two Indian Customs officials who were standing on the rear passenger platform and were the possessors of well-tanned skins, hotly took him to task. Whereupon poor Huck, a mild, inoffensive man, unwittingly exacerbated the situation by retorting, 'I was talking to those two black bastards up there,' and he pointed to the tailpin on which two mean-looking crows were perched. 'Not you two black bastards,' he added.

1962 was a quietly important year. During April Cathay Pacific's first pure jet went into service, and by December we were equipped with a Convair 880, two prop-jet Electras and VR-HFF our Skymaster and work-horse supreme. The Osaka authorities were obdurate in keeping Itami airport unavailable to our Convair, and it was mid-1964 before they relented. The stated reason was the objection of the local population, which could have seemed reasonable, but it was somewhat coincidental that by the time they relented all our competitors possessed jet aircraft. To this day Osaka maintains a 10 p.m. jet curfew, possibly the earliest anywhere in the world, and the authorities have combined this with a noise-abatement procedure so exacting that many pilots consider it to border on the dangerous, especially during the summer months when the hot, humid atmosphere gives only restricted lift.

Higher salaries and better fringe benefits sought by Philippine Air Lines pilots stranded 300 Manila-bound travellers at Kai Tak. In April 1963 Cathay Pacific carried full loads to Manila and it was common to see thirty passengers bargaining among themselves for a cancelled seat.

The same month our engineering director Jack Gething resigned from the Board and was replaced in May by Michael Yorke Twistleton-Wykeham Fiennes, a Director of John Swire and Sons. Michael has of course retired, but he remains the Company's Archivist, on a labour-of-love basis.

On July 6, 1964 Captain Lawrence Gerard King and I were involved in an incident which, though it ended well and without injury to any of our 53 Manila passengers, could easily have brought disaster to us all. He had been scheduled to make a route-check of my technical knowledge of the Convair 880 and general flying ability. As part of the check I flew a complete sector from the right-hand, or co-pilot's seat. Everything had gone nicely until, at the appropriate moment, when stabilized on the Kai Tak glide-path, I instructed him to lower the undercarriage. A red light indicated a malfunction in the nose-wheel. Before aborting our approach we retracted the main wheels and again attempted a normal extension of the gear, an operation which merely aggravated the fault by jamming the up-latch linkage even more tightly, though we did not know this at the time.

We spent the next one hundred minutes orbiting Stonecutter's Island in Hong Kong's western harbour trying to lower the gear, with Don Brown, our flight engineer, spending a great deal of time in the 'hell-hole', a compartment containing electronic and other instrument equipment accessible from a trapdoor near his seat. When he ascertained that the nose-wheels were fully retracted we raised the main wheels, placed the landing-gear lever in neutral and activated the device which lowered the gear under emergency. We pulled a moderate amount of 'G' force to assist with the extension, but without success. Don then attempted to release the up-lock through a small inspection window using a special bar provided to force the nose-gear strut to a down position if it did not safety under its own sequence, but with the nose strut retracted the up-latch was inaccessible.

We followed other advice from our engineering experts with whom we were in radio contact, but the up-latch remained jammed. Daylight was fading fast and after preparing the cabin for an emergency landing we jettisoned fuel down to 5000 pounds in Numbers One and Four tanks, giving us a landing weight of 110,000 pounds. By this time all the passengers had been moved to the rear cabin to help keep the nose from contacting the runway for as long as possible. A final briefing to the passengers emphasised that the touchdown would be normal until the speed was reduced and the nose contacted the runway, and that they could expect some sensations of impact then. The cabin crew had stowed all loose articles and erected the emergency chutes at each door. Then in the failing light we crossed the threshold of Runway 31 at 124 knots. The nose contacted the runway at 80 knots with hardly a bump, but with a flurry of sparks so intense as to temporarily obstruct forward vision. The passengers were evacuated without problem or injury, though the tail remained extremely high.

On October 13 Mr Ralph Winship retired from the DCA, depriving the company of one of its most enthusiastic supporters. Another loss was when our chairman, Mr. W.C.C. Knowles retired in September. He had joined the Board in 1950 and chaired it since December 1957, and during those fourteen years had entertained few thoughts except those in pursuit of the company's welfare; to me he clearly qualified for the appellation 'A Man's Man'. After he retired from the company he accepted the post of Vice-Chancellor of the University of Hong Kong. On New Year's Day 1966 he became Executive Director of Lloyd's Register. In his sixty-first year he visited Hong Kong in the course of a world tour on behalf of the Register, and renewed old friendships. He then proceeded to Djakarta where on Monday, January 13, 1969 he suddenly died, barely a week after leaving Hong Kong.

The anniversary which brought the greatest joy to our commercial administrators was reached on October 20, 1964 when Mr Ong Tjoe Kim, a well-known Singapore businessman, became our millionth passenger.

Captain Dave Smith, my associate of Burma days, took his seat on the Cathay Pacific Board of Directors on March 5, 1965. Born in Morayshire in the Highlands of Scotland in 1918 he served with the RAF during World War II, worked on a vast mapping project immediately after being demobilized, and took part in the Berlin airlift in 1949. When Air Burma was liquidated Cathay Pacific's Operations Manager Pat Moore hired him in January 1951.

During Dave's tenure as flight superintendent he suffered a burst ulcer while taxi-ing an aircraft at Kai Tak for a local training flight. Some amongst us would have questioned the ability of the trainee pilot to get the aircraft back safely to the ground, had this happened later in the flight. This trainee later resigned and obtained a command with a small charter outfit but was killed when attempting a landing somewhere on the Continent during bad weather. Dave Smith retired from Cathay Pacific on November, 30, 1971.

More publicity came my way in September 1965 when, during a takeoff run at Taipei, an engine of the Convair I was flying was wrecked, ingesting a large bird. A translation of a Chinese language newspaper which reported the incident reads rather quaintly:

> 'A case of an old hawk which suddenly flew into the Number Two jet engine rendering trouble to the aircraft and almost causing an accident of overshooting the runway. Through the calm control of Captain Eather emergency brakes were applied and six tyres were blown with a loud bang.'

We had been bound for Osaka with 96 passengers. Our ground speed was V1, otherwise known as the critical engine-cut speed—should an engine fail after this point the takeoff should be continued. Suddenly there was a fearful bang accompanied by a violent swing to port. It felt as though I had lost part of the port wing, so I did not carry on with the takeoff and applied maximum emergency braking. The tyres did not, as reported, blow out. They slowly deflated after we returned to the terminal ramp, due to the heat the braking generated in the wheels.

Because of an incident on Christmas Eve that year, saturation publicity showered on one of our pilots, Captain Leonard Dudley Cadogan Cowper. While on the landing run at Saigon's Tan Son Nhut airport his Electra experienced an asymmetrical propellor reverse situation and veered off the runway. After clipping an elevated marker board with the Number One prop the Electra came to rest with the nosewheel and port main wheels off the runway. Crash vehicles and fire crews of the USAF arrived before the dust had settled. The airport was considered the busiest in the world, with a movement every twenty seconds, for the Viet confrontation was at its height. After a half-hearted attempt was made to tow the plane free a mean-looking USAF airport commandant gave the skipper thirty seconds to move his aircraft, otherwise he would order in the bulldozer. The commandant's tone clearly indicated his sincerity and Len managed to move the Electra under its own power and clear the runway.

That incident raised some excitement in the Press. But in the previous

October it had brought his name into almost every home in the Colony when he became the bridegroom of Miss Joy Drake, the reigning 'Miss Hong Kong'.

After considerable haggling our third Convair 880 was bought from Venezolana Internacional de Aviacion SA. This chapter, as well as 1965, comes to a close with the retirement of Mr J.K. Swire, 'Mr Cathay Pacific' himself. An aviation era had ended.

CHAPTER SIXTEEN
HAIL AND FAREWELL

'Farwel my book and my devocion'
A Legend of Good Women . . . Geoffrey Chaucer

1967 was anniversary year. On Saturday January 7 Butterfield and Swire hosted two days of celebration to mark its centenary; on September 24 Cathay Pacific came of age and celebrated its twenty-first anniversary. The centenary celebrations commenced with a dinner party and variety show in the City Hall, followed next evening by a ball at the Hong Kong Club where 500 staff members and their partners danced the night away. Festivities concluded with Mr John Swire presenting a cash gift of $HK500,000 to the University of Hong Kong and the Chinese University of Hong Kong for scholarship foundations. Mr John Browne, Chairman of Butterfield and Swire (H.K.) Ltd was present. His local Board of Directors had donated a fifth of the total. Later it contributed a similar sum towards a Chinese-English Dictionary of Modern Usage compiled by the brilliant Dr Lin Yutang, Research Professor of the Chinese University.

Dr Lin received his Doctorate of Philology at Leipzig. He was the first Chinese to found a Chinese language literary magazine known for its wit and humour, and he also produced a number of books in English. In his spare time he invented a Chinese typewriter. His dictionary, completed in 1971, is still considered to be the best.

Our fourth Convair went into service on January 25, an indication that Duncan Bluck's deadline of March 1 for a pure jet operation would be achieved, but the withdrawal of the remaining Electra with its short field landing capabilities necessitated our withdrawal from the Brunei service. By the time our fifth Convair went into service in September, Calcutta, Naha, Okinawa and Seoul either received revised routing or had been added to the list of destinations. October records showed that we were now operating 88 flights in and out of Hong Kong each week.

Such expansion demanded a complementary increase in flight personnel, especially air hostesses. Naturally the intakes included some who were cute rather than beautiful, but these had attributes which more than amply compensated. Some girls of education and background could be among the less sharp and alert. Others with little higher education were efficient to the highest degree.

One particularly pompous captain actively disliked one of the less attractive girls and never missed an opportunity of declaring that anyone taking her to bed was just too lazy. One of the less bright girls once sought the advice of the flight crew on preparing a 'very dry' martini a passenger had requested. Her preliminary training had taught her the correct way to mix a martini, but the 'very dry' stipulation had thrown her. The crew told her it should be placed in the oven at 320 degrees for 45 seconds. She followed these instructions and later returned to the cockpit with a beaming smile. Her passenger, she said, had told her it was the very best martini he had ever enjoyed.

A sharp hostess brought 'Captain Pompous' a bowl of fruit in complete disarray; he told her to take it away and bring it back more tastefully arranged. She returned with a tray on which was a plate with a large banana and two red plums in phallic design and in a soft demure voice enquired whether the skipper thought that better. The skipper, with a serious countenance, thought it was indeed!

Of all flight crew the air hostess division supplied the company's fastest turnover. Of several dozen young ladies only few stayed for a year or more and as the company became larger many of the just-recruited girls resigned before a captain could get to fly with them. The exploits of one stick in my memory despite the fact that she was not with the company for an extensive period.

She was a Japanese national of rather buxom proportions who had had some success in the noble art of judo—a somewhat alarming combination. Attractive in an earthy way, she never lacked for male companionship. Her stated ambition was to sleep with every one of the expatriate crew! To eliminate confusion—a distinct possibility, for there were more than 200 of us—this methodical lass decided to keep a record.

I never saw this book but I have it on the authority of a colleague perhaps more fortunate that he had not only seen it but had been permitted to appraise his own entry. When he attempted to turn to other pages the lass admonished him, telling him it was not ethical; nevertheless he was delighted to confirm that he had obtained a satisfactory pass.

Our Electra fleet's Flight Captain John Carrington retired at the beginning of April 1967, ending an association which had begun in September 1951. I enjoyed an article he wrote on a pilot's paperwork that appeared in *Shell Aviation News* the following year. A couple of extracts:

> 'The first requirement for any young man aspiring to be a commercial pilot is the ability to write the Lord's Prayer on the head of a pin. Without this skill, after a year or two in the business and the attainment of quadruple figures there will still be no prospect whatever of filling in Form CA24—his flying log book. The design of this slim volume is such that while there is plenty of room for remarks about the flight, the columns for almost every other detail are, like the cargo-holds of most modern aircraft, strictly space-limited . . .

> 'Forms fascinate me. The ones I particularly like are those which ask date of birth, and in the next column age. One of the most curious I ever filled in was at an airport in Southern Japan. I had been diverted there with a full load of passengers and, having refuelled, was ready to depart for my normal destination in rather a hurry, as the hot breath of Flight Time Limitation was beginning to fan the back of my neck, when the health officer of the port

suddenly arrived on a bicycle and presented me with a form the size of *The Times*. All details had to be completed, including such items as: height of masts, draught, beam, number of cabins and tonnage, both gross and net. I wonder what he did with it . . .'

A unique type of cargo was featured in a May issue of *The Post*. The headline read: FISH OUT OF WATER LIVE TO REACH HONG KONG TABLES. The first sentence: 'Ever hear of live fish travelling 1100 miles to market, out of water and live on arrival?'

About seven years earlier one of Cathay Pacific's salesmen on a short holiday in Phnom Penh saw elephant fish on sale—Suen Hok Yu, as they are known to Chinese. Since they are a great delicacy he bought some direct from a market fish tank just before his return to Hong Kong, slipped them in a plastic bag and brought them home where, to his great surprise, they completely revived after he placed them in a bucket of water. This discovery obviously had promise and before long Cathay Pacific brought a trial shipment to Hong Kong where a local distributor had no difficulty in selling them to several gourmet Chinese restaurants.

Looked upon as a biological freak the fish are caught in Tonle Sap, a huge muddy and shallow lake which often dries up, this being the reason the fish have found the ability to survive out of water. The lake has a higher fish content than any other in the world—eight tons to the square kilometre. From the lake trucks brought the fish 100 miles to the Phnom Penh airport, where they were loaded into the livestock hold of a Convair in shallow aluminium pans with clip-on lids. Air holes in the sides were the only concession to fish comfort. At the time the article appeared Cathay Pacific was bringing two tons of the fish on each of its thrice-weekly flights.

Most airline operators produce a traffic manual which lists regulations covering the carriage of pets and prohibited articles. The durian was one such prohibited article, a large oval fruit of the East Indies. It has a hard prickly rind, a soft cream-coloured pulp, a most delicious taste and an odour which even the addicts have to describe as ghastly. It was the one fruit no captain would allow aboard his ship; its terrible stink permeated the whole aircraft in minutes. Though this is well known it's surprising how many Asian passengers try to sneak one aboard. Invariably olfactory perception traces the culprit and the offending article is despatched with alacrity.

I clearly remember the furore, tantamount to a Press horse-whipping when that wonderful bandleader Xavier Cugat managed to smuggle his chichuahua undetected into the Colony. Even that most gentlemenly of men, airport commandant Owen Hamilton went into print and close to a fit over the matter.

Politically things were less than promising this year. During May communist organisations in Hong Kong sought to impose their will on the Government and the man in the street by intimidating workers, by fomenting work stoppages, by demonstrations and rioting and indiscriminate violence. This stemmed directly from China's cultural revolution with the dedicated Maoist armed with the Little Red Book and the belief that he would be invincible. On May 11 serious rioting broke out in many a Kowloon street. For three days mobs battled the police, attacked and set fire to buses and other vehicles and looted Government offices in an orgy of senseless destruction. Many were paid to take part. A curfew was imposed during the nights of May 11, 12 and 13. On the day after that the police firmly restored order without having to call on Army support. The period brought great credit to the name of Chief Superintendent Peter Godber who was seen at the head of his men in almost every trouble spot; unfortunately in the years ahead this courageous officer would lose public respect when he was imprisoned on charges of corruption.

Confrontation continued throughout the year and scarcely a day passed without several bombs having to be deactivated. Once Judy and I were drawn to the window of our tenth-floor flat by the shrill of police whistles just in time to see a man blown to pieces by a bomb he had intended to fasten to the wall of the police station close by. I turned away with the callous remark: 'Serve the bastard right!' For that was a time when only the most charitable could turn the other cheek.

In early July a note from Staff Manager Terry asked me to present myself for the issue of an Essential Service Warrant authorising me to move around should a curfew be reimposed. I never used it, for the police kept a firm hand on the situation and my only unhappy surprise during the whole of this dreadful period occured a few minutes after I had left the Miramar Restaurant in the Kai Tak terminal building on November 27, when a bomb exploded and tore a gaping hole in the ceiling. No one was injured, but thirty people protected by a stout wooden wall will not forget that day.

Friday June 30 found me taxi-ing out to Runway 13 for takeoff in a heavy thunderstorm. Intense rain reduced visibility to a minimum. Conditions demanded a ground-monitored radio control departure and I was instructed to line up on the runway and hold until the controller had me on contact in his scope. Suddenly an hysterical voice ordered me to clear the runway immediately, and as I scuttled off I intercepted through the headset the tidings that a Thai Caravelle jet had just struck the water near Channel Rock, just 300 yards short of Runway 31's threshold point. The airport closed immediately and soon RAF helicopters were bringing bodies and survivors to the runways and to where a field hospital had been established.

I returned to my home a very chastened pilot. I knew many had died, but would not learn till next day that only 56 of the 80 souls aboard had survived. What upset me most was that barely five mintues after the accident the thunderstorms had passed leaving a clear blue sky, for with a short delay to his approach Captain Vigor Thorsen, pilot of the ill-fated Caravelle, would have logged another incident-free sector.

One accident seems to trigger another. On August 31 Captain Len Cowper again became newsworthy when the Number Three engine of his Convair jet exploded and caught fire on takeoff at Hanada, Tokyo's International Airport. Len brought his stricken craft to a stop on the remaining yards of the runway, and thankfully there were no injuries.

That year ended on a note which, without a little bit of luck might have meant disaster to one of our Japanese hostesses. On the clear wintry night of December 29 a mean Arctic wind was cutting across the tarmac and keeping the temperature down to three degrees Celsius. I had almost finished my pre-flight walk-around inspection and had reached a point adjacent to the port wing root when I looked up to see a body tumbling through the air. Miss Aki Koyano glanced off the left fender of the motorized passenger stairs and hit the tarmac with a resounding thud—a sound I never want to hear again.

All we could do was keep her warm until the ambulance took her off to hospital—she made a full recovery. The ground servicing crew had moved the steps a distance of about four feet away from the door lip, a favourite ploy which gave them just that little extra working space as they serviced the forward areas. But they never would remember to erect a safety bar across the door entrance.

By April 1968 the introduction of the company's sixth Convair enabled it to operate 185 jet flights each week to seventeen cities within its Far Eastern network. This Convair (VR-HGA) was 'the Mandarin Jet' with a palatial eye-catching, specially-designed Chinese interior decor. Passengers publicised it far and wide, for a satisfied customer is still the world's best public relations agent. Our financial wizards had paid Taiwan's Civil Air Transport $HK18,480,000 for it. CAT introduced jet services with this aircraft, to become the first airline to operate pure jet scheduled passenger service on regional routes in the Far East.

This short ferry flight was followed by the longest, which brought Cathay Pacific's seventh Convair from VIASA in Caracas, Venezuela in November, with Bob Howell in command. During 1970 Cathay Pacific added two more Convair 880s to its fleet, both purchased from JAL. This meant that in the period the company operated this type there had been nine of them on the Hong Kong register, but mishaps had reduced the figure to seven, and this was the number available for sale when the company withdrew the type from service in 1975.

All seven Convairs, including all spares plus all spare engines but excluding the simulator were purchased by Compagnia Inter-Americana Export-Import Incorporated SA of Panama, a subsidiary of International Air Leases Inc., of Miami, Florida. The figure they paid is quite unbelievable and I hesitate to record that it was a paltry $US500,000; but it was that or the breaker's hammer so the company accepted it. The figure came from Bob Dewar, Director of Airlines operations, and he should know. Cathay Pacific excluded the simulator, planning to use sections, including the computer for their proposed Boeing 707 simulator.

With the expertise gained from operating the Convair 880 simulator and experiencing the immense saving in fuel and insurance costs Cathay Pacific became a firm advocate for this type of ground training, and after only a brief interval signed a contract with the Mitsubishi Precision Company for a Boeing 707-320B simulator at an agreed cost of $US1,400,000. The unit was delivered to Cathay Pacific's ground training centre during late 1972 and was soon installed and calibrated under the watchful direction of Ian Bartlett, Manager of Simulator Training and Maintenance. Before the year ended experts from the British Civil Aviation Authority had flight-checked and approved it.

31st October 1968
Cathay Pacific's 32 year old Senior Purser Chir Yung-Mur (Johann)
proudly displays the APA's Safety Award he received from William A
Jennings. The citation read "for outstanding performance and exceptional
discipline during an emergency following a take-off accident at Hong Kong
on 5th November, 1967."

CV 880 VR-HGA 1969
Recently CPA's Famous Mandarin Jet

CPA's Convair 880-22M . . . VR-HFZ
Previous registration YV-C-VIA. Entered CX Service September 22, 1967, purchased
from VIASA July 4, 1967 for HK$17,130,000. Destroyed June 15, 1972: A bomb
detonated in passenger cabin near Pleiku, Vietnam.

1975

Ground level shot of four of the seven CPA Convair 880's 'cacooned' and awaiting a buyer.

1975

Aerial photograph of a 'cluster' of CPA Convair 880's 'cacooned' and awaiting a buyer.

For its Lockheed Tri-Star L1011 simulator Cathay Pacific authorised a contract with Redifon Flight Simulation Limited of the UK, the price tag 1,600,000 pounds. It was in use by July 1976.

With this wonderful ground equipment, and with Cathay Pacific conditions, first-class men filled the positions of instructor. Two come readily to mind: the pipe-smoking Ronald Walter Brown and the ever-helpful John Barry Perkins. Captain Chris Bushe was appointed the company's manager of Simulator Training.

Long before the departure of the Convairs the company's Boeing 707 fleet had stabilized at twelve of these magnficent planes, all of them procured from North West Airlines. I was one of twenty-two aircrew chosen for the initial course which commenced in North West Airlines training building in Minneapolis in June 1971. This unique building was without a single window, designed for maximum concentration. Inside I felt as though I were in another world. But trainees are still old-fashioned enough to be diverted by Nature's glories or a quick glimpse of femininity in motion. At a later period, when I was involved in delivery flights I entered this building on a brilliantly sunny morning, and when I left the swinging door just three hours later, two feet of snow had fallen to cast a white mantle over everything.

Our first Boeing 707, VR-HGH arrived in the Colony in July 1971 and entered service on August 24. Between these dates she was used to train crews both in Hong Kong and in Kuala Lumpur, where the circuit was less busy. Subang, the new $Straits 52,000,000 international runway at Kuala Lumpur had been officially opened in 1965 replacing the old 4,800 foot strip located just to the south of the city. That old strip was a nightmare, surrounded by many obstructions. Even in clear weather there were problems. I have been on final approach and a steam train crossing the end of the runway has pumped so much smoke into the air that my forward visibility decreased to nothing and I had to go round again. This frequently happened. For the record, the biggest aircraft our company operated to that small strip was the Lockheed Electra L188.

On the new Subang runway we were taken through the same series of 707 exercises as we had mastered in the North West Airlines simulator at Minneapolis. The pilots had a trio of exceptionally talented instructors in the persons of Captains Jerry Frederickson, Bill Halverson and Bill Rowe; our flight engineers learned their trade under the expert eyes of Don Abbot and Howard Glenna. Bill Rowe was responsible for my training.

The procedure adopted by our company for takeoff has the captain with his left hand on the nose-wheel steering control. The first officer monitors the instruments and calls out the speeds during the takeoff run. At 80 knots the captain puts his left hand on the control column and at a certain speed designated 'V1' has both hands there. The flight engineer adjusts the throttles to maintain maximum power and monitors that the throttles do not vibrate from the required setting.

One senior captain just could not get on with a certain senior flight engineer. The feeling was mutual. The flight engineer had developed the annoying habit of monitoring the throttles by gripping them at the tops rather than the trailing edges. The captain, when making his initial power reduction after takeoff would find the engineers hand's under his, and had developed the habit of pulling it off and throwing it towards the first officer. This annoyed the engineer though he was in the wrong, and one day in Tokyo he purchased a 'bleeding hand' from a magicians supply shop.

On the next flight with his enemy the takeoff proceeded, the captain reached across to make the first power reduction, found the engineer's hand where it should not have been, plucked it from the throttles and threw it aside. A contrived bellow of agony was rent from the engineer. The captain, from the corner of his eye, saw a hand sailing towards the first officer who was not in the ploy and ducked in alarm. Momentarily under shock, the captain over-controlled the plane, which in turn produced some interesting gyrations. Naturally the aftermath included some straight talking, but the strangest effect of all this, was that these two men who had hated each other's guts then became the closest of friends. The skipper became more mellow in regard to procedures, while the engineer followed the proper hand drill to the inch.

Bill Sowrey joined HAECO as Sales Manager from the Concorde project at the British Aircraft Corporation. He had considerable experience as a flight test engineer as well as a pilot. In aviation the Sowrey family name was legendary. On September 23, 1916 Second Lieutenant Frederick Sowrey, a 23-year-old pilot of 39 Squadron, RFC, destroyed German Zeppelin LZ 32, which was under the comman of K.Lt Werner Peterson. Lieutenant Sowrey's mount was a tiny BE2c armed with a machine-gun and it was battling a leviathan 521 feet long, kept aloft by 935,000 cubic feet of dangerous inflammable hydrogen and armed with four machine-guns. The Zeppelin wreckage came roaring down near Billericay, a village near London, incinerating its crew. Seconds after it hit the ground K.Lt Peterson staggered from the furnace, a fightfully burnt man screaming 'Dreizehn!' It was his thirteenth raid. At that time Lieutenant Sowrey had two brothers in the RFC. He finished his career as a Group Captain decorated with the DSO, DFC and AFC. His son rose to the rank of Air Vice Marshall.

Bill Sowrey gave me some photocopies of his uncle's RFC training manual. What interesting reading it makes! My eyes fastened on the instruction for the BE:

'The BE is a tractor machine possessing a good range of speed, 70 to 40 mph. It is capable of climbing, fully loaded, at a rate of 500 feet a minute.' What a contrast to the Convair 880's maximum speed of 615 mph! One section of the little book is as applicable today as it was then. It reads:

'An aeroplane can never be too clean. Rust, mud, dust and superfluous oil must at once be removed when it returns to the shed.' Our past Director of Engineering and Maintenance D.S. Delaney insists that all Cathay Pacific aircraft get a good rinse and polish every 220 hours, for an unwashed plane can cost a lot in reduced speed, which adds to fuel consumption.

To the Vietnamese 'Tet' signifies their Lunar New Year, which they celebrate for three or four days during January or February, but to the Allied servicemen 'advising' the Vietnamese forces in 1968 'TET' meant nightmare, for at 0300 hours on January 31 seventeen battalions of elite Vietcong sappers infiltrated Saigon and after vicious fighting penetrated the U.S. Embassy and General Westmoreland's headquarters at Tan Son Nhut Airbase. By February 23 the infiltrators had been driven off. To Cathay Pacific 'Tet' meant the suspension of their Saigon service for a fortnight.

The appointment of Brisbane-born Keith Sillett as General Sales Manager in 1970 seemed to bring a new drive and vigour into the marketing side of the company. In addition to many other sales ploys he revitalised the 'Discovery' project. An advertisement in the *Sydney Morning Herald* in 1960, publicising the Electra service to Hong Kong had used the slogan 'Discover a new world—discover the Orient'. At that time the slogan did not click, but Keith's publicity made 'The Discovery Airline' a recognisable description of the company.

The commercial and marketing departments now pursued an active expansion policy, opening new offices and broadening network coverage. Less successful routes and agencies were discarded or temporarily suspended. An expected winner did not pay off with the Siem Reap, Angkor Wat route. Opened on April Fools Day 1970 it was discontinued the following month as the war came ever closer to these beautiful ruins. Soon thereafter mortar shells and rifle fire were smashing sickening gaps into this one of the world's treasures.

In March 1969 we resumed Djakarta services, and I freshened, as it were, a memory of early morning departures from there. On the way to the airport we would pass several of the foul-smelling 'klongs', the waterways which criss-crossed the city. Fringing them, a line of brown bottoms pushed out over the water in response to calls of nature. Since the poorer Indonesian is quite uninhibited about his natural processes this occasioned little surprise. More off-putting were those amongst them using the water to brush their teeth.

Our first Boeing 707's inaugural flight was to the new Itami runway at Osaka which paralleled the old, short and slippery strip. It had been opened during February 1970 and with its well-calibrated instrument landing system in operation our days of bloodshot eyes, straining for landmarks through the industrial haze above Japan's second largest city became a bad memory.

Building that new airport had not been without its problems for it was constructed on large tracts of ancient farmland, but the opposition was quite insignificant compared with that which faced the authorities building the new Tokyo airport complex at Narita, and still does. Even though the $US2,280,000,000 facility was ready for its scheduled opening in 1971, it did not become operative until seven years later.

In the intervening years the opposition developed into a well-trained army which at times mustered 1000 farmers and radical students who fought pitched battles with the famous Tokyo Riot Police, with death and maiming common. When not fighting, the dissidents kept the airport closed by cutting the main electric supply cable, preventing the storage of fuel supplies, and building high-level obstruction towers on approach centre line. Even on the morning of May 21, 1978 (the day Cathay Pacific's first flight there landed) more than 6000 leftists marched on the airport and there confronted 14,000 police guards, many of whom

13th November, 1972
Snr. Captain Charles 'Chic' Eather.
Boeing 707 Aircraft of CPA.

were seriously burned in a continuous fusillade of flaming petrol bombs.

Scheduled services to Den Pasar, the airport of the exquisite island of Bali, were introduced from October 17, 1971, and with the commissioning of Japan's fifth international airport at Kagoshima, Captain Nev Hall took our initial non-scheduled flight there.

Following a six-year break and the enlargement of the landing strip a Brunei, Cathay Pacific returned there in 1973. What was more pleasing, especially to the Australian crews, was the reintroduction of the Sydney service, and from October 21 the Cathay Pacific flag became prominent again at Kingsford Smith Airport. Our equipment the B707 was competitive with Qantas, perhaps with a slight edge in our favour for our flight was direct, while Qantas transitted Manila. Many travellers go to great lengths to avoid these brief stops.

The 707 delivery flights had continued, and I had to make the last three. My first, the tenth ferry flight, was beset with problems that tested my ability to the utmost. It had me thinking the honour, for honour it was, might more happily have been conferred on somebody else.

Stripped of all colour right down to its silvery skin, and showing only the black stencilled Hong Kong registration VR-HHD the Boeing rose from the Minneapolis runway on March 29, 1974 into a sinister atmosphere that hid conditions worse than the minimum visibility, freezing rain and slick, greasy runway we had just left. By the time we arrived abeam of the Great Falls measuring station conditions had improved sufficiently to let us have our first cup of coffee. From this point onward the weather improved rapidly and we looked forward to a reasonable flight the rest of the way, but it was not to be. It continued as though jinxed, and when we approached Seattle we could see a violent thunderstorm bearing down on the airport. We scuttled into a landing, just vacating the strip before the fury of the storm broke. We spent the night there while Brian Thompson, Cathay Pacific's engineering manager supervised the loading of our Boeing's wide-body kit.

In the morning we continued on to the glittering beauty of Hawaii's islands, which were lit by brilliant sunshine. We negotiated the busy circuit at Honolulu International Airport with an outward show of familiarity which no one aboard really possessed. The morning of April Fools' Day dawned with the type of day the Hawaiians expect, rather than hope for, but our problem was a heavy plane and we had to take off before air temperature rose too high. With this objective perhaps we rushed things more than usual.

Captain Len Cowper, acting as my co-pilot had completed our pre-start check list and we were just sitting there waiting for a start clearance when Bruce Holyman, the Chief Flight Engineer said that neither he nor Flight Engineer Barry Cawthorn could reconcile the traffic compiler's takeoff safety index. After Len and I pored over the load sheet for several minutes it was obvious that our flight engineers were correct; the traffic compiler had made an error. The problem lay with the floor weight of two particularly heavy security check canopies. These items, which resemble the frame of a door, detect metal substances when a passenger passes through, illuminating a series of lights and activating a buzzer.

The intensity of light and sound depends on the amount of metal the traveller is carrying.

The two canopies had been loaded at Seattle under the care of Flight Engineer Ken Barnes who had also joined the flight there, but they had caused no concern at that time in relation to our takeoff index since our fuel load was far from maximum. With full tanks at Honolulu the index had moved out of the safe range.

We all got into the job of rearranging the load and brought it within the required range, but this delay of almost three-quarters of an hour meant that by the time we reached the end of the longest runway the outside temperature had risen to 31 degrees centigrade, putting us barely within our weight for takeoff distance range. But our final calculations indicated that all was well, and our heavily-laden Boeing handled like a thoroughbred.

However, that lost time probably saved us from even greater trouble. Later in the day an Air India 707 approached Hong Kong from the southwest and, on landing at Kai Tak in the middle of some terribly squally conditions, suffered undercarriage damage. The runway had to be closed and we were diverted to Taipei with barely enough fuel for the flight and little or no holding reserved. So our delay out of Hawaii proved to be a blessing in disguise.

Navigator Ray Broadhead produced some interesting statistics: the flight time of 12 hours 23 minutes was a company flight time record and almost a Boeing 707 record for any company. We had avoided the direct route between Honolulu and Hong Kong because of 100-knot headwinds and chosen a longer route to the north which gave only 30- to 40-knot headwinds, and despite an increase of 300 nautical miles in the distance flown we had saved time. The distance of 5250 nautical miles (6060 statute miles) approximated a quarter of the distance round the earth and one-fortieth of the distance to the moon. Takeoff weight was 316,000 pounds; the weight of the plane, cargo and passengers 161,000. The fuel loaded weighed 155,000 pounds, and when we dipped the tanks at Taipei we confirmed we had burned off 142,500 pounds of fuel which was almost equal to the weight of the 707 with cargo and passengers, and 74 per cent of the weight of a fully-loaded Convair 880-22m.

Cathay Pacific crews were terminating their flight duties at certain cities in Japan which, without a daily flight service, meant there could be a slip pattern of several days. So as to get a better crew utilisation the company had the crews commute to places more frequently serviced. During the previous year crews were commuting from Osaka to Fukuoka or vice-versa on JAL's Boeing 727. We were now commuting on the 'Bullet' train from Osaka to Nagoya. This was quite an experience. We usually occupied the Club Car where the public speedometer hung. The distance is about 220 kilometres and the train covered the trip at 210 kilometres an hour in just four minutes over the hour, completely stable and free from vibration.

Looking forward and planning for the future is, of course, what big business is all about, but when I read a *Post* report in May 1968 that Mr Peter Mingrone, Lockheed's export sales manager was in Hong Kong to sell 'Next generation' aircraft—a product still on the drawing-board—I did feel that this planning ahead was being taken just a little too far. How wrong I was! His sales pitch was for that regal conception the Tri-Star L1011. Its price tag at that time was $US15,000,000.

The company signed the contract in 1974, a decision made only after surviving a vigorous sales campaign from McDonnell-Douglas and the persuasive ability of Danny Kaye, the world-famous entertainer, this time in the guise of supersalesman. His product was the estimable DC10. The first Tri-Star arrived at Kai Tak on September 2, 1975. Its registration VR-HHK is a little more than coincidental, the last two letters being the abbreviation for Hong Kong.

It entered service on September 15, just fifteen days after my retirement. It had been flown from California under the command of Captain Bernie Smith, who was about to make a meteoric rise in the John Swire and Sons organisation, which really occurred through the Bahamas Airways takeover.

Following intense negotiations John Swire and Sons acquired Bahamas Airways in 1968. Through Bahamas Airways (Holdings) Limited, BOAC retained a 15 per cent interest. Duncan Bluck was the obvious choice to control the new enterprise. Shanghai-born and educated in England he had joined Butterfield and Swire in 1948 and served in its shipping department before being seconded to Cathay Pacific. He spent 1952 as Cathay Pacific's Bangkok manager, and then went to traffic manager in 1955, commercial manager in 1958 and was finally promoted to the Board in April 1964.

On October 1 1968 he took over the reins of Bahamas Airways as Chairman and Managing Director, based at Nassau on New Providence Island. He announced a two-stage expansion plan for the international service which linked Nassau with the United States at Miami and West Palm Beach. In the first stage, up to mid-December, Tampa and Fort Lauderdale would be added to the network. Then he hoped to introduce flights to New York and Montreal, extending possibly to Chicago and Washington later. The plans envisaged service to Jamaica and other Caribbean areas and possibly to South America, but Bahamas Airways was liquidated in late 1970.

When Bernie Smith was Director of Flight Operations for Cathay Pacific he gave me the reasons for the liquidation:

'They were straightforward. We were running into problems with the Bahamas Government concerning work permits right from the beginning. It took up to a year to process a permit, especially for a pilot, and though their policy of giving Bahaman citizens first opportunity was admirable in itself, no experienced local pilots were available and the short-term prospects were not promising. We started a cadet scheme, and had two trainees at Oxford at the time of liquidation.

'Then, although we had been nominated as the National flag-carrier with consequent reciprocal parallel sector rights with all other countries, we found these rights were being eroded when the Prime Minister, a partner in a local law firm, had set up another airline aligned with sterling currency. Although this existed merely on paper it was obvious that something untoward was happening.

'About May 1970 the Prime Minister made a clear statement that as far as the Government was concerned the Bahamas would be following an open-sky policy, which meant that anyone could parallel our routes. This was of course unacceptable to the company. It would be rather akin to the Hong Kong Government allowing another airline to set up in competition with Cathay Pacific on the routes it had pioneered usually with years of financial loss. This would mean economic disaster to the original operator and give him no opportunity of recovering his invested capital.

'At this stage our company gave the Government the ultimatum of either taking over Bahamas Airways, or we would have to proceed to voluntary liquidation. This must have been the best-kept secret in the Bahamas. It came as a complete surprise to everyone when, in October that year we announced the liquidation of the airline. It was a great tragedy, for the airline had terrific potential and could have become far bigger than Cathay Pacific.'

Some aspects of Bernie's stint in Nassau presented their own surprises. He was working in his office one day when a chap burst in and sat down. In Hong Kong, among the Chinese who are always most respectful, this could never happen.

'His first words were extremely pointed,' Bernie said. 'With glaring eyes and accusing finger he told me he would have my work permit withdrawn and send me off the island before the day was out. He was the brother of a girl who had applied for a flight stewardess job and failed the initial test. His outburst carried on for some time, and as soon as he left, I phoned Duncan Bluck and told him to expect this character. Sure enough he stormed into Duncan's office and gave him the same treatment. Then he scuttled off to the Minister of Labour's office, and we had to write later, explaining why we had not employed the girl.

'Interviewing for stewardesses, one of the first questions we asked a girl was "Are you married?" Her reply was invariably "No". The next standard question was, invariably, "How many children do you have?" Just as invariably, the answer was "Four". This gives an indication of the open-ness, in all respects, of the island girls, but it did give me something of a shock the first time I heard the interviewer asking what were standard questions.

'The night I arrived at the Nassau International Airport (once named Windsor Field) Tony Capell and Phill Cheetham met me and took me to my accommodation at the Nassua Beach Hotel. We were standing at the bar having a few beers and when Tony mentioned someone or other I said, "Of course, he was always the nigger in the woodpile," an expression I did not habitually use and one I had not used for years. Looking up I saw the barman glaring at me homicidally. Capel burst into hysterical laughter and Cheetham visibly paled and commenced coughing furiously. From that moment I found this expression rising to my lips on every possible occasion though I knew its use was quite boorish; nor did I mean any disrespect by its use. I finally geared myself to banishing it from my vocabulary.

'About a week later Duncan Bluck hosted a large cocktail party at his house. Shortly before I had left Hong Kong the newspapers were running a series of articles dealing with unsolved crimes. One of these was the Sir Harry Oakes slay-

303

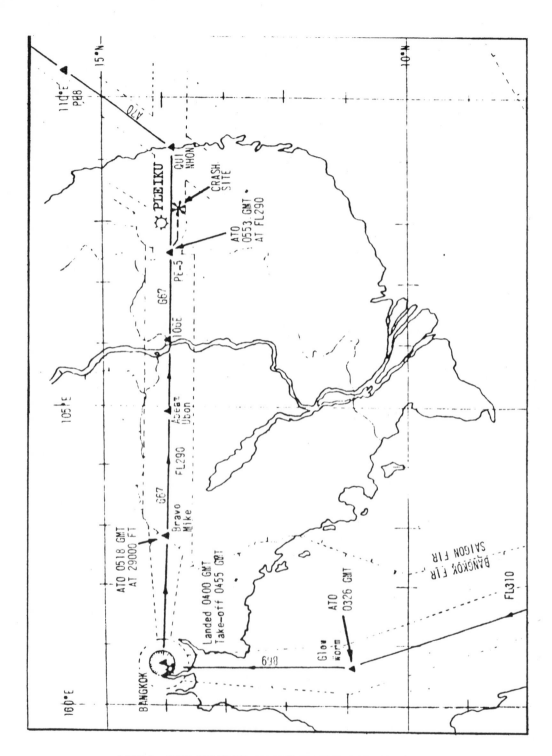

MAP 6: THE CONVAIR 880-22M VR-HFZ CATASTROPHE

ing, a crime that occurred while the Duke of Windsor was Governor-General of the Bahamas during the war years.

'I was standing in a large group of businessmen when I asked if the crime had ever been solved. Suddenly everyone stopped talking—there must have been a hundred and fifty people thereabouts—and almost at once my group of about thirty had dwindled to three. A chap came up and in a quiet voice said, "My dear chap, that is one of the things we don't discuss in the Bahamas." I had dropped the heaviest brick imaginable.'

Bernie Smith's first association with Cathay Pacific was on Boxing Day 1952, after his resignation from the RAF in which his last posting had been with 26 squadron at Kai Tak. He resigned in 1957 seeing little prospect for promotion to captain rank but returned the following year, and for the next eighteen years made spectacular progress. At the beginning of February 1976 he was still a person of great consquence in the company and throughout the Colony, but on the 10th of that month he resigned, following his alleged involvement in the great Lockheed scandal which tainted some of the most influential people throughout the world. It was a distressing finale to the career of a charming young man widely admired and respected.

Many individuals, both expert and lay, were involved in investigating the destruction of VR-HFZ with all aboard, which may have been Cathay Pacific's most heart-rending disaster. On June 15 1972 at 1354 hours Saigon time the Saigon Area Control Centre acknowledged this aircraft's routine report from point PE5, 29,000 feet up on the Asian Air Corridor (Airways Green 67). This airspace had a lower limit of 24,000 feet and an upper one of 39,000. Most of the higher and more efficient flight levels were blocked off then by USAF B52s en route from their base at Sattahip, 70 miles south southeast of the airport at Don Muang, Bangkok, in their vain attempt to bomb North Vietnam into submission.

Soon after the message a Viet Nam Air Force aircraft sighted the crashed and still-burning airliner 27 miles southeast of the township of Pleiku in Central Vietnam. Two helicopters of the Rescue Co-ordination Centre landed beside the wreckage, recovered two bodies and flew them to Pleiku.

The airliner had carried 81 people, ten of them in the operating crew. The pilot in command, Henry Neil Morison was the company Flight Captain of the Convair fleet. Senior First Officer Lachlan Campbell Mackenzie occupied the captain's seat and was under command instruction. Leslie Albert Boyer was in the co-pilot's seat and the company's senior Convair check flight engineer was also on the flight deck. Cabin crew consisted of two pursers, Kar-wah Dickey Kong and Hok-man William Yuen, and four hostesses, Winnie Chan, Kwong-Yiu Ellen Cheng, Lai-Har Tammy Li and Lai-Kuen Florence Ng. Ten bodies including those of Lachlan Mackenzie and Winnie Chan were never recovered. It was assumed they were either incinerated or were scatted in the Agent Orange-defoliated highlands jungle some miles from the wreckage site. The entire area was subject to war activity. One engine was never found. The early discovery that the undercarriage had broken into two pieces immediately narrowed the field of investigation.

Examination located many small velocity impact craters and explosive 'splash' typical of that found in other aircraft subject to explosive blast. They constituted the first positive evidence that an explosion had occurred, most probably inside the passenger cabin. X-rays of all recovered bodies showed metal particles consistent with them having been exposed to the effects of an explosive device, and nine bodies found to contain a heavy concentration of particles were retained for additional laboratory examination.

The black box (flight data recorder) showed the accident had occurred 64 minutes and two seconds after takeoff from Bangkok, a bare five minutes after Saigon had received the Convair's last transmission. Medical and pathological analysis indicated that all passengers and crew were probably rendered unconscious by the massive decompression which followed the detonation of a high explosive within the passenger cabin.

The world's media gave the crash full coverage. The *South China Morning Post* of June 16 discarded the original belief that the airliner had been in collision with a U.S. military jet. The report concluded with distressing descriptions of the heartbreak of those waiting for loved ones, and the stories of those who had switched flights and survived.

Not until July 2 did the *Sunday Times*, a Kuala Lumpur paper, report that CPA CONVAIR WAS BLOWN UP BY A BOMB. The *Post* of August 8 reported that the body of Miss Somwang Promprin, common-law wife of Police Lieutenant Somchai Chaiyasut had been impounded for further investigation. It contained suspected bomb fragments. This was the only body the Thai Police Department retained. The other eight originally held over had been released to their families, including that of Lieutenant Somchai Chaiyasut's eight-year-old daughter. At the time of this report the Lieutenant, attached to Thai Police Aviation Division, was not being held in custody but payment of insurance policies he had taken out was being withheld. They totalled $US220,000.

On September 2, Lieutenant Somchai Chaiyasut was charged with mass murder. It was alleged he handed a package to his fiancee (originally described as common-law wife) who was travelling with his eight-year-old daughter of a previous marriage, and told her it was a present for a friend in Hong Kong. Somchai had taken out more than $3,000,000 in insurance policies on the lives of his fiancee and daughter.

When Somchai's trial got under way in September the following year he apparently became so bored with proceedings that he frequently dropped off to sleep. During March 1974 when called upon to testify Somchai stated he thought the plane was not only overloaded but travelling too fast and too high. For a man reputed to have a knowledge of aviation these were thoroughly ridiculous statements and something of an insult to the Court's intelligence. On May 30, 1974 the defence and prosecution delivered their final statements. The three-judge panel withdrew to consider the verdict, a process expected to take several months, but that same day they delivered a 'not guilty' verdict to a packed court after eleven months of what was termed Thailand's most sensational trial.

Mr Foi Malikhao, who headed the Government's five prosecutors, lodged

The Convair 880-22M VR-HFZ Wreckage
15th June 1972
27 miles SE of Pleiku, Vietnam

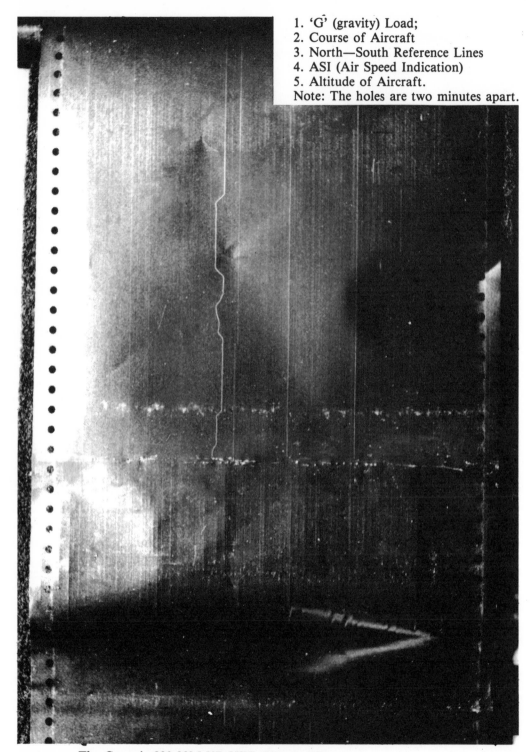

1. 'G' (gravity) Load;
2. Course of Aircraft
3. North—South Reference Lines
4. ASI (Air Speed Indication)
5. Altitude of Aircraft.
Note: The holes are two minutes apart.

The Convair 880-22M VR-HFZ Catastrophe
15th June 1972—27 miles SE of Pleiku
Vietnam. Fairchild 5424-241A Flight Data Recorder Tape (Black Box)

an appeal. He had a brilliant reputation to protect, for until this trial he had never lost a case, but Somchai's defence team, which also consisted of five lawyers and included his own father, continued to prove more than a match. Although the police authorities were alleged to have stated that they thought Somchai guilty, they conceded that under Thai law the circumstantial evidence, strong though it was, was not enough for a conviction. On December 22 1976 we learned from a Bangkok press release of the previous day that Lieutenant Somchai had won his claim against the insurance companies.

The P.R. man's lot during times of adversity becomes particularly distressing, for then he must be an accomplished psychologist in his handling of grief-stricken people. Fortunately with the advance and recurrent training methods required for aircrew. and the reliability of modern aircraft, such periods are rare. With the exception of its initial appointment Cathay Pacific has been remarkably fortunate in its choice of Public Relations people, for they have included the legendary Australian author Alan Marshall, a fine lady named Valentine Pope, and Tim Rossi, with David Bell bringing an experienced approach to a position which embraces the whole Hong Kong Swire Group.

Valentine Pope told me one of the outrageous stories for which Peter Waitt was famous, this one concerning a dinner he arranged to celebrate the inaugural flight to Nagoya in March 1966.

'This dinner was held at a Hong Kong restaurant, and in honour of the Japanese dignitaries a special dish had been ordered. The *piece de resistance* a large crayfish, still alive, was set in the middle of the table and hot sauce poured over it. The crayfish snatched a table napkin, briskly wiped itself, and walked off the plate to the edge of the table, much to the horror of the guests.'

As the decade progressed two costly systems brought benefits to the Cathay Pacific traveller. 'CPARS' is a computer-based reservation system which became operational during October 1971 and 'LOPOC' is a $HK4,250,000 computerised departure control system which speeds up all aspects of passenger, cargo and catering handling on the ground, and reduces check-in congestions. It came into operation in 1977.

From the marketing aspect the company was elated when on March 14, 1973 CPARS pinpointed the name of T. Saito as the five millionth passenger since it began operations in 1946. 'Mr Five Million' was presented with a specially inscribed wrist-watch to signal this landmark. The following year the name 'Butterfield' disappeared into history and hencefort the company has been John Swire and Sons (HK) Ltd. No Butterfield had been associated with the group since the Shanghai days of 1866.

1976 established our most distant westerly destination. On November 16 the Brunswick-green livery of Cathay's 707 made its first appearance in Bahrein, the tiny island State in the Persian Gulf. The Melbourne scheduled service opened the following month. Expansion continued in 1977 and from April 4 the picturesque city of Penang was included in our timetable. Dubai, the commercial and trading centre of the United Arab Emirates followed in November. In November of the following year both Kaosiung (Taiwan) and Nagoya were added to the system, and then three days later Port Moresby, capital of the newly independent State of Papua New Guinea received once-weekly coverage.

This record of what is probably the world's most successful regional airline reaches it conclusion during 1979, which seems the optimum time to stop, for this was when Cathay Pacific became equipped with the superlative Boeing 747 jet, the Jumbo. Likewise this was the year Roy Downing was honoured with an O.B.E. and concluded his career with Hong Kong's Department of Civil Aviation.

Of all the people who came to the Roy Farrell Export-Import Company none now remains with Cathay Pacific. The last was Lyell Louttit who retired in August 1975. Cathay Pacific has had some wonderful and long-serving employees. Mr Chester Yen, regional manager, Man Chi Yau (Ah Man) the company's first and only office boy in 1948, Mr Lam Kwok Wai, the courier of the company mail-bag whose duty took him across the harbour four times a day—I considered every one a worthy workmate. Closer to me, Chan Pak Chi, our crew transport driver and Tong Kit, who did practically everything: worked at check-in, issued tickets, compiled airway bills, released and accepted cargo, dealt with cables and letters, and handled money. Wei Chin Ching—'C.C.' to his legion of friends—was another fine Chinese. Equally fine was Portuguese Miggie Miguel, who devised an ingenious balance computer which found an aircraft's centre of gravity within seconds and made obsolete our previous method of drawing dozens of lines on a load-sheet. Miggie had attained the position of Freight Superintendent when he died in September 1969. Mr Fung Hon's first job was aircraft boy on the DC3s. At that period we had no cutlery or even glasses, and one of his duties was to ensure sufficient plastic substitutes were aboard.

The names continue to come to my mind: John Dick and Jock Campbell of the Commercial department; Marie Bok and Alma O'Hoy, secretaries *extraordinaire*; Remi Aromin and Chester Wong of the Operations division, and dozens of other fine people each contributing in his own way to the fortunes and smooth running of our company.

Changes were made within the commercial administration as people resigned and were replaced by others of equal ability. Unfortunately promotion changes too often are the prelude to retirement. The company has always been a close-knit family. Any member of the group could always get right into the presence of the Taipan to express his point of view, suffering a minimum of delay. I cannot recall such a direct line of approach being available in the other Hongs, but while this attitude is fostered I feel that the group will continue its astonishing prosperity.

In the New Year's Honours list of 1976 the Queen awarded the OBE to the Hon. J.H. Bremridge, Chairman of the Group, and the CBE to A.G.S. McCallum, President of John Swire and Sons (Japan) Limited, both for meritorious service to the public. Within the group Edward Scott was appointed chairman of the Swire empire in Australia with Dick Large going to a similar position in Japan. H.M.P. 'Mike' Miles became Deputy Managing Director of Cathay Pacific and another respected cricket mate of mine H.B. 'John' Olsen was appointed General Manager South East Asia, with headquarters in Singapore.

VR-HGP B707 Kai Tak, 1974

VR-HGH over Hong Kong, 15.3.1975

VR-HGH Boeing 707 over Hong Kong 15.3.1975

VR-HGU approaching Kai Tak 15.8.1975

L1011 Tristar just after roll-out at Palmdale, U.S.A. 17.6.1975

Cathay Pacific's first Lockheed Tristar VR-HHK parallels the skyline
of Central Hong Kong prior to landing at Kai Tak Airport.
2nd September, 1975

L1011 Tristar. 13th July 1975 on Test Flight

Sadly, a wonderful era in the life of the Group came to a close during 1978 when Jock Campbell, Eddie Brown, John Dick and Captains Keith Brady and Gus Walker reached retirement age.

Cathay Pacific in its 34th year is an airline of substance, the envy of many others in the highly competitive field. It retains its remarkable reputation of never having received a Government subsidy. The quality and popularity of its service can be gauged by the statistics for 1979, especially compared with those recorded 31 years before:

1948:	Passengers carried 9,000	Freight	40,000 kilos
1979:	Passengers carried 2,629,536	Freight	18,229,796 kilos

What magnificent equipment the company operates—eight Boeing 707-320s (all C Models), a similar number of Lockheed Tri-Star L1011s, and three Boeing 747-200Bs. The Jumbos, registered VR-HKG, VR-HIA and VR-HIB cost a massive $US54,000,000 each—a contrast to the $HK159,000 Butterfield and Swire paid de Kantzow and Farrell's Cathay Pacific for their first DC3 on July 1, 1948.

My pre-retirement flight into Kai Tak took place on August 28, 1975. Just as we rounded the checkerboard on final approach to Runway 13 we were suddenly confronted with a thunderstorm which had sneaked across the airport from the east. The storm had somehow eluded Civil Aviation's radar operator and our first indication of any bad weather around was the wind's sudden gusting to more than 40 knots with an accompaniment of blinding rain. Visibility remained just within landing limits, and then when the elements realised their prey was safely out of danger the weather immediately cleared, and we taxied to the terminal under a brilliantly star-studded sky. Where had the storm come from? Where had it gone?

As I walked with the crew away from the Boeing 707 and my final Cathay Pacific command I told them of a similar situation which materialised just as rapidly and just as unheralded during an approach I was making into Taipei some months before, when the weather had deteriorated even more dangerously.

Just before midnight on April 5 I was settled on the Taipei ILS glide-slope. On this beautiful calm night there was no moon, but visibility was first-class and the lights of Taiwan's capital were twinkling just to the right of a clearly visible airport. Suddenly the voice of the tower controller advised a change of runway direction; the wind commenced to gust and a landing from the opposite direction was more favourable. We were instructed to break right and call in on the downward leg.

As we joined this downard leg we were violently buffeted and my first officer said we were just below an extensive nimbo-status roll-cloud which was producing the severe turbulence. Throughout the final approach and touch-down the driving rain progressively reduced visibility, but it remained just clear enough until the moment our wheels were rolling along the Sanshing airport. Then the heavens opened with a downpour that brought our forward visibility to zero. The accompaniment of thunder and lightning was so severe that not only was I hunching my shoulder muscles as though I expected a blow, I was clenching my teeth.

We completed the landing run with much slipping and sliding and came to a stop almost on the very end and the extreme left-hand side of the strip. My flight engineer recorded our touchdown time as 2352 local time, which meant that the very moment which subjected us to this most dangerous condition would have been 2350, the precise time at which Taiwan officials recorded the death of their President, the Generalissimo Chiang Kai-Shek.

Cause and effect I think not; but one could not but think that Nature at her most ferocious had brought a fitting finale to this turbulent and tangled period of China's political turmoil, for I can recall no other time where there were more cross-currents. No one knew precisely where he stood from day to day—yet, for all that, in no other modern period have the Chinese people achieved more.

Close down all engines, for I have reached

THE END

EPILOGUE

Anniversary followed anniversary and Cathay Pacific celebrated yet another birthday on the 24th September 1982—it is now in its 37th year of operation.

Competition (Laker Airways) had thundered into its sphere of operation and just as swiftly thundered out again, however the world-wide spectre of spiralling fuel costs haunts the company to where the percentage of operational expenditure attributed to this item has increased 60% since February 1976, while actual fuel costs have risen 330% during the same period.

Britsh Airways, has produced some interesting fuel consumptions. Throughout their fleet they have calculated that $65 million a year could be saved by flying four knots slower; $43 million if pilots retrimmed aircraft instead of relying on the auto-pilot, and other staggering savings in other minor areas of general operation.

Cathay's approach to this operational nightmare was to set up a Fuel Sub-committee under the chairmanship of Lew Roberts, who quickly acknowledging a situation where fuel invoices represent 25% of total operational expenditure, tackled this task with such vigour that in 1979 (the first calendar year of the sub-committee's charter) saved the company $US1.8 million.

This was accomplished by introducing a weight reduction on each item, such as using thinner paper for inflight magazines, changing the material of pillowcases to man-made fibre, utilising lightweight cutlery, meat trays, and blankets. For, as he points out—'the cardinal rule is that you have to burn fuel to carry extra fuel which becomes almost the original chicken and egg situation. For the extra weight you need extra fuel which is in itself extra weight which needs more fuel which continues *ad infinitum*.'

Having done everything possible to handle this "bogey" the company resumed the basic task of directing their airline by up-dating established routes and dilligently seeking new extensions wherever there appeared sufficient inducement.

During 1978 Cathay opened its 21st, 22nd and 23rd destinations to Nagoya, Kaohsiung, Taiwan, and Port Moresby. Frankfurt and Shanghai (after an on-and-off start) was serviced the following year. However, the route which brought the most satisfaction to 'Mr Cathay Pacific' John K. Swire (now in his 89th year) was the introduction of the Hong Kong to London extension. This was a cherised ambition fulfilled, but not without some disappointment for early in the year Cathay's application for this route had been refused.

On July 16, 1980, VR-HIA, Cathay's 2nd Boeing 747, with Captain Ron (Jacko) Jackson-Smith at the controls, and assisted by F/O B.E. Taylor and F/E John Voysey, roared off the Kai Tak runway precisely on time.

Captain Geoff Gratwick took over command at Bahrain and brought her in on schedule at London's Gatwick Airport.

Mr Duncan Bluck, the then Deputy Chairman of the HKG Swire Group, was met on arrival by Mr Adrian Swire, with Adrian's beautifully preserved Spitfire aircraft forming an historical counterpart. John Olsen, Regional General Manager

January 1, 1982
Mr. Duncan R. Y. Bluck, the present Tai-Pan of the Swire Group of companies in
Hong Kong.

The Hon. Sir J. H. Bremridge, the immediate past Tai-Pan of the John Swire & Sons Hong Kong Group, the present Financial Secretary for the Colony of Hong Kong.

Europe and Middle East, was in attendance with John Dick, who had returned from his 1978 retirement, to become CX station manager at Gatwick. With the passing of time the Air Transport Licensing Authority, relaxed the restriction on the number of flights that could be operated there per week and almost immediately a fourth frequency was commenced. In early December, it was announced that a 5th weekly service would start on 8th January and the service became daily from 1st July 1981.

The latest route addition is a non-stop service Hong Kong to Brisbane which was inaugurated on 4th August, 1982.

With such vast distances to circumnavigate, equipment has to be of prime importance. Cathay's choice of the magnificent Jumbo fulfills this requirement and they presently control one of the finest wide-body fleets in the aviation world, and while several of the Lockheed Tri-Stars are leased their Boeing 747 fleet represents a major financial outlay.

The total value of the six 747's, including Rolls-Royce engines, is HK$1,800 million, while the RB211-525 engines, with engine support, are valued at HK$480 million. A breakdown shows the 5th Jumbo represented an investment of HK$301 million, of which HK$75 million was for the purchase of engines, galleys and seats from Rolls-Royce and other companies in the United Kingdom.

Nevertheless, having stressed the importancce of the correct equipment the basic element for every worthwhile enterprise must revolve around people. Those who presently direct the fortunes of the company have been shrewdly chosen for their business acumen and aviation expertise, however, one must also spare a thought for those, of an earlier era, who brought the company to the standard where others continued to forward its welfare and success.

Space does not permit a comprehensive listing of the current regime who continue to direct the diverse phases of what is one of the most successful of present carriers, for it is worth repeating that Cathay has never received a government subsidy, which is a proud statement to be able to make in the face of a type of competition which is regarded as one of the most brutal in our modern industrial society.

On the last day of 1981 John Bremridge retired from the Chairmanship of the John Swire & Sons Group in Hong Kong. Being of a restless nature there was no way that he could really retire, thus it came as no surprise when he accepted the Hong Kong Government's invitation to become Financial Secretary for the Colony.

On New Year's Day Duncan Bluck reached the peak of a spectacular career when he became the Group's Hong Kong Taipan. Later the then Governor, Sir Murray MacLehose (now Baron MacLehose) appointed him to chair the H.K. Tourist Association. In the 1982 New Year's Honours, Adrian Swire was created a Knight Bachelor for his service to the shipping industry.

All these were well earned and timely appointments, and a source of pride to most of us older hands, however, we quickly returned to sobering thoughts when it was remembered that C.C. Roberts had died on the 24th May 1980. 'C.C.' to everyone including wife Mary, was one of the 'Greats', who sustained the Firm through every kind of trouble. When the Pacific War became inevitable it fell to C.C. to take charge of B & S H.K. and to face the fighting and internment. He had a great share in laying the new foundations of company policy after the war and building on them. He was Chairman of the Board of Directors of Cathay which followed the Butterfield & Swire purchase way back in late forties.

So what of the 'old hands'—Queensland's fair climate has attracted a goodly number. Don Delaney, Bob Howell, Geoff Johansen, Pat Moore, Harry Smith, Dave Smith, Lucy—Ken Steele's widow (now Tait), Ina—Charles Terry's widow, Vera—Jack William's widow (now Davis), live nearby. Further north near the Brisbane area reside Geoff Arnold, Joe Bridgett, Len Cosgrove, Dennis Field, Merv Houston, Bill Jones, Barney Smith and Alex Wales.

Just south of the border live Eric Aylwood and Alan Gifford. Continuing further south into New South Wales and in the Newcastle area are Bob Smith, sister Daisy now the wife of Jack White, while in and around Sydney are Bo Egan, Ken Begg, Don Brown, Harry de Leuil, Tom Heywood, Keith Sillett, 'Pinky' Wawn, John Warne and the two heroes of the Hainan shoot-down Ced Carlton and Phil Blown.

The other Australian States have attracted a lesser number – Victoria hosts Vic Leslie, Norm Marsh and Keil Mast – the West looks after Jutta – Jim Hargraves widow, Sam Smith and Gus Walker.

Many who have forwarded the interests of Cathay returned to the old country such as Fred Lillywhite, Bill Pepperell and Stan Pain.

Canada attracted its share like Brian Jones, Fred Melbye, Peter Waitt and the families of Betty-Jane and Gilbert Tsui and Ruth and Philip Tsui—ex-cabin staff supreme. (In late 1979 CPA topped the 1,000 Cabin Attendant mark.)

Bob Sutherland is in New Zealand, Ken Wolinski in Singapore, Nancy and Dan Holeczy in West Germany, Alan Pratt in Honolulu, Ed Berry, U Sway Tin and Roy Farrell still in Vernon, Texas, USA.

Finally, what of the future?

True the Bamboo Curtain is still in unobtrusive existence, but no longer the formidable barrier it once was. A traveller can now, with few obstructions, take the train across the border to Canton; air travel is a daily event and thus a greater number of tourists can enjoy the magnificent scenery with which inner China is blessed, even the indigenous folk of Hong Kong make regular trips to their Homeland a state of affairs which would not have been chanced a short while ago, but for all this the Crown Colony is looked upon as an "Imperalistic pimple on the backside of China".

The New Territories lease expires on 30th June 1997 and while the large "Hongs" outwardly reflect a confidently vocal front its frequent repetition breeds a certain suspicion. True they are plowing staggering millions of dollars into rebuilding and expansion, but what assets do they really hold outside the Colony; sometimes it is prudent to sacrifice millions to protect hundreds of millions. Mr Denis Bray, Secretary of Home Affairs, recently stated '1997 is in no way influencing our future plans for Hong Kong', and whereas a recent poll showed only 4% want China to take back control of the Colony it would be interesting to learn just what portion of the 5¼ million of its inhabitants was sampled to obtain that figure.

The Chinese are a resilient race and hold a splendid optimism for the future and what it might bring. They have a saying that 'whenever business is bad paint the counter'. I have found that provided his rice-bowl is full he gives little or no trouble and is quite contented to let the few trouble makers get on with their own nefarious deeds.

Attempting to forecast what a political climate might be by 1997 is mind bending; for the lease question will decide the whole future of Hong Kong and not just the Territories, for regardless of the past Cultural Revolution, China is a proud and highly cultured nation who is progressively gaining in modern industrial expertise and with each day strengthening its position in this competitive world—they are so astonishingly adaptable and thrive on hard work—so how will this giant and wonderful Dragon jump—this intriguing and complex answer remains known only to the Lords of Time.

GLOSSARY OF ABBREVIATIONS

AB	Air Burma
ANA	Australian National Airways
AVG	American Volunteer Group (Flying Tigers)
BOAC	British Overseas Airways Corporation (Now BA)
BA	British Airways
BAF	Burma Air Force
BCPA	British Canadian Pacific Airways
B&S	Butterfield and Swire
CAB	Civil Aeronautics Board
CAT	Civil Air Transport
CATC	Central Air Transport Corporation
CIA	Central Intelligence Agency
CNAC	China National Aviation Corporation
CPA	Cathay Pacific Airways Limited
CPAL	Canadian Pacific Air Line
DCA	Department of Civil Aviation
ETA	Estimated Time of Arrival
fei gei	Cantonese for aeroplane
FAA	Federal Aviation Agency
'GEORGE'	Auto-pilot
HAECO	Hong Kong Aircraft Engineering Co Limited
HKA	Hong Kong Airways
JAMCO	Jardine Aircraft Maintenance Co Limited
JAL	Japan Air Lines
JS&S	John Swire and Sons Limited
KLM	Koninklijke Luchtuaal Maatsehappij NV (Royal Dutch Airlines)
KMT	Kuomintang (Nationalist China)
MATCO	Macao Air Transport Company
NWA	North West Airlines
PAL	Philippine Air Lines
PAMAS	Pacific Air Maintenance & Supply Co Limited
POAS	Pacific Overseas Airlines (Siam) Limited
PSP	Perforated Steel Plate
QANTAS	Queensland & Northern Territory Aerial Services Limited
RAAF	Royal Australian Air Force
RAF	Royal Air Force
RFEIC	Roy Farrell Export-Import Company
TAA	Trans-Australia Airlines
TAAS	Trans-Asiatic Airlines (Siam)
tael	Chinese weight (a tael of gold weighs 1.3 ozs)
THAI	Thai International Airways

UBA	Union of Burma Airways
USAF	United States Air Force

BIBLIOGRAPHY

Books:
History of RAF Kai Tak 1927—1971 by GLD Alderson
HK DCA Annual Departmental Reports
Flying Tiger—Chennault of China by Robert Lee Scott Jr
Virtue in Flying by Joan Priest
The Dragon's Wings by William M Leary Jr
The Fall of Hong Kong by Tim Carew
Hong Kong—Borrowed Place—Borrowed Time by Richard Hughes
Colony in Conflict by John Cooper
Wings of Gold by James Sinclair
The National Geographic Magazine
Shell Aviation News
Air World—ESSO
Canton Barrier by Andrew Geer
Freedom At Midnight by Collins and Lapierre
Chinese Looking Glass by Dennis Bloodworth
Pagoda by James A Phillips

Newspapers:
The Tiger Standard—Hong Kong
Hong Kong Telegraph
Sing Tao Man Pao
The China Press—Shanghai
Mindanao Times—Philippines
Daily Telegraph—Sydney
Sydney Morning Herald
China Mail
South China Morning Post
Wah Kiu Man Po
Shanghai Evening Post
Manila Bulletin
Daily Mirror-Sydney

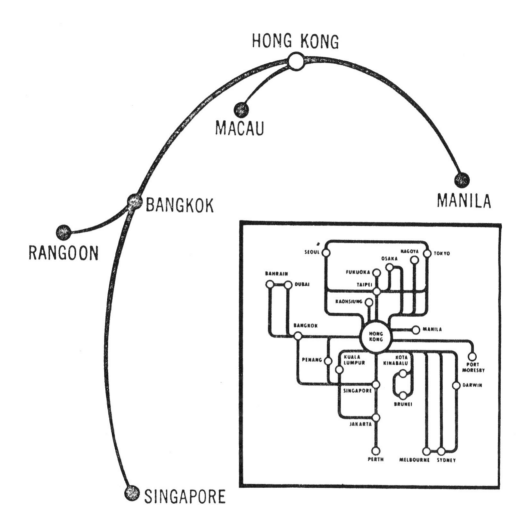

FIGURE 11. *CATHAY PACIFIC'S ROUTE NETWORK IN 1948 and 1979*

DOUGLAS DC3

VR-HDB (C47A) Previous Registration NC 58093
    Entered CX service—September 24, 1946.
    Taken over by B & S (C.P.A.) July 1, 1948 for HK$159,000.-
    Sold to Mandated Airlines, Lae, New Guinea (W.R. Carpenter) for HK$320,000.- on August 6, 1955.

VR-HDA (C47B) Previous Registration VH-ASJ
    Entered CX service—September 24, 1946
    Taken over by B & S. (C.P.A.) July 1, 1948 for HK$259,400.-
    Sold to Societe Royal Air Laos, Vientiane on July 24, 1961

VR-HDG (C47A) Previous Registration
    Entered CX service— 1947
    Taken over by B & S (C.P.A.) July 1, 1948 for HK$268,321.-
    Crashed Braemar Reservoir, Hong Kong, on February 24, 1949.

VR-HDI (C47A) Previous Registration PIC-24
    Entered CX service—1947
    Taken over by B & S (C.P.A.) July 1, 1948 for HK$206,400.-
    Sold to Australian National Airways on July 7, 1951.

VR-HDJ (C47B) Previous Registration
    Entered CX service—1947
    Taken over by B & S (C.P.A.) July 1, 1948 for HK$199,700.-
    Sold to Malayan Airways, on April 6, 1951.

VR-HDW (C47B) Previous Registration
    Entered CX service—1947
    Taken over by B & S (C.P.A.) July 1, 1948 for HK$267,800.-
    On Charter to Air Burma, crashed at Anisakan September 13, 1949.

VR-HEN (C47A) Previous Registration PIC-199
    Entered CX service—1947
    Taken over by B & S (C.P.A.) July 1, 1948 for HK$102,000.-
    Sold to Compagne Aerienne De Transport Indochinois, Hanoi, Indo China, on December 5, 1950.

C47 NC 58093 (VR-HDB).

CATALINA

VR-HDS (PBY/5A) Previous Registration PIC-258
              Entered CX service—1947
              Sold to Macao Air Transport on July 1, 1948.

VR-HDT (PBY/5A) Previous Registration
              Entered CX service—December 5, 1947
              Taken over by B & S (C.P.A.) July 1, 1948 for HK$173,400.-
              Pirated en route from Macao, July 16, 1948.

VR-HDH (PBY/5A) Previous Registration
              Entered CX service—February 1948
              Taken over by Macao Air Transport on July 1, 1948.

AVRO-ANSON

VR-HDX (Mk.1) Previous Registration VH-BFL
      Entered CX service—January 1948
      Purchased from McIllree, U-Drive Pty Ltd., Sydney on December 27, 1947.
      Written off at Sandoway, Burma, on February 9, 1948.

VR-HDU (Mk.1) Previous Registration VH-BFK
      Entered CX service—January 1948
      Purchased from McIllree, Sydney on December 17, 1947.
      Sold to Major A.S. Cannon, Peacock Motors, Rangoon Burma, in November 1950.

DOUGLAS DC4 (SKYMASTER)

VR-HEU (C54B) Previous Registration PH-TLO
        Entered CX service—September 23, 1949
        Purchased from K.L.M. on September 7, 1949 for HK$803,800.-
        Shot down by Chinese Military aircraft off Hainan, en route from Bangkok to Hong Kong, July 23, 1954.

VR-HFF (C54A) Previous Registration CF-CPD
        Entered CX service—August 1954
        Purchased from C.P. Air in August 1954 for HK$2,333,233.-
        Sold to Starways, Liverpool, January 18, 1963.

DOUGLAS DC6

VR-HFG (DC6) Previous Registration N 90876
>Entered CX service—April 1955
Purchased from Pan American Grace Airways in April 1955 for HK$5,699,663.-
Sold to Air Vietnam, Saigon, December 20, 1962.

DOUGLAS DC6B

VR-HFK (DC6B) Previous Registration
>Entered CX service—June 22 1958
Purchased from Douglas, June 1958, for HK$6,736,860.-
Sold to Braathens, Oslo, Norway, November 29, 1962.

LOCKHEED ELECTRA
VR-HFO (L188) Previous Registration
        Entered CX service—April 1959
        Purchased from Lockheed, April 1959 for HK$11,546,657.-
        Sold to Convair Div. G.D., June 1, 1965.

VR-HFN (L188) Previous Registration
        Entered CX service—June 1959
        Purchased from Lockheed, June 1959 for HK$11,546,657.-
        Sold to Rifia Corp. Miami, March 22, 1967.

CONVAIR 880—22M

VR-HFS (22M) Previous Registration
Entered CX service—April 8, 1962
Purchased from Convair, March 29, 1962 for HK$25,207,908.-
Withdrawn from CX service—November 9, 1973.

VR-HFT (22M) Previous Registration HB-ICL
Entered CX service—November 14, 1964
Purchased from Swiss Air, October 18, 1964 for HK$22,762,194.-
Withdrawn from CX service— March 25, 1973.

VR-HFX (22M) Previous Registration YV-C-VIC
Entered CX service—February 2, 1966.
Purchased from VIASA, November 22, 1965 for HK$20,035,889.-
Crashed into sea near end of the Kai Tak runway, November 5, 1967.

VR-HFY (22M) Previous Registration N 8477 H
Entered CX service—January 25, 1967 .
Purchased from Alaskan Airways, November 5, 1966 for HK$20,387,766.-
Withdrawn from CX service—February 5, 1974.

VR-HFZ (22M) Previous Registration YV-C-VIA
Entered CX service—September 22, 1967
Purchased from VIASA, July 4, 1967 for HK$17,130,000.-
Destroyed June 15, 1972—bomb detonated in passenger cabin near Pleiku, Vietnam.

VR-HGA (22M) Previous Registration B 1008
Entered CX service—March 1, 1968
Purchased from C.A.T., January 10, 1968 for HK$18,480,000.-
Withdrawn from CX service—April 10, 1974.

VR-HGC (22M) Previous Registration YV-C-VIB
Entered CX service—February 7, 1969
Purchased from VIASA, November 26, 1968 for HK$14,275,000.-
Withdrawn from CX service—June 15, 1974.

VR-HGF (22M) Previous Registration JA 8022
Entered CX service—March 15, 1970
Purchased from J.A.L. January 8, 1970
Withdrawn from CX service—September 15, 1975.

VR-HGG (22M) Previous Registration JA 8024
Entered CX service—August 28, 1970
Purchased from J.A.L. June 28, 1970
Withdrawn from CX service—September 15, 1975.

Entire Convair 880 fleet of 7 aircraft sold to Cie. Intermericana Export-Import Inc., a subsidiary of International Air Leases Inc., of Miami, Florida, U.S.A.

BOEING 707—320

VR-HGH (351 B) Previous Registration N 351 US
        Entered CX service—August 24, 1971
        Purchased from N.W.A., July 2, 1971
        Sold to Far East Air Transport for US$3,157,000.00
        Deregistered August 28, 1977
        Subsequently written off by Lan Chile.

VR-HGI (351 B) Previous Registration N 352 US
        Entered CX service—February 18, 1972
        Purchased from N.W.A., December 31, 1971
        Sold to Laker Airways December 1, 1977 for US$4.2 million.

VR-HGN (351 B) Previous Registration N 354 US
        Entered CX service—July 4, 1972
        Purchased from N.W.A., April 30, 1972
        Sold to Laker Airways April 2, 1978 for US$4.2 million.

VR-HGO (351 B) Previous Registration N 353 US
        Entered CX service—October 20, 1972
        Purchased from N.W.A., August 27, 1972
        Sold to Euro Airfinance Ltd. September 10, 1978 for US$4.5 million.

VR-HGQ (351 C) Previous Registration N 362 US
        Entered CX service—January 23, 1973
        Purchased from N.W.A., November 18, 1972.

VR-HGQ (351 C) Previous Registration N 363 US
        Entered CX service—July 28, 1973
        Purchased from N.W.A., May 25, 1973.

VR-HGR (351 C) Previous Registration N 361 US
        Entered CX service—October 27, 1973
        Purchased from N.W.A., August 8, 1973.

VR-HGU (351 C) Previous Registration N 364 US
        Entered CX service—January 24, 1974
        Purchased from N.W.A., November 7, 1973.

VR-HHB (351 C) Previous Registration N357 US
        Entered CX service—March 27, 1974
        Purchased from N.W.A., January 20, 1974.

VR-HHD (351 C) Previous Registration N 358 US
        Entered CX service—Juen 2, 1974
        Purchased from N.W.A., April 2, 1974.

VR-HHJ (351 C) Previous Registration N 360 US
        Entered CX service—August 5, 1974
        Purchased from N.W.A., June 2, 1974.

VR-HHE (351 C) Previous Registration N 359 US
        Entered CX service—October 2, 1974
        Purchased from N.W.A., August 5, 1974.

LOCKHEED L1011

VR-HHK (L1011) Previous Registration (Dash 100 version)
       Entered CX service—September 15, 1975
       Purchased from Lockheed, September 2, 1975.

VR-HHL (L1011) Previous Registration (Dash 100 version)
       Entered CX service—November 1, 1975
       Purchased from Lockheed, October 22, 1975.

VR-HHV (L1011) Previous Registration G-BAAA (Dash One version)
       Leased from Court Line, in service April 8, 1977
       Converted to purchase November 4, 1977.

VR-HHG (L1011) Previous Registration N328EA (Dash One version)
       Bought from Eastern, in service May 8, 1977.

VR-HHX (L1011) Previous Registration N326EA (Dash One version)
       Leased from Eastern, in service September 26, 1976
       Converted to purchase December 4, 1977.

VR-HHW (L1011) Previous Registration G-BAAB (Dash One version)
       Bought from Court Line, in service October 30, 1977.

VR-HHY (L1011) Previous Registration (Dash One version)
       Bought from Eastern, in service August 18, 1978 at cost US$18,750,000.00.

VR-   (L1011) Previous Registration N321EA (Dash One version)
       Leased from Eastern, in service November 8, 1978.

BOEING 747

VR-HKG (B 747) Previous Registration
      In service
      Cost US$54 million.

VR-HIA (B 747) Previous Registration
      In service
      Cost US$54 million.

VR-HIB (B 747) Previous Registration
      In service .
      Cost US$54 million.

A Britannia 102 was wet leased from British Airways (then BOAC) from December 1960 to February 1961 an operated the following round trip flights. During the period the Lockheed L188s were being modified,

Hong Kong—Manila	28 trips
Hong Kong—Bangkok—Singapore	9 trips
Hong Kong—Manila-Darwin-Sydney	16 trips
Hong Kong—Saigon—Kuala Lumpur-Singapore	5 trips
Hong Kong—Bangkok—Kuala Lumpur—Singapore	11 trips
Hong Kong—Taipei	8 trips
Hong Kong—Singapore	2 trips
	79 trips

THE CATHAY PACIFIC AIRWAYS FLEET SEPTEMBER 1983

LOCKHEAD TRI STAR L1011S VR-HHK
VR-HHL
VR-HHV
VR-HHW
VR-HHX
VR-HHY
N   -314
N   -316
N   -321

BOEING 747-200B Series: Passenger VR-HIA
VR-HIB
VR-HIC
VR-HID
VR-HIE
VR-HKG
VR-HIF

Freight VR-HVY

In September 1983 Cathay Pacific re-purchased their first DC3, Reg. No. VR-HDB and at time of print is in transit back to Hong Kong, and will be presented to the Hong Kong Museum of Science and Technology to commemorate the founding of the airline.

25th July 1982
CPA took delivery of their latest 747

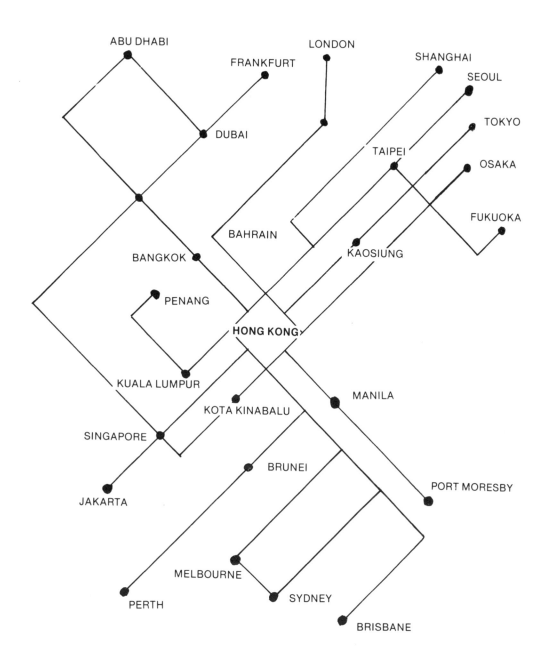

Figure 12: CATHAY PACIFIC'S ROUTE NETWORK 1982

THE AUTHOR

Charles ('Chic') Eather although chronologically young, attained statutory senility on 2nd August 1975, when after 34 years of flying, 25 of them with Cathay Pacific, and with well over 24,000 flying hours behind him, relinquished the job he loved and did so well. His was an adventurous career. If it didn't happen to Chic, it never happened (that is, short of total destruction). He was and is highly regarded, both professionally and personally.

In spite of his great (avionic) age, he has an active and arduous interest in sport. Black belt graded in Judo and also Jodo (a Japanese martial art using stick and sword), he still had the audacity to open the batting for his local eleven. He could easily go round the 24,000 odd hours again!

In his retirement Chic resides at Sorrento, a suburb of Surfers Paradise, Queensland, with his lovely Chinese wife Judy (a porcelain doll if ever there was one), and his children Edward and Alica.